You Are Not a Kinesthetic Learner

You Are Not a Kinesthetic Learner

The Troubled History of the Learning Style Idea

THOMAS FALLACE

The University of Chicago Press
Chicago and London

The University of Chicago Press, Chicago 60637
The University of Chicago Press, Ltd., London

Published 2025
Printed in the United States of America

34 33 32 10 30 29 28 27 26 25 1 2 3 4 5

ISBN-13: 978-0-226-84136-6 (cloth)
ISBN-13: 978-0-226-84138-0 (paper)
ISBN-13: 978-0-226-84137-3 (e-book)
DOI: https://doi.org/10.7208/chicago/9780226841373.001.0001

Library of Congress Cataloging-in-Publication Data

Names: Fallace, Thomas D. (Thomas Daniel), author.
Title: You are not a kinesthetic learner : the troubled history of the learning style idea / Thomas Fallace.
Description: Chicago : The University of Chicago Press, 2025. | Includes bibliographical references and index.
Identifiers: LCCN 2024043186 | ISBN 9780226841366 (cloth) | ISBN 9780226841380 (paperback) | ISBN 9780226841373 (ebook)
Subjects: LCSH: Learning, Psychology of. | Cognitive styles. | Education—Curricula—Social aspects—United States. | Racism in education—United States.
Classification: LCC LB1060 .F34 2025 | DDC 370.15/23—dc23/eng/20241106
LC record available at https://lccn.loc.gov/2024043186

♾ This paper meets the requirements of ANSI/NISO Z39.48-1992 (Permanence of Paper).

Contents

INTRODUCTION

The Learning Style Idea

Probably everyone reading this book has some basic conception of the learning style idea. The theory is that everyone has a style of learning through which they learn best, and that learning through one's style will be more efficient and effective than learning through a less compatible style. Also called *learning modalities*, *learning preferences*, *thinking styles*, *intellectual styles*, and/or *cognitive styles*, the learning style idea has slowly spread throughout schools, media, and popular culture over the last fifty years. One study from 2014 found that well over 90 percent of teachers from around the UK, the Netherlands, Turkey, Greece, and China subscribed to the learning style idea, and a 2015 study confirmed that nearly 90 percent of teachers in the US and Canada agreed with the statement "Individuals learn better when they receive information in their preferred learning style (e.g., visual, auditory, kinesthetic)."[1] A 2014 study of higher-education faculty found that 64 percent of professors agreed that teaching to a student's learning style enhanced learning.[2] The same year, a study of thirty-nine institutions of higher learning found that 72 percent of them taught the learning style idea to teachers as part of professional development, and a 2019 study confirmed that 80 percent of introductory texts in education and educational psychology introduced the learning style idea to teacher candidates.[3] A search for the term *learning style* in the ERIC educational research database garners more than seven thousand studies, and the same term typed into the Google Scholar search engine returns more than 400,000 results. As one set of scholars commented in their review of the validity of the theory: "The learning-styles concept appears to have wide acceptance not only among educators, but also among parents and the general public."[4]

Scholars have developed dozens of learning style classifications since the 1970s, but the most popular version since the 2000s has been the VAK model, which suggests that all learners can be classified primarily as either a visual, auditory, or kinesthetic (VAK) learner. According to this typology, visual learners allegedly learn best through reading or viewing images and videos. Auditory learners allegedly learn best by listening to lectures and absorbing verbal explanations of things. Kinesthetic learners allegedly learn best by doing, building, or interacting physically with things. I used the term *allegedly* because since the inception of the learning style idea in the early twentieth century, the science behind it has been problematic. As the cognitive psychologist Daniel Willingham concluded in 2010, learning styles might exist, "but after decades of trying, psychologists have not been able to find them."[5] Although the existence of learning styles has not held up to scientific scrutiny, decades of anecdotal, practitioner-based, and experimental research has demonstrated that students at all levels of education from kindergarten to graduate school have benefited from learning style–based curricula.[6] It is difficult to parse out whether these successes can be attributed solely to the implementation of learning styles themselves—as opposed to the introduction of more personalized, student-centered, and engaging approaches to teaching in general. What cannot be denied, however, is that the learning style idea has grown exponentially since its inception early in the twentieth century, and that it continues to grow in popularity.

This book traces the troubled history of the learning style idea. As implied in the title, I approach the topic with skepticism. Generally, I think the learning style idea has probably done some good in American schools, because the theory has inspired millions of educators to make their teaching more engaging, student centered, and relevant. However, many of these teachers would have employed student-centered methods anyway, so learning styles became a way to justify their predetermined, intuitive pedagogical commitments. Unfortunately, as I argue in this account, many well-meaning advocates have used the learning style idea to label and silo the very students who need to be challenged and supported with a rigorous curriculum. That is, learning styles became more than a way to recognize student difference; they became unwarranted labels and identities that steered students away from the kind of learning that would have served them best. Accordingly, advocates have repeatedly attempted to align specific racial and socioeconomic groups with learning styles—a well-intended effort aimed at creating a liberating, engaging, and relevant experience for these marginalized students, but one that often comes dangerously close to racial stereotyping and social sorting.

The origins of the learning style are complex and opaque. Unlike the related theory of multiple intelligences, which has a single originator—Howard Gardner—the learning style idea does not have a single founding scholar, nor does it have a single line of development. The ideas that individuals have specific personalities and that students differ in their learning tendencies can be traced back centuries; the idea that children employ all their senses when learning can be traced back to the nineteenth century; and the idea that students differ in abilities and interests was a cornerstone of the progressive education movement of the early twentieth century. However, the idea that individuals can be aligned with specific learning styles that clashed with that of many teachers and schools did not emerge until the middle of the twentieth century, and even then the idea was applied solely to students who were struggling to read. Not until the 1970s did educators begin to construct learning style assessments meant for *all* students in *all* subjects. Not until the 1970s did educators attempt to assess students formally and align them with permanent and dangerous labels such as "kinesthetic learner."

By the 1970s, educators had created more than a dozen learning style inventories.[7] By 2004, according to one review, there were more than seventy learning style typologies in existence.[8] Generally, these learning style inventories can be sorted into five groups. First were the VAK-based models, based on differences or preferences in sensory channels. Even though VAK-based approaches have had the weakest scientific support, they have been the most popular since the turn of the twenty-first century, due to the intuitive and simplistic nature of the scheme. Second were the cognitive or thinking style approaches that built on the research of the psychologist Herman Witkin. Under Witkin's classification, one is either field dependent or field independent, based on one's ability to separate an item from its surrounding visual field. Witkin's scheme inspired educators in the 1970s and '80s to pursue the idea of a Black or Latine learning style that clashed with the presiding White culture of schools. Witkin's typology has the most rigorous and scientific research base of all the learning style typologies. In fact, the twenty-first-century learning style advocates continued to build on Witkin's work. However, Witkin's work is the least known by practitioners. Third were personality-based learning style models that drew inspiration from the Swiss psychologist Carl Gustav Jung. The popular Myers–Briggs typology drew upon Jung's eight personality types (e.g., introverted feeling type, extroverted thinking type) and explored the pedagogical implications of the role of personality in classroom interactions. Fourth was the experiential learning typology of the business professor David Kolb, whose scheme was most popular with college professors.[9] Under Kolb's classification, one is primarily an assimilator, an accommodator, a converger, or a diverger, based on how one prefers to process new information. Finally, one of the most popular learning style typologies was never intended to be learning theory at all: Howard Gardner's theory of multiple intelligences.[10] Under a common misapplication of Gardner's theory, one is either a musical, linguistic, logical-mathematical, kinesthetic, spatial, interpersonal, intrapersonal, or naturalistic learner. Gardner spent much of the latter half of his career trying to distinguish his intelligences from learning styles—with limited success, because teachers and educational authors have consistently conflated Gardner's intelligences with learning style types.

As we can see from even this partial list of typologies, the learning style idea has always lacked coherence and consistency. How could five models of learning all be true? Whereas some learning style advocates sought to absorb and synthesize all the schemes into a comprehensive model, others simply ignored competing models and contradictory research altogether; Gardner in particular has attacked the entire learning style enterprise, with focus directed particularly at the VAK-based version of the theory. Thus, the learning style idea was never really a single idea so much as it was a cluster of ideas. Moreover, the learning style idea reflects a cluster of critiques about the shortcomings of teacher-centered instruction and the one-size-fits-all curriculum that has failed to meet the needs of millions of students.

Across the twentieth and twenty-first centuries, advocates offered many critiques of the schools that the learning style idea sought to remedy. They argued that student difference was a fundamental aspect of a healthy democratic society and that schools failed to address these differences by treating all students the same. Others argued that bureaucratic public schools and norm-referenced standardized tests were not as fair and objective as they claimed to be; instead, these structures reflected the values of the able-bodied, White, middle-class society to which minoritized, impoverished, and disabled students were expected to adjust. "The cognitive style of most educational institutions is not consonant with that of most Mexican-American and Black children," researchers concluded in 1973. "This lack of consonance may be contributing to the failure which members of these groups experience in school."[11] These norm-referenced standardized tests also emphasized students' weaknesses and deficiencies instead of focusing on their strengths and differences. Thus, addressing the learning styles of students not only recognized the humanity of individual students in ways that supported a thriving democratic society, but it also disrupted the assimilationist impulses of American schools that had been systemically oppressing students of color. When education policymakers switched their focus from educational opportunity to equitable educational outcomes in the 1960s and '70s, the learning style idea served as both an explanation for gaps in achievement among racial groups and a possible remedy for how to close these gaps. With the adoption of high-stakes testing in the 1990s and beyond, the learning style idea offered a potential way to raise test scores for struggling students. As one learning style advocate remarked in 1990, standardized testing had educators "looking for answers" and made them "more likely to be open" to new ideas.[12]

The educational research establishment—as represented by its most prestigious and rigorous journals—initially embraced the learning style idea, and it continued to spread the idea through practitioner-oriented journals, professional development workshops, textbooks, and the popular media. The field of teacher education has tolerated and at times embraced the learning style idea because it aligns with a general aversion to teacher-centered methods, though it was not solely responsible for perpetuating this aversion. To a large extent, advocates for learning style inventories circumvented the educational research establishment altogether by going straight to the teachers and administrators themselves without waiting for validation from cognitive scientists and peer reviewers. As one critic pointed out in 1990: "The tendency among the learning style researchers has not been to pursue the necessary iterative pattern of hypothesis-investigation-modification but rather to rush prematurely into print."[13] Despite these problems, college professors and teachers in graduate and professional schools have also adopted and implemented the theory. Therefore, the learning style idea cannot be attributed merely to the "bad ideas" of "ed schools," as one critic charged, because it originated in the discipline of cognitive psychology, had only a tangential relationship to colleges and schools of education, and was embraced by college and graduate school professors, including those in medical and business schools, who, according to some critics, should have known better.[14] Even ski instructors and wrestling coaches found use for the learning style idea.[15]

So why and how is the history of learning style idea dangerous and troubled? To be honest, when I first began my inquiry, I was expecting to discover a narrative in which the research community originally supported the promise of the learning style idea, but then became skeptical over time as additional research emerged. However, this is not what I found. To the contrary, from the idea's inception, researchers expressed skepticism, practitioners ignored numerous caveats and cautions issued by learning style advocates about labeling students permanently with learner identities, and educators overextended and misapplied the idea in a multitude of ways. In fact, the godfather of personality studies, the sociologist Gordon Allport, first warned against the formation and application of typologies in 1937: "A typology is always a device for exalting its author's special interest at the expense of individuality of the life which he ruthlessly dismembers. All typologies place boundaries where boundaries do not belong. They are artificial categories."[16] The VAK-oriented learning style typology emerged from an unwarranted extension of techniques in remedial reading instruction, and researchers employed Witkin's field dependence/independence typology to develop race-based learning style theories in the 1970s while overlooking Witkin's own research, which failed to establish a strong link between race/culture and cognitive styles.

Despite these overapplications, missteps, and setbacks, the learning style idea continued to grow in popularity throughout the 1980s, 1990s, and 2000s as national and international networks formed to support its spread. Even more troubling and dangerous was the act of labeling students with learning style–based identities such as "kinesthetic learner" and then providing these students with a less-rigorous curriculum. In fact, one 2023 study found that teachers, parents, and students considered visual learners to be "smarter" and kinesthetic learners to be "sportier"—demonstrating the anti-intellectual assumptions of the "kinesthetic" label.[17] Since the 1970s, learning style advocates disproportionately identified students of color as kinesthetic learners and, as a result, offered them lower-level activities and materials.

This history of the learning style idea not only traces the troubled history of a dangerous idea that never really had the full backing of the scientific community, but it also demonstrates how ideas enter the educational discourse, how these ideas enter the classroom, and how they become conventional wisdom. It further demonstrates how difficult it is to unseat these ideas once they have been accepted and espoused by practitioners, especially when they have such intuitive appeal. The history of the learning style idea, however, reveals an even bigger truth about American schools. As educators were asked to do more and more to meet the needs of a racially and ethnically diverse student population, as well as accommodate students identified with disabilities, they were looking (and hoping) for a panacea to alleviate the rising expectations that society was placing on the schools—a pressure that only increased after the implementation of high-stakes standardized testing after the passage of No Child Left Behind in 2001.

Now that most of the punitive aspects of educational accountability introduced by No Child Left Behind have been removed, I believe the time has come for educators to abandon the learning style idea. This will be difficult because it took decades for the idea to emerge, and, I fear, it may take decades for it to fully disappear. "A new scientific truth does not triumph by convincing its opponents and making them see the light," the physicist Max Planck once observed, "but rather because its opponents eventually die, and a new generation grows up that is familiar with it."[18] Planck's observation points to the generational nature of clinging to deep-seated and cherished beliefs, even when they are proven to be wrong. His quotation also points to the need for a new theory to replace the old one before advocates "see the light." The *science of reading* and the *science of learning* are popular phrases currently being employed by critics to counteract the kind of thinking espoused by learning style advocates and could serve as replacements for the learning style idea.[19] Nevertheless, it is too premature to declare or even predict the fall of the learning style idea because many continue to defend it.

The goal of my historical study is to demonstrate that the theoretical and empirical support for the learning style idea was never very strong to begin with, that the practical applications of the idea were far narrower than most educators ever realized, and that identifying students with permanent labels and identities such as "kinesthetic learner" was and is dangerous. The impulse toward inclusivity that drove the learning style was a noble one, and the critiques of the one-size-fits-all curriculum were often warranted; but in many cases, the learning style idea has led to faulty assumptions about group and individual characteristics that were more dangerous than the one-size-fits-all pedagogy they sought to replace.

1

Sensory Channels and Personality Types

There were no major turning points in the early history of learning styles. The idea emerged incrementally over decades and synthesized other ideas from a variety of fields and disciplines, most of which were completely unaware of one another. This was one of the reasons the learning idea spread so successfully—there was no single figure, book, or study that captured the public imagination at a particular moment in time in the way the publication of Howard Gardner's *Frames of Mind* (1983) would do for the idea of multiple intelligences.[1] This slow development allowed the idea to enter the public and educational discourse stealthily and largely free from scrutiny.

One turning point occurred in 1966 when the sociologist Frank Riessman boldly asserted in a journal for the National Education Association (NEA) that "everyone has a distinct style of learning, as individual as his personality." These individualized styles, he continued with no sense of irony, "may be categorized principally as visual (reading), aural (listening), or physical (doing things)." Further, Riessman linked the "disadvantaged child"—which readers in the 1960s would have understood as a Black or Latine student—with the "physical approach to learning." He argued that all teachers ought to "identify the learning strengths in his pupils and then how to utilize them to overcome weaknesses."[2] With these assertions, Riessman became one of the first scholars to offer a broad generalization about the learning style of entire groups of students, and he was also one of the first to introduce the VAK learning style typology to an educational audience. There is no evidence that Riessman's article caused much of a stir at the time, and, because he provided no citations, it cannot be determined where he got his ideas from. Nevertheless, the fact that his reference to the existence of personalities and learning styles made it through some form of editorial or peer review suggests that the idea was at least plausible by the mid-1960s. How had this happened?

For Riessman's assertion about personalities and VAK-based learning styles to be plausible, several sub-assertions would have had to have been established: First, that there was some significance to the visual, auditory, and kinesthetic division of sensory channels. Second, that all students could be identified with a strength in one sensory channel. Third, that a strength in one channel could be substituted for a weakness in another. Fourth, that a student's personality could in some way impact their learning. Fifth, that all students could be aligned with a semipermanent "type," based on either their personality and/or their sensory-channel strength. Finally, that entire groups of students could be assigned with a particular learning style that was somehow linked to their personality and/or sensory-channel strength. In this chapter, I unravel the origins and development of these assertions and how they came together in the work of Herman Witkin and Frank Riessman—the first two scholars to suggest that differences in students' learning style types could help explain disparities in learning outcomes.

Visual, Auditory, and Motor Types

Two major tenets of the VAK learning style typology were that students learn best through one of three sensory channels—visual, auditory, kinesthetic—and that a weakness in one sensory channel could be substituted or supplemented by a strength in another channel. The development of this substitution theory was significant because it marked the point when the personality theory was translated into a learning theory. It took decades for this conceptualization to fully emerge, and even when it did, advocates intended the idea to be applied solely to students who had been identified with a learning disability.

The idea that students learned through their visual, auditory, and kinesthetic senses stretched back well into the nineteenth century, and it was a key ingredient in the student-centered methods that emerged during the nineteenth and early twentieth centuries. European educators such as Johann Heinrich Pestalozzi and Friedrich Froebel emphasized the importance of tactile learning by having young children manipulate objects as part of a student-centered pedagogy that catered to children's natural curiosity. The Italian physician and pedagogical innovator Maria Montessori also encouraged students to work with all their senses when solving educational problems, and even suggested isolating senses, such as handling objects while blindfolded so the sense of touch could be engaged before the other senses were; as Montessori observed, "Many children who have not arrived at the point of recognizing a figure by looking at it, could recognize it by touching it." However, Montessori never suggested having students learn solely through a single sensory channel. In fact, the combination of senses is what made her method effective. "Undoubtedly, the association of the *muscular-tactile* sense with that of *vision*," she insisted, "aids in a most remarkable way the perception of forms and fixes them in memory."[3] The Harvard professor Henry W. Holmes, who authored the introduction to English translation of *The Montessori Method* (1912), was uncomfortable with Montessori's method and warned that "the isolation of senses should be used with some care" because "to shut off light is to take one step towards sleep." Holmes worried that "strain involved in mental action without the usual means of information and control" could be harmful to students.[4] This was far from an endorsement for the isolation of sensory channels in learning.

Concurrently in the United States, the progressive educator John Dewey famously defined education as "a process of living and not a preparation for future living," and so he too encouraged the fusion of the cognitive, moral, and physical aspects of the learning process, especially for young children.[5] However, Dewey never suggested that student learning be isolated to one sensory channel or focused on one cognitive approach. In fact, he opposed such methods. "Training by isolated exercises [of senses] leaves no deposit, leads nowhere; and even the technical skill acquired has little radiating power, or transferable value," Dewey asserted in his 1910 classic *How We Think*. "Such methods of training . . . compare very unfavorably with the training of eye and hand that comes as an incident work with tools in wood or metals, or of gardening, cooking, or the care of animals."[6] In other words, Dewey argued, adults did not isolate their senses in their day-to-day problem solving and activity, so there was no reason to isolate the senses of young children, because such activities were unnatural, artificial, and disconnected from the real-world problems they would face. Learning style advocates in the 1970s would cite Dewey and Montessori in support of the VAK learning style idea, but both directly opposed the isolation of sensory channels. Thus, despite a recognition of engaging all the senses in learning, it was not student-centered pedagogical progressives who first successfully introduced the VAK-based learning style idea. The specific identification of this typology—and, more significantly, the idea that individuals had a strength in one sensory channel that could be used to supplement weaknesses in other channels—had more complicated and convoluted origins that emerged slowly from remedial reading instruction.

Early discussions of visual, auditory, and kinesthetic learners centered around how literacy and the role of mental processing, or what psychologists at the time called *mental imagery*, in learning new material. Building on the work of the German psychologist Wilhelm Wundt, most pre-progressive psychologists believed that the learning process involved the movement from *sensation* to *perception* to *image*, which was the form in which new knowledge became permanently embedded in the mind. Imagery, according to the thinking of nineteenth-century psychologists, constituted the semipermanent mental furniture of memories, imagination, recall, and thinking. They recognized that individuals differed in how they stored their mental imagery, particularly when recalling information. The German psychologist Ernst Meumann identified three "ideational types . . . an auditory, a motor, a visual type" in his book *The Psychology of Learning*, which was translated from German to English in 1913. As Meumann explained, the ideational types could be distinguished by how individual learners "recalled verbal images to consciousness." According to Meumann, an auditory type "hears the auditory images of words," a motor type "has a mental revival of the muscular sensation," and visual type sees "the visual images of written or printed words." Regarding the development of literacy, Meumann continued, the visual type "imprints upon his consciousness a picture of the printed word," but the "individual who belongs to the auditory or the motor type immediately transforms the visual pictures, obtained from reading, into heard or spoken words."[7]

Meumann's VAK-based theory might look like the origins of the VAK learning style idea, but this is not quite the case, because his relatively brief discussion of the "ideation types" was preceded by a longer, six-page discussion of "learning types," which he divided into "rapid learners" and "slow learners." As Meumann explained, "The rapid and the slow learner each represents a characteristic mental type which may be determined experimentally in its essential attributes . . . [and] these typical differences are present even in children."[8] Thus, although Meumann's visual-auditory-motor ideation typology was an antecedent to the later VAK model, it was related to, but distinct from, the "learning types" he had introduced earlier in the book. In other words, Meumann had indeed introduced a learning style theory in his book, but the visual/auditory/motor ideational typology was not it. Instead, his dualistic learning style theory centered around slow and fast learners. Even if Meumann had offered up the VAK typology as a learning style theory, it would have been of limited use, because his "recall" process related only to words that had already been learned; he did not introduce it as a method for learning new vocabulary.

Around this time, Stephen Sheldon Colvin, a psychologist at the University of Illinois, elaborated on Meumann's ideation types and its relevance to literacy instruction by suggesting that these types needed to be taken into consideration by teachers. Colvin cited Meumann's ideation type theory throughout his textbook, *The Learning Process* (1911): "A method of instruction in reading . . . which will be effective for the child possessing strong visual imagery may be of very doubtful merit when used in instructing the child of the motor type." Colvin looked forward to the time "when certain standard tests may be devised to determine the sensory and intellectual differences of children, to the end that instruction may be modified and adapted to suit individual rather than general needs." Not only did Colvin see a potential benefit in testing students for imagery type to instruct them better, but also to sort students by their anticipated future occupation. Testing for "sensory differences" such as visual, auditory, and motor processing, Colvin explained, "is likewise important in ascertaining the interests and capacities of children and adolescents for various kinds of school work and for various kinds of occupations outside of school."[9] Despite Colvin's hope, no general-use sensory assessment emerged before World War II. However, during the 1920s, intelligence tests were widely adopted and administered by school principals, who used students' intelligence quotient (IQ) scores to sort them based in part on their anticipated future occupation, just as Colvin had suggested.

Intelligence testing in the US began during World War I when, in 1916, Lewis Terman published the *Measurement of Intelligence*. Terman's study was based on data on the administration of the Binet–Simon intelligence test on thousands on schoolchildren, including Black, Latine, and Indigenous American students. The administration and results of the IQ tests reflected the racism of the period. For example, Terman identified a general "dullness" among the "Spanish-Indian and Mexican families of the Southwest and also among negroes," whose average mental age was allegedly three years lower than the average White student. Terman insisted that "children of this group should be segregated in special classes and be given instruction which is concrete and practical." In case study of a Black boy with an IQ of 80, Terman predicted that his mental capacity would never exceed that of an average twelve-year-old boy.[10] Beyond dismissing the intellectual capacity of students of color, Terman's data confirmed that students whose parents came from Western European descent and who held professional positions consistently scored higher in intelligence than those White students whose parents were of non–Northern European descent and/or of working-class background. Thus, Terman's data justified the existing racism of the period and traced social inequality to innate and hereditary differences, as opposed to differences in environment, language, values, or education. Through books such as *The Intelligence of School Children* (1919) and *Intelligence Tests and School Reorganization* (1922), Terman encouraged wider use of his tests in the public schools to identify "retarded" and "feeble-minded" students and endorsed a policy of segregating them into special classes.[11] During the next decade, IQ tests became very popular with school administrators. One survey conducted in 1925 found that 64 percent of elementary schools, 56 percent of junior highs schools, and 40 percent of high schools were not only administering IQ tests to all their students, but also using the results to sort and homogenously group them.[12] Terman also participated in designing the Scholastic Aptitude Test (SAT), which became a common entry requirement for colleges and universities after World War II.

The norm-based standardized testing created and administered during the first decades of the twentieth century recognized differences among students but traced these differences to innate, biological, and racial divergences in intelligence. Psychometricians such as Terman made no attempt to relate these differences in intelligence to cultural, environmental, or contextual factors, nor did he address the kind of sensory differences among students proposed by Meumann and Colvin. Other than using the results of the IQ tests to align students with their projected future occupations, Terman had little to say about pedagogy and even less to say about how to address learner differences. Although teachers unofficially (and privately) labeled students as "slow" or "bright" based on their IQ scores, these norm-based assessments did not create official labels in the way that learning style inventories later would. The idea that a student's learning weakness in one sensory channel could be substituted with another sensory channel emerged from a separate line of thought: the field of remedial reading instruction.

The Kinesthetic Method

In 1921, Grace Fernald and Helen B. Keller of University of California at Los Angeles published an innovative instructional model based on use of the kinesthetic channel. Fernald and Keller reported seven cases studies in which "the kinesthetic method" successfully taught students to read who previously "failed to learn to read after three or more years in the public school." The kinesthetic method involved having students trace the letters of self-selected words written on the blackboard repeatedly with their fingers over and over until they could do so by memory. After several rounds of the finger-tracing process, the students wrote the word out by hand until they could do so by memory. Finally, they were shown the word in print and asked to recognize it. After learning dozens of words through this hands-on, kinesthetic method, students repeated the trace/write/read process, using entire sentences instead of words. According to Fernald and Keller, as students gradually built up their vocabulary through the kinesthetic method, their literacy skills began developing at a faster rate and their fluency improved exponentially.

Fernald and Keller were struck by the kinesthetic aspects of learning for students who struggled to learn through visual and auditory means. "Children who have to trace words in the early learning stages continue to make slight hand and arm movements in attempting to recall difficult words or to learn new words," the authors reported. "All the children make marked movements of articulation during the process of learning a new word, even after reading has been well developed." Based on these observations, Fernand and Keller concluded that "the kinesthetic elements seem to be the essential link between the visual cue and the various associations which give it word meaning."[13] Although Fernand and Keller recognized the significance of using the kinesthetic channel to reach these struggling students, they did not refer to these students as kinesthetic learners, nor did they suggest that all students should be assessed for whether or not they were a kinesthetic learner.[14]

By 1943, when Fernald expanded her research into the book *Remedial Techniques in Basic School Subjects*, the idea that an individual recalled images visually, auditorily, or kinesthetically had apparently become common sense for teachers of struggling students. "Every student of psychology knows that some people tend to get visual images, that is picture experiences that they recall," Fernald explained. "Other people either get no visual images at all or very vague ones, [and] . . . other remember things in terms of their own movements." Like Colvin, Fernald suggested that certain imaging strengths in visual, auditory, or motor images could be used to supplement weaknesses in other imaging channels: "Normal perception, retention, and memory could be developed by individuals whose failure seems to be due to the inability to learn through visual and auditory channels, if tactile and kinesthetic methods were involved in the learning process." Again, Fernald did not suggest that *all* students should be classified as visual, auditory, or kinesthetic learners and then be taught exclusively through those methods. Rather, Fernald insisted, the kinesthetic method she described should be employed only for those students who had "failed to learn to read by visual and auditory methods."[15] Furthermore, she observed that the students she successfully taught using the kinesthetic method often used a mix of kinesthetic, auditory, and visual methods. In a passage that seemed to repudiate the entire concept that students could be aligned with only one VAK-based learning style at a time because they quickly moved from one learning channel preference to another, Fernald noted:

> One of the most interesting things about the work has been the way in which individual differences were evident in the methods of learning used by different children. Some traced just long enough to get the letter form and then learned any new word by merely looking at it; and then writing it apparently from the visual image. Other children seemed very dependent upon some sort of auditory image and said the word over and over to themselves while they looked at it, repeating it as they wrote it. . . . One point that cannot be emphasized too strongly is that each child was allowed to use the method by which he learned most easily.[16]

Although Fernald's book also addressed remedial techniques in arithmetic and other school subjects, her discussion of VAK-oriented methods was limited to the subjects of reading and spelling, or the techniques related to other subjects only to the extent that they required learning vocabulary. In other words, the kinesthetic method was appropriate only for language acquisition and not for the development of mathematical algorithms and/or the learning of scientific, literary, or social concepts, which limited the utility of the idea beyond learning to read.

A focus on the role of the senses in remedial reading concurrently emerged from the field of psychiatry as well. In 1925, a neuropsychiatrist and pathologist, Samuel Orton, identified a condition in which children of average intelligence were struggling to learn to read due a disability that had previously been identified by James Hinshelwood as "word-blindness."[17] Orton broadened the definition beyond extreme cases identified by Hinshelwood to include more students and tried to rename the disability *strephosymbolia*, but eventually the condition came to be known as *dyslexia*. Not only did Orton identify one of the most common conditions in the field of special education, but he also suggested a remedy. Drawing upon the work of Marion Monroe, who had earlier created a disability assessment based in part on visual, motor, and auditory senses, Orton directed teachers to "capitalize on [students'] auditory competence by teaching them the phonetic equivalent of the printed letters."[18] In other words, when teaching dyslexic students, Orton suggested that teachers substitute and/or supplement the visual cue with auditory and kinesthetic ones, as Montessori and Fernald had also suggested. Working with Orton, the psychologists Anna Gillingham and Bessie Stillman created a set of instructional materials for dyslexic students that combined and sequenced visual, auditory, and kinesthetic elements of learning to read. The "multisensory" method of teaching dyslexic students to read came known as the Orton–Gillingham reading program, a popular approach that is still in use today.[19]

Despite that approach's role in promoting the VAK model of learning styles, it must be noted that these groundbreaking works by Colvin, Fernald,

Meumann, and Orton and Gillingham were not centrally about learning styles, and all these scholars were careful to apply the theory only to the recognition and recall of words, not to the learning of subject matter in general. Meumann even seemed to think that his (now forgotten) slow/rapid learning style typology was more significant to overall learning patterns than his three ideation types that aligned with the VAK model. Fernald designed her kinesthetic method for use with *all* struggling readers, not just those who were identified as kinesthetic learners. The Orton–Gillingham program combined all three VAK modalities into "multisensory" instructional materials. Furthermore, the whole theory of ideation types was based on an outdated cognitive model of "imagery" and "apperception" that progressive psychologists later dismissed because it sounded too much like the disproven faculty psychology of the nineteenth century—the idea that the mind was composed of mental faculties such as attention, imagination, and so on that could be independently strengthened, like muscles.[20] From the purview of the twenty-first century, one can see why behavior psychologists, who first came to prominence during World War I, sought to impose some precision and scientific rigor upon these convoluted discussions of cognition. Behavioral psychologists such as John Watson and later B. F. Skinner had no use for non-observable concepts such as "auditory images" and "imprints upon consciousness," and "the ideational types." Instead, behavioral psychologists focused solely on stimulus-response bonds in the environment that could be easily observed and quantified and empirically verified through replicable laboratory studies.[21] Terman's intelligence tests promised to bring objectivity to student assessment through the application of quantitative methods. Postwar educators of students with disabilities employed both intelligence testing and VAK-based assessments to help struggling readers, and they did not originally view IQ testing and learning styles as incompatible.

In 1954, a new disability designation was identified that drew further attention to the role of senses in learning: the *auditory processing disorder*. The psychologist Helmer Myklebust first identified children who "can hear but . . . cannot structure the auditory world and select the sounds which are immediately pertinent to adjustment."[22] That is, Myklebust identified students whose hearing was not physically impaired in any way, but who nevertheless had trouble perceiving, separating, and processing the sounds into meaning. Some experts estimated that as much as 15 percent of school- age children had some sort of undiagnosed auditory processing disorder, which inhibited their learning across all subjects. Since most teachers taught through auditory methods, this put students with this disorder at a huge disadvantage. Advocates did not recommend that teachers apply VAK-based learning style inventories to catch these undiagnosed cases. Nevertheless, rising awareness of auditory processing disorder drew further attention to the role of the senses in learning.

In 1954, Robert E. Mills developed an evaluation instrument called the Learning Method Test that identified which method—visual, phonic, kinesthetic, or a combination—worked best for teaching word recognition. Predictably, he discovered that different methods worked best for different groups of students differentiated by intelligence. He found that "children of low intelligence" learned best through kinesthetic methods, children of average intelligence learned best through visual and combination methods, and children with high intelligence learned best through visual methods. Mills concluded that his research "indicates the need for concentration of energies on finding out which method is best for which children rather than developing a recipe or a best method that will serve all children all the time."[23] Mills did not refer to students as visual learners, auditory learners, or the like, yet he was the first educator to assess the effectiveness of aligning specific methods with specific students, and the first to align groups of students with preferred learning styles to their IQs.

Building on the work of Fernald and of Mills, the identification of learning styles via the VAK typology arose in concert with the growing field of special education. To provide more-useful feedback for students with special needs, Samuel Kirk and James McCarthy developed the Illinois Test of Psycholinguistic Abilities (ITPA) in 1961. This popular assessment was designed to move beyond the single scores provided by IQ tests to indicate areas of learning strengths and weaknesses. The ITPA assessed three dimensions of student learning: channel, level, and process. The "channel" referred to "the sensory-motor path over which the linguistic symbols and received and responded," and the channel categories aligned with the learning modalities of the VAK typology—what they identified as "auditory input, vocal output, and visual input and motor output."[24] Based on data from multiple administrations of the test, the educational psychologists John D. King and Larry Masat issued pedagogical recommendations based on these sensory-motor pathways. "Retarded children have more difficulty understanding what they hear than what they see," King and Masat explained. "They also have more difficulty with auditory than with visual ideas."[25] They suggested that teachers use images to accompany spoken words for students with a deficiency in the channel of auditory learning. Just as Mills had done, King and Masat aligned students of low intelligence with "motor" learning, as opposed to visual and auditory learning, which they aligned with students of higher intelligence.

In summary, prior to the 1970s, no educator had yet constructed a formal VAK-based learning style typology or assessment, yet researchers in psychology, remedial reading, medicine, and education were beginning to develop literature and assessments that drew attention to the significance of the sequence and isolation of the visual, auditory, and motor/kinesthetic senses. The terminology for referring to the senses was inconsistent, as researchers used the terms *imagery type*, *channel*, and/or *sensory path*. None of them used the terms *learning modality* or *learning style*. Nevertheless, Fernald, King and Masat, and Mills all suggested that aligning VAK-based teaching methods with VAK-based student learning styles would lead to better results, but their research was mostly limited to the areas of remedial reading instruction for struggling students and students with learning disabilities. They also emphasized that most students used multiple or sequential VAK channels when learning, and that students should not be limited to using just one channel. None of them offered a compelling case for the existence of learning styles as a legitimate approach to teaching all students. So when Riessman and others introduced the VAK learning style typology in the 1960s and '70s, they were extending the implications of this research far beyond what was warranted or intended by those who first identified the significance of learning channels.

Personality Studies

The early research on sensory channels was obscure and likely read only by specialists and educators of students with disabilities. The research on personality, on the other hand, had far broader appeal among scholars and public school educators. Although scientific interest in personalities emerged in the 1930s, the idea that individuals had different personalities based in part on biology stretches back centuries. Pre-modern medicine was rooted in the idea that an individual's personality would display the predominance of one of their four humors: black bile, phlegm, yellow bile, and blood. Those with an excess of black bile had a personality that was melancholic, those with too much phlegm were phlegmatic, those with too much yellow bile were choleric, and those with too much blood were sanguine.

In modern times, the Harvard psychologist William James referred repeatedly to personality in his highly influential two-volume text, *Principles of Psychology*, published in 1890. James considered personality to be part the "stream of thought" that constituted the workings of the human mind. In his book *Pragmatism* (1907), James identified two "types of mental make-up," which he dubbed the "tender-minded" and the "tough-minded"—the former was idealistic and dogmatic, the latter pluralistic and skeptical.[26] More significantly, the Swiss psychologist Carl Gustav Jung published his classic text *Personality Types* in 1921, which introduced four psychological functions (thinking, feeling, sensation, and intuitive) and two life attitudes (introversion and extroversion). According to Jung's typology, the two functions and the four attitudes combined into eight possible personality types; for example, one could be an extraverted thinking type or an introverted feeling type. Jung's theory was dismissed by many American psychologists at the time because it was not based on the scientific methods of laboratory research, which was becoming dominant in American universities and laboratories. However, Jung's theory did inspire one significant person, an intelligent and ambitious housewife named Katharine Cook Briggs, to develop a personality test that would steadily grow in popularity over the next half century.

In the mid-1930s, Briggs became obsessed with Jung's personality type and began applying the theory to her friends and family. She corresponded with Jung and developed his ideas into a formal personality test in the 1940s. Despite Jung's apprehensions about Briggs's misapplication of his theory, she fanatically pursued publication of the *Personality Type Inventory* she had developed. Katherine's daughter, Isabel Briggs Myers, made a few revisions to the test and finally secured a publishing deal. In 1944, the *Myers-Briggs Type Indicator Handbook* was made available to the public for the price of fifty cents. The first major organization to adopt the Myers–Briggs handbook was the Office of Strategic Services, a government organization that trained spies for the Cold War. The Myers-Briggs Type Indicator was later adopted by Educational Testing Service (ETS) in Princeton, New Jersey, where it would eventually reach millions of users and become the most popular personality test in the world. However, in the 1940s and '50s, it was just one of many personality tests available.[27] With the rise of office work after World War II, corporations became more interested in sorting and assessing the happiness of its employees based on personality tests. One researcher estimated that 60 percent of US corporations in 1956 were using personality tests to assess their workers.[28]

With the publication of *Personality: A Psychological Interpretation* in 1937, Gordon Allport had established himself as the nation's leading scholarly authority on the topic. As the second-youngest scholar to ever be elected president of the American Psychological Association (APA), Allport was one of the most influential psychologists of the mid-twentieth century. He conceptualized a three-tiered model of personality made up of cardinal traits, central traits, and secondary traits. Through such an approach, Allport balanced the scientism of a universal typology with the subjectivity of individual expression. Unlike the typologies of Jung and Myers and Briggs, Allport was careful not to define personality as fixed. Instead, he cast it in dynamic and evolving terms. "Personality is less a finished product than a transitive process," he insisted in a passage ignored by many of his followers. "While it has some stable features, it is at the same time continually undergoing change." More significantly, Allport made no attempt to create personality types; in fact, he directly opposed the practice. By creating and applying personality types, as James, Jung, and Myers and Briggs had done, Allport objected, "the author is imposing his own interests on human nature . . . divisible according to *his* scheme." These labels were mere "abstractions created by taking bits of people and forcing them into a category of special delight to some investigator." Allport had earlier generated a list of hundreds of terms used to describe human personality in the literature through the years, thus demonstrating the futility of limiting the messiness of human nature to two or four types. "The real mischief of the doctrine of empirical types is that it implies that a personality is wholly subsumed under a type," Allport concluded, "but . . . this is never the case."[29]

There was a sociopolitical element to Allport's psychology as well. As authoritarianism continued to spread across the globe in the late 1930s and '40s, Allport considered the study and celebration of personality to be an antidote to the rigid, assimilationist thinking of authoritarians. To "avoid authoritarianism," Allport pleaded in his presidential address to the APA in 1939, "we [must] keep psychology from becoming a cult from which original and daring inquiry is ruled out by the application of one-sided tests of method."[30] This was a criticism of the then-prevalent behavioral psychology that reduced all human interaction to stimulus-response connections and rejected any non-observable concepts—such as thinking, feeling, and personality—as unscientific. Behavioral psychologists such as Watson and Skinner did not recognize the study of personality as legitimate, because they believed the study of personality involved the non-observable aspects of mind that could never be studied and verified with scientific precision. In response, Allport aligned behavioral psychology with the authoritarian ideologies of fascism and communism, due to both these ideologies' rejection of creativity, morality, and individual expression. He was not alone in doing so. In fact, many of early advocates for cognitive psychology contrasted their approach with behavioral psychology and cast it in political and ideological terms.[31]

Fears of authoritarian tendencies and their relationship to a maladjusted personality continued to grow during the early years of the Cold War. Writing in the 1940s, the historian Arthur Schlesinger Jr. warned that there was potentially "a Hitler, a Stalin in every breast."[32] In 1950, the psychologists Theodor Adorno, Else Frenkel-Brunswik, Daniel Levinson, and R. Nevitt Sanford published *The Authoritarian Personality*, one of the most important and cited studies of the period. Adorno and his associates' book underscored the importance of the scientific significance of personality and its relationship to the social and political health of the nation. "It seems apparent that any attempt to appraise the chances of a fascist triumph in America must reckon with the potential existing in the character of the people," the authors stated. "Here lies not only the susceptibility to antidemocratic propaganda but most dependable sources of resistance to it."[33] Based on a battery of tests (including the famous F-scale assessment), the authors discovered that many Americans did, in fact, demonstrate a preference for authoritarianism. Psychologists, including Herman Witkin (see below), would continue to employ the F-scale to assess authoritarian tendencies in their subjects for decades.[34] Adorno and his coauthors warned that the prevalence of the authoritarian personality was a potential time bomb that could be exploited by a ruthless political leader. Others feared that the excessive desire to fit in was conducive to authoritarianism. For example, in *The Lonely Crowd* and other critical essays, the sociologist David Riesman argued that Americans were developing a personality that was too "outer-directed." By this he meant the American citizen submitted easily to "the pressure to *join*, to submerge himself in the group—any group—and to lower still further not only the feeling that he can, but that he has a right, to stand on his own." According to Riesman, Americans were too eager to "surrender any claim to independent judgement and taste," and he worried too that such an outward-directed attitude was dangerous for a healthy democracy.[35]

This postwar concern about the American character and personality carried over to schools. In the 1940s and '50s, American educators began to take more notice of this emerging work on personality, especially as it began to overlap with developmental psychology. "The problems involved in investigating personality development and social development are so closely related," an educational psychologist concluded in 1950, "that it is difficult, if not impossible to separate them."[36] However, it was mental hygienists who expressed the greatest concern for the potential threat posed by students' personalities. The mental hygiene movement was part of a growing therapeutic ethos among educators that sought to treat pathological mental conditions at the individual and group level.[37] This trend aligned with the systems-based thinking of social scientists who employed school administration to attack broader social, psychological, medical, and moral problems. As American high schools were consolidated following World War II so they could offer more gifted, advanced placement, vocational, and elective course offerings, school counseling and administrative bureaucracies expanded to address and sort these larger populations.[38] Furthermore, as the historian Christopher Lasch has argued, psychologists during this period began to reconceptualize problems that were once considered family and religious matters into psychological and social deficiencies requiring systemic therapeutic intervention. In 1960, approximately 130 million psychological tests were administered to students to screen their psychological well-being.[39] As Lasch wrote: "Therapists, not priests or popular preachers of self-help or models of success like the captains of industry, became [people's] principal allies in the struggle for composure."[40]

Following the lead of Allport and Adorno, mental hygienists correlated good mental health with a well-adjusted personality, and poor mental health with an authoritarian personality. As the educational psychologist George Stevenson put it, "In this contest [between democracy and authoritarianism,] mental hygiene as now conceived is identified more closely with democratic aims." Therefore, Stevenson elaborated, improving the mental health of American students was necessary for the maintenance of democracy in the face of foreign and domestic authoritarianism. "The ultimate test of the principle of democracy lies not in its vulnerability to outside attack," Stevenson noted in 1940, "but in the strength of the individual to withstand aggressions from within himself and his own society."[41]

Postwar cognitive psychologists considered the study of personality to be not only a legitimate area of psychological study, but an indispensable ingredient in the preservation of democratic life itself. Allport stated that scholars of personality sought to rescue the "nexus of individuality" from the impersonal "laws of learning" and "genetic principles" that dominated the field.[42] As Allport explained in 1955, behavioral psychologist such as Watson and Skinner had "imitated the billiard ball model of physics . . . [and] delivered into our hands a psychology of an 'empty organism,' pushed by drives and molded by environmental circumstances." In contrast, cognitive psychology—and studies of personality in particular—accepted that "man possess[ed] a measure of rationality, a portion of freedom, a generic conscience, propriate ideals, and unique values" that were needed for a "theory of democracy."[43]

Although educators took the research on personality very seriously, they were initially less concerned with aligning students with personality-based learning styles than they were with identifying students with personality disorders that could make them susceptible to totalitarianism during the Cold War. Despite Allport's repeated pleas to avoid reducing personality to permanent identities and types—which, he suggested, subsumed individuality into overgeneralized and unfounded categories—psychologists plowed ahead anyway by constructing personality tests that aligned individuals with specific types. One of the most significant and influential postwar personality typologies was constructed by the psychologist Herman Witkin.

Herman Witkin and Perceptual Styles

In the late 1940s, Witkin, a psychologist at Brooklyn College, began studying how human perception might change under certain conditions. He was less interested in which sensory channels were used to collect information than he was in how this information was perceived and processed by the mind once it had been collected. He was particularly interested in how people orient themselves in space. Witkin had heard stories about fighter pilots who flew into a cloud and then exited upside down without any sense that they had reoriented themselves while flying through it. He asked: When determining whether they were upright in relation to the ground, did people depend more on the pull of gravity to orient themselves, or did they rely on their visual field? To study this obscure topic, Witkin and his associates developed a small, tilted room and a chair that could be turned right or left to match the orientation of the room. Participants were asked to determine when they felt upright as the visual field of the room remained in a tilted position as their chair titled left or right. To test this further, Witkin later developed a slightly more complicated apparatus called the rod-and-frame test that consisted of a glowing rod, a glowing frame around the rod, and a movable chair for participants, all of which could be tilted at different angles independent of one another. Participants were asked to make the luminous rod stand upright as the chair and luminous frame tilted right and left, thus throwing the subject, the rod, and surrounding frame out of alignment with one another. Through these experiments, Witkin discovered that people's space orientation differed, but did so in a consistent pattern. Some participants could straighten the rod out in relation to the ground, regardless of the angle of the chair or glowing frame around it. However, others were too fixated on the angle of the glowing frame around the rod to straighten it out in relation to the ground.

To further study perception and its relationship to one's surrounding field, Witkin developed a much cheaper and easier paper-based task called an embedded-figures test. This test asked participants to recognize an image that was embedded inside of another image—for example, participants were asked to identify the image of a three-dimensional rectangle embedded inside a far busier and more complex image of boxes, colors, and lines. Just like his results from the tilted-room and rod-and-frame tests, the embedded-figures test revealed that some participants could find the embedded image easily, whereas others struggled. More significantly, Witkin found that the participants who struggled to separate the orientation of the glowing rod from the glowing frame around it also struggled to find the embedded figures in the busy image. As Witkin explained, "The finding of the significant relationships between performance in the orientation tests and performance in the embedded-figures test helps us define more precisely the nature of the individual differences we had observed." What Witkin and his associates had initially thought were differences in perception and bodily orientation, they now reconceptualized as global differences in the subject's relationship to their surrounding visual field. Based on these findings, he determined that there were two types of people. Field-independent people were "those who showed a capacity to differentiate objects from their backgrounds." Field-dependent subjects were "those whose performance reflected relatively passive submission to the domination of the background, and the inability to keep an item separate from its surroundings." Having established the psychological differences between field-independent and field-dependent individuals, Witkin set out to determine how and when this differentiation occurred, conducting his rod-and-frame and embedded-figures tests on children ages eight to twenty over the course of several years. He discovered that "children's perceptual style tends to be established early in life and remain relatively stable," although there was a slight tendency for maturing children to become more field independent over time. Perplexed by the origins of this psychological differentiation, Witkin speculated that the origins of perceptual styles could possibly be found in the "experimental study of personality."[44]

The scientific study of personality and the Cold War ideology of resisting authoritarian thinking inspired Witkin to study human perception in the late 1940s. He aligned himself with leading cognitive psychologists such as Jean Piaget, Heinz Werner, and Jerome Bruner, all of whom rejected the stimulus-response psychology of behavioral psychologists such as B. F. Skinner and embraced the Gestalt and Freudian traditions of Europe.[45] Specifically, cognitive psychologists considered the ways that preexisting cognitive schema and social context affected the process of learning, thus blurring the line between individual and group consciousness. Both Piaget and Bruner questioned the immutability of intelligence and emphasized the importance of early childhood education on future learning. Furthermore, Piaget and the anthropologist Claude Lévi-Strauss aligned themselves with the "structuralist" movement of the 1960s, which sought to describe mental systems and mechanisms that all humans shared, regardless of culture, content, or context. For Piaget, all humans past and present have developed along a unilinear path through the sensorimotor, preoperational, concrete operational, and formal operational stages. For Lévi-Strauss, all human societies past and present have organized their myths around binary oppositions such as male-female, raw-cooked, and life-death. These structures were not considered contextual, contingent, or relativistic; they were immutable and universal, and they described ongoings systems at work.[46] "Before the 1950s, talk of 'systems' or 'structures' was uncommon," the historian Hunter Heyck has pointed out. "By the 1960s, system and structure and associated words, such as *function* and *process*, were widely used terms."[47] Although Witkin did not draw directly upon these theories, he shared an interest in underlying schemes of mental organization with the structuralists and system-based theorists.

As a cognitive psychologist, Witkin was interested in studying the mental processes and qualitative differences inside the mind, not the environmental reinforcements outside the mind. He had carefully developed his field dependent/independent model of cognitive functioning over a decade and half, and he cautiously publishing his findings in peer-reviewed journals. In addition to these articles, he presented his field dependent/independent framework in the book *Personality through Perception*, published in 1954.[48] However, his model reached a much larger audience, when he presented his later research on development of the cognitive styles in the book *Psychological Differentiation: Studies in Development*. The book was widely reviewed and would be recognized as one of the hundred most-cited books of the 1970s. Based largely on the reception of this groundbreaking book, Witkin would go on to be included on a list of the hundred most-cited social scientists of the twentieth century.[49] So does Witkin's widely read and highly regarded book mark the origins of the learning style idea? Not quite.

Although Witkin discussed the different "cognitive functioning" of field-dependent and field-independent people throughout *Psychological Differentiation*, he did not use the term *learning style* a single time.[50] He also completely ignored the theory and research on sensory channels and VAK-based learning. In fact, he barely addressed learning at all. Although the field dependent/independent model was easy enough for anyone to understand, the contents of the book itself were highly technical, full of statistical charts, and flush with scholarly citations. His audience was other psychologists, not educational professionals. Witkin was a slow and meticulous scholar, which is why his field dependent/independent typology held up to scholarly scrutiny for so long. But this careful approach meant that it would take him an additional decade to even begin to speculate on what the educational implications of his idea might be. By the time he did formally introduce his theory to American educators, others had taken the lead to introduce their own learning style typologies. And the first to do so was the sociologist and educational reformer Frank Riessman.

The Culturally Deprived Child

As a graduate student in the late 1940s, Riessman objected to the way that working-class and poor people were being depicted in sociological studies such as Adorno's *The Authoritarian Personality*. He thought the F-scale assessment that Adorno and his associates used was biased against less-educated subjects and depicted them as more racist and authoritarian than they really were. He thought improved methods could bring about more accurate depictions of the working class, who thought differently—but not worse—than their middle-class counterparts.

Riessman completed his doctorate at Columbia University in 1955 with a dissertation on worker attitudes toward participation and leadership. In the late 1950s, he began collaborating with S. M. Miller on a series of studies that used the Social Perception Test they developed as a substitute for more commonly used assessments such as the F-scale.[51] Based on their findings, Riessman and Miller sought to correct the simplistic depictions of the working class as authoritarian, impulsive, and depraved. Indeed, their depictions of working-class Americans were more affirmative and descriptive, and avoided merely listing the ways that they diverged from middle-class norms. "The America worker today . . . is traditional, 'old fashioned' and somewhat religious," they related in a 1961 article on working-class subculture. "He is stubborn in his ways, concerned with strength and ruggedness, interested in mechanics, materialistic, superstitious, holds an 'eye for an eye' psychology, and is largely uninterested in politics." The working class, they continued, "reads ineffectively, is poorly informed in many areas, if often quite suggestible, although interestingly enough he is frequently suspicious of 'talk' and 'newfangled ideas.' "[52] The stability of these class attributes and their imperviousness to intervention, Riessman and Miller speculated, was what made it so difficult for working-class people to adapt and aspire to the middle-class lifestyle.

Although Reissman and Miller did not cite the work of Oscar Lewis, their perspective mirrored that of Lewis's "culture of poverty" thesis, which had been introduced in 1960. Based on his study of impoverished people in Mexico City, Lewis argued that generational poverty created a self-perpetuating set of pathologies—such as lack of impulse control, chauvinism, sense of resignation, and fatalism—that impoverished people transmitted from generation to generation, making upward mobility very difficult, if not impossible. Similarly, in his pivotal book, *The Other America* (1962), Michael Harrington described poverty in America as "a culture, an institution, a way of life" that "was different from that of the rest of society."[53] The description of the working class by Miller and Riessman was allegedly meant to be an improvement over the negative depictions of their sociological forebears such as Adorno, but it still did not depict them in a particularly positive light, nor did it make them seem any less impulsive, conservative, ignorant, or closed-minded. For these reasons, historians would later group Riessman, Lewis, and Harrington together as purveyors of the "culture of poverty" thesis.

When Miller and Riessman published their article surveying the traits of the working class, Riessman had already completed a draft of his controversial book, *The Culturally Deprived Child*, eventually published in 1962. In this book, he not only first introduced the idea that economically disadvantaged students may have a different learning style, but he also continued to pursue this paradoxical approach of moralistically demanding more respect for lower-income Americans while simultaneously cataloging a list of their shortcomings and negative attributes. According to Riessman, it was the "push from Civil Rights movement" that inspired him to pivot his scholarly focus from working-class White people to urban students of color. As Black leaders such as Martin Luther King Jr. won political and legal victories, they soon shifted their attention to issues of economic and social inequality. To combat these social and economic inequalities, President Lyndon Johnson's Great Society and War on Poverty initiatives funded compensatory educational services such as the Head Start preschool program. The Great Society drew federal funding and research dollars to previously neglected urban areas populated by people of color. "You have the Civil Rights movement demanding that education be changed, and you have the Federal government paying for it," Riessman later explained. "You have in a sense, the pressures of both the negative and the positive." These pressures created "a positive context for change" and rewarded "people working with the disadvantaged" like him.[54] The engagement of urban, Black youth became a central concern for Riessman and other educators looking to bring equitable outcomes to these students. Policymakers designed Head Start and other preferential and compensatory programs to address the perceived cultural deficiencies of poor students to close the achievement gap between White and Black students. However, many of the well-meaning volunteers, workers, and researchers who answered the call to address urban poverty applied middle-class biases to urban youth, which further perpetuated the view that Blacks were culturally deprived or deficient.

It is unclear how or when Riessman came up with the controversial phrase *culturally deprived* that he unfortunately used in his title. He had used the phrase the year before in the endorsement of another book, but upon publication of his book in 1962, he immediately regretted the "bad" title; only a few years later, he would comment: "I think it would be well if the controversy wasn't on the question of whether *The Culturally Deprived Child* is a good title or not. There isn't any, because I don't like the title either."[55] The controversy over the title and its connection to the "culture of poverty" thesis has long overshadowed the fact that this book was the first conspicuous and widely read use of the learning style idea as a potential means increase student achievement. In the book, Riessman also identified poor Appalachian Whites, Puerto Ricans, Mexican Americans, and Indigenous Americans as culturally deprived, yet the examples in the book focused almost exclusively on urban (and particularly male) Black youth, who, he argued, had a different style of learning than White students and teachers. Riessman used the terms *cognitive style*, *type of thinking*, *style of learning*, and *style of thinking* interchangeably. Under the heading "Another Style of Thinking," Riessman asserted: "Deprived children are capable of developing abstract, symbolic thinking. They appear to develop this type of thinking in slower, more direct fashion; that is they require more examples before 'seeing the point.'"[56] Riessman attempted to point to the untapped potential of urban youth and to advocate for addressing their particular learning style, writing:

> The underprivileged child has a cognitive style or way of learning that includes a number of features that have unique creative potential: his skill in non-verbal communication (his is not word bound). His proclivity for persisting along one line (one track creativity), his induction emphasis on many concrete examples, and his colorful free association feeling for metaphor in language, perhaps best seen in his use of slang. These potentialities, indigenous to his cultural heritage, must be fully explored in any program concerned with developing talent among underprivileged groups.[57]

Elsewhere in the book, Riessman decried the "anti-intellectualism and narrow practicality of the deprived," echoing the language he had used to describe the working poor the year before, and demonstrating that he was operating, at least partially, through a deficit lens that emphasized what these students lacked instead of how their behavior merely differed from middle-class norms.[58]

Riessman's book received criticism from both those who rejected his cultural relativism as well as those who thought he had overemphasized the cultural deficiency of urban Black students. As Cynthia Deutsch pointed out, "Riessman's argument on cultural relativism does not take into consideration the increasing industrialization of our society and the consequent greater dependence on verbal communication which lead to a greater need for facility in verbal skills such as reading and writing."[59] Drawing on the literacy research of Martin Deutsch, she insisted that language acquisition was critical to learning and that the urban Black youth had verbal deficits that needed to be corrected, not catered to or celebrated. Dismissing Riessman's relativistic approach to culture as too empathetic and irrational, Kenneth Johnson, an educational consultant for the Los Angeles public schools, likewise identified a learning style of the culturally disadvantaged. However, Johnson was more overt in his deficit language: "The learning style of the culturally disadvantaged is not efficient. . . . It is slow, physical, nonverbal, problem-centered, and concrete-oriented—like the learning style of a young child." Johnson listed further deficits of culturally disadvantaged youth, such as "negative attitude towards intellectual tasks," "inability to recognize adults as information sources," "ineffectiveness to verbal stimuli," "present-oriented," "slowness with intellectual tasks," and "inability to deal with multiple problems."[60] Johnson's assertion that the learning style of the culturally disadvantaged was "like the very young child of any culture or social class" linked his assessment to the largely debunked ethnocentric theory of recapitulation—the idea that the development of the individual retraced the sociological/psychological history of the human race, and that non-White cultures/minds represented earlier childlike stages of White cultures/minds. Anthropologists in the early twentieth century used the theory of recapitulation to justify domination over non-White and premodern cultures that were characterized as childlike, undeveloped, inchoate, and savage.[61] By adopting the "child" metaphor, Johnson unwittingly linked his approach to the hierarchical theory of culture he was trying to challenge. "The term culturally disadvantaged . . . is a relative term," Johnson noted. "The disadvantage materializes when the child leaves his primary cultural group to function in the dominant culture."[62] Thus, according to Johnson, the deficits of the culturally disadvantaged were contingent, not absolute. Nevertheless, Johnson approached Black and Latine students as ontologically less formed than their White counterparts, and he espoused cultural assimilation in lieu of cultural preservation.

On the other end of the spectrum, many challenged Riessman's idea that Black students were culturally deprived in any way. The Black author Ralph Ellison insisted there was "no such thing as a culturally deprived kid." Suggesting that Black students were culturally *different*, not deprived, Ellison argued that poor Black children could draw upon a rich "social fabric" based on "basic ingenuity" that had been overlooked by White educators. He implored educators "to find out what [Black children] have," and asked, "What do they have that is a strength?" He observed that, instead of language deficits, Black children had "great virtuosity with the music, the poetry of words."[63] Citing Ellison, Janet Castro likewise questioned Riessman's assertion that Black students had verbal deficits, and she demonstrated the consistencies in the language patterns of Black youth, which she had studied in her research by using drama and games to access the students' rich linguistic knowledge.[64] The education professors Bernard Mackler and Morsley Giddings also took issue with Riessman's idea that urban Black students were in any way culturally deprived: "Persons whose behaviors and beliefs do not conform to the dominant American cultural patterns, are by no means without a culture. Realizing this central fact has implications education of high importance."[65]

In an article for the *Journal of Negro Education*, Riessman attempted to respond to both critiques of his approach—that he was too dismissive and not dismissive enough of urban Black culture. Carefully replacing the term *culturally deprived* with *economically disadvantaged* and/or *educationally deprived*, Riessman again outlined "the content-centered, not form-centered mental approach" of urban youth and their "physical and visual style in learning." He also listed additional deficits of the educationally deprived, such as "poor auditory attention, poor time perspective, inefficient test-taking skills, and limited reading ability." Thus, Riessman seemed unable to get out of his own way by trying to separate himself from the "culture of poverty" thesis of Lewis and Harrington by repeatedly demanding that educators recognize the positive attributes of Black culture, then repeatedly applying the adjectives of *poor*, *slow*, *inefficient*, and *anti-intellectual* to describe Black students. Would anyone view these traits as positive?[66]

Riessman had introduced the learning style idea cautiously in *The Culturally Deprived Child*. However, a couple of years later, he had somehow become certain that these learning styles existed, and he continued to preach about the potential of learning style idea to teach low-income urban students. In a 1964 article in *Teachers College Record* (with no citations), he again speculated on possible outcomes of identifying and exploiting students' learning styles. He was vague about exactly what the specific learning styles were and how many there might be, but he was nevertheless comfortable enough to align "disadvantaged" children with what he called a "physical style of learning." A student with a physical style of learning, he explained, "learns more slowly; he learns through the physical (that is by doing things, touching things); he learns visually, and he functions in a rather one-track way in that he doesn't shift easily and is not highly flexible in his learning." A physical learner "has to get one's muscles into it, and this takes time."[67] A couple of years later, in an article in the *NEA Journal* (also with no citations), Riessman was even more assertive about the existence of VAK-based learning styles.

Where did Riessman get the idea of learning styles? Since he cited no research or scholarship, it is difficult to determine with certainty. As explained above, the field of special education had been exploring the effectiveness of teaching struggling students to and through different sensory channels (auditory, visual, motor) for decades. Even Allport listed "*visual-kinesthetic-auditory* types" as an example of the personality typologies he opposed, but he did not specify exactly who the psychologists were that supported the idea, beyond "psychologists interested in imagery."[68] To some extent, the VAK learning style typology likely grew seamlessly out of Riessman's research on the characteristics and mentalities of the working class. Like Allport had done during World War II, Riessman contrasted his learning style approach with the behavioral psychology of B. F. Skinner, which Riessman dismissively characterized as "abstract, molecular concepts of learning derived from pigeons and rats" that missed the more "wholistic [*sic*] or global dimensions of learning operative at the phenomenal level." He did not seem to have any awareness of Witkin's work on cognitive styles, nor was he impressed with the research on perception and personality in general. In fact, he pitted his learning style approach directly against research on personality: "When one does borrow from psychology, it may be better to concentrate on learning and cognition rather than personality and motivation."[69]

A decade later, in 1976, the publisher asked Riessman to update *The Culturally Deprived Child*, but he decided to write an entirely new book instead. As he explained in the preface, the "old title was entirely inappropriate" and "so much new material and thinking [had] evolved in the last decade and a half." He called his new book *The Inner-City Child*.[70] As a centerpiece to the book, he reproduced his 1964 *Teachers College Record* article on learning styles nearly word-for-word. In 1976, he also published portions of this chapter on learning styles in the practitioner journal *Today's Education*, in which he cited a couple of studies that had recently been published supporting the learning style idea and how to assess it.[71] However, he again failed to clarify what the specific learning styles were or to explain what research supported the learning style idea when he first introduced it in the 1960s. By the 1970s, Riessman had mostly moved past his interest in teaching inner-city children anyway. No longer convinced that educational interventions alone could alleviate poverty, he helped paraprofessionals unionize, founded the journal *Social Policy*, and researched the possibilities of full employment and self-help as alternatives to education. As the learning style idea continued to spread in the 1970s, it did so largely outside Riessman's purview, and few recognized him as one of the original purveyors of the learning style idea.

Not all scholars who employed the idea of learning styles linked the idea to cultural differences and deficits. Conversely, not all scholars using the cultural deprivation paradigm adopted or discussed the idea of learning style.

For example, one medical school instructor writing in 1964 used the learning style idea to describe students' different study habits.[72] Even other scholars who applied the learning style idea to urban youth, such as Robert Strom, used it in inconsistent ways. As Strom put it in his 1965 book *Teaching in the Slum School*, "Not only is instruction influenced by different types of learning but recent studies suggest that children differ in their preference of learning styles." However, instead of outlining the divergences between middle class and culturally deprived learning styles, Strom pointed to an "authoritarian method of learning" versus a "spontaneous style of learning in which trial and error, experimentation, and idea modification are utilized."[73] Strom suggested that the "authoritarian" and "spontaneous" learning styles cut across class and racial types, thus paving the way for the race-blind learning style inventories that would emerge in the 1970s.

Although Witkin published his first article on his perception tests in 1950, his first peer-reviewed article on the implications of his cognitive style model on teaching and learning did not appear until 1977—over a quarter century later.[74] The article, a coauthored review of the literature on his cognitive style theory, appeared in the *Review of Educational Research*. The article was well received and won an award as the best review article of the year from the prestigious journal. Witkin's late-career pivot toward the educational applications of his idea was likely inspired by his move to Educational Testing Service (ETS) in Princeton, New Jersey, in the early 1970s. His first scholarly foray into education explored the relationship between field dependence/field independence and the selection of academic majors and elective courses at the college level. He discovered that field-independent students tended to gravitate toward math and science majors, whereas field-dependent students tended to prefer the helping majors such as psychology and education.

By the 1970s, Witkin's former graduate students, collaborators, and disciples began applying his cognitive styles theory to a range of educational topics and experiments. By 1972, he was beginning to summarize this work and to issue generalizations about the role of cognitive style on student-teacher relations. For example, several studies found that students who were field dependent preferred teachers who were field dependent and vice versa.[75] These findings added additional evidence to the cultural mismatch theory suggested by Riessman and others about the problem of student learning styles not aligning with teaching styles, although no attempts were made to align entire racial or ethnic groups with a particular learning style. In fact, since the 1950s, Witkin had made careful and qualified generalizations about the different cognitive styles of men and women, but he rarely addressed race or class. Witkin seemed far less interested than Riessman was in the racial and class aspects of learning, and rarely included race as a category of analysis for his field dependent/independent typology (see chapter 3).

One notable exception to Witkin's evasion of race was a 1975 paper he delivered at a conference. In this paper, Witkin cited a 1970 study by Max Rennels published in the *Journal of Negro Education* about the role of teaching style in engaging "disadvantaged urban black children."[76] As Witkin reported, Rennels identified Black students at both extremes of the field dependence/field independence continuum and then taught them with field dependent– and field independent–aligned art methods. Rennels found that "contrary to expectations," the style of learning made little difference for students, because all the students, regardless of cognitive style, learned best through an analytic teaching style—a teaching method Rennels had specifically designed to align with field independence. The analytic art method based on field independence involved having students take multiple photographs of an object and then use the photos to draw a three-dimensional representation of it on their own, whereas the synthetic method based on field dependence involved using step-by-step directions that gradually built up to a three-dimensional drawing. Not only did Rennels's study produce counterintuitive results regarding the efficacy of aligning specific teaching styles to specific learning styles, but it appeared to undermine the validity of cognitive/learning styles altogether. Witkin's 1975 review article clearly served as an early draft of his award-winning article for *Review of Educational Research*.[77] However, for unknown reasons, the published version of the Witkin's award-winning article removed the reference to Rennels's study altogether. Despite its evasion of race, Witkin's review article further pushed his field dependent/independent model into the educational consciousness.

*

The learning style idea emerged from two streams of thought: research on the role of sensory channels in remedial reading instruction and research on personality. The two approaches were not incompatible, but they did not necessarily add up to a comprehensive theory. Some theorists would attempt to merge these two strands with limited success; most pursued either the VAK-based learning style model of Riessman or the global personality typology of Witkin. However, identifying the intellectual roots of the two major learning style approaches does not really answer the broader question of how and why the learning style idea became so appealing to researchers and education during the second half of the twentieth century. To answer that question, one needs to consider a broader transformation in educational thought that occurred in the 1960s.

Looking back from the purview of 1969, the educational researcher James Coleman argued that a fundamental change had taken place in American education over the last decade. Coleman had been the lead author of the widely read 1966 report, *Equality of Educational Opportunity*, so he had been studying the role of educational inputs and outputs for nearly a decade (see chapter 3).[78] For most of American history, Coleman argued, educators had focused on "equality of educational opportunity" by encouraging more students to attend school and to attend for longer. To achieve this goal, he continued, education had been made free, local, religiously and (after 1954) racially integrated, and based on "a common curriculum for all students." However, by the 1960s, equality came to mean "equality of results given different individual inputs," such as race, class, gender, and disability status. As a result, the school's responsibility shifted from "equalizing distribution of [its] quality to the quality of its students' achievements."[79] That is, instead of offering access to a common curriculum and allowing all students—regardless of background—to compete and struggle to master it, the school was now charged with ensuring that *all* students of *all* backgrounds mastered the common curriculum. As President Johnson explained in his famous speech at Howard University in 1965: "We seek . . . not just equality as a right and a theory but equality as a fact and as a result."[80] The new goal was equitable outcomes for all groups, not merely educational access. Whereas disadvantaged, racially oppressed, and learning-disabled students had formerly been dismissed as unprepared or unfit when they did not achieve academic success, under the new equity outlook, these students were expected to achieve academic success at the same level as those students without these challenges and setbacks. This was a radical development, and one that placed enormous pressure on American schools. The learning style idea came to prominence during this shift as American classrooms diversified and schools were faced with the challenge of ensuring success for all students, regardless of background, culture, ability, status, or race. After 1969, the federal government began a national testing regime called the National Assessment of Educational Progress (NAEP) to track national trends in learning. Prior to NAEP, the government collected and reported data on educational inputs only, but after 1969, the focus shifted to educational outputs. Since the results were disaggregated by race, the NAEP results brought further attention to the achievement gap between White students and students of color.

The second major shift took place in educators' view of culture. The anthropological understanding of culture had shifted from a hierarchical outlook that placed all cultures on a universal scale of development (i.e., savage, barbarian, civilized) into a pluralistic outlook that celebrated cultural difference. Rather that treating White and able-bodied approaches as the educational standard and dismissing those that diverged from this standard as deficient, the pluralistic outlook approached these divergences as equally valid. As the philosopher Horace Kallen put it in 1957, cultural pluralism embraced "equality of the unlike, not only of the like or the same."[81] The pluralistic outlook had existed for decades among anthropologists, but as discussed in the next chapter, the civil rights movement further pushed it into the center of the educational discourse. As a result, educators approached struggling students as different, not deficient. "'Equal educational opportunity' may not mean that all learners address the same goals or pursue the same curriculum, the same textbook, the same time blocks, and the same teaching style," one educator explained in his justification for learning styles. "Those learners who comply with the teacher's preferred style may receive favoritism while their counterparts are reprimanded for their individualities."[82] Educators attacked standardized tests and the one-size-fits-all curriculum for sorting all students against a universal norm, and they sought alternative explanations for why some students did not achieve as well as others. The learning style idea emerged from this broader context of trying to ensure success for all students regardless of their race, culture, or disability status. It grew out of a frustration with a public school system that was systemically underserving millions of students with an excessively rigid and standardized approach.

2
Diagnosing Learning Styles

Historians have linked the 1940s and '50s to the ideology of consensus liberalism.[1] Social scientists celebrated the merits of assimilation, adjustment, and conflict resolution, which they aligned with democratic dispositions, and they shunned ideological rigidity, abnormality, and extremism, which they aligned with totalitarian dispositions. The scholarly and educational focus on personality emerged from this context as psychologists constructed assessment instruments to identify dangerous pathologies and/or to find ways to have different personalities work harmoniously. By the 1960s, this consensus outlook began to thaw. New Left leaders celebrated individual self-expression, conflict, and principled disruption as necessary components of a healthy and thriving democracy. As a result, public schools were criticized during the '60s and '70s for their failure to recognize student individuality and diversity, their overreliance on norm-referenced tests, and their inflexible and irrelevant curricula that did not directly address pressing student concerns, such as the Vietnam War, civil rights, and Watergate. New Left critics cast public school's bureaucracy and objectivism as part of the problem rather than part of the solution. The critics demanded a more flexible curriculum, localized control of schools, and alternatives to the one-size-fits-all approach that marginalized millions of children.[2]

In January 1980, *US News and World Report* published a story on a school district in Worthington, Ohio, with a new economic program pedagogical program that recognized student differences. The program, based on a learning style typology called the Learning Style Inventory (LSI), "tailored instruction to the needs of individual students in ways never before possible." The Worthington High School principal who implemented the new program equated the outdated, traditional, one-size-fits-all curriculum of the past to "a doctor who sticks his head into a full waiting room and says 'All of you take two aspirin and come back tomorrow.'" Pushing the medical metaphor even further, the principal considered the traditional approach to teaching as "educational malpractice, because it [didn't] fashion a remedy for a special need." Instead, he argued, an educational approach based on learning styles better recognized and addressed a diverse student population: "We can't head into the 80s teaching only to the kids in the middle." The article quoted further praise for the LSI, including an endorsement by Scott Thomson, executive director of the National Association of Secondary School Principals (NASSP). "The ability to map learning styles is the most promising development in curriculum and instruction in a generation," Thomson exclaimed. "It is the most scientific way we know to individualize classroom education." By invoking *science*, Thomson was not referring to research from the scientific community that supported the learning style idea, because no such research existed. Instead, he was referring to the application of a scientific system for identifying the needs of students and aligning them with the appropriate learning methods. This "scientific way" of sorting students based on learning styles fused the bureaucratic systems thinking of the 1950s with the individualized, humanistic instruction of the 1960s. The article concluded by asserting that the learning style approach could potentially be "the key educational improvement of the decade."[3]

At the center of the LSI was the idea that all students learned primarily through a visual, auditory, or kinesthetic (VAK) modality or sensory channel. As the *US News and World Report* article related, the authors of the LSI found that "between 20 and 30 percent of schoolchildren are auditory. They learn best from what they hear. Another 40 percent are visual and remember those things best that they see or read. The remainder depend heavily on tactile senses and require mobility, physical activity and touching of objects in order to learn."[4] The article implied that the idea of catering learning to the individual's learning style was based on a recent scientific or technological breakthrough. It also implied that the learning style idea was based on rigorous and sound research. However, as demonstrated in the previous chapter, the research on learning channels up to that point was suggestive as best, and there were very few studies in which substitution of one channel for another was rigorously tested. Those studies that did exist on learning channels applied solely to reading instruction and in no way suggested that the VAK-based methods be applied to other subjects. Even the study that assessed Herman Witkin's field dependent/independent typology questioned the efficacy of the approach, because the research found that teaching strategies fostering field independence were superior for *all* students, not just those who were identified with that label. All of this suggests that, despite Scott's assertions to the contrary, the early research on identifying and teaching to learning styles was not promising. Nevertheless, the idea continued to spread, and new learning style typologies continued to proliferate. The general idea that students differed in their learning styles was so intuitive to teachers, and the failures of the one-size-fits-all approach to schooling were so apparent to parents and students, that the idea was enthusiastically expanded and embraced.

The Learning Style Typologies of Kolb and Gregorc

The celebration of difference that accompanied the civil rights movement and emergence of the New Left spilled over to the college curriculum, where demands for relevance and electives by students was largely met. Although Witkin and his peers had conducted some research on how his field dependent/independent typology affected college students, the primary focus of learning style advocates had been on K–12 education. The exception was David A. Kolb.

Kolb earned his doctorate in social psychology from Harvard University in 1964, the same year that Riessman published his article on learning styles in *Teachers College Record* and two years after the publication of Witkin's *Psychological Differentiation*. However, there is no evidence that Kolb was aware of either Riessman's or Witkin's work. Instead, his interest in learning styles emerged from his own experiences in the college classroom. As Kolb was teaching a class on management theory at the Massachusetts Institute of Technology (MIT) as an associate professor in the late 1960s, he was struck by the fact that many of his students learned the material most effectively through his lectures, whereas others learned better through more engaging activities such as class discussions, role playing, and simulations. Fearing that if he accommodated some students who learned one way then he would then be limiting his students who learned in other ways, Kolb decided to try to accommodate all his students through a variety of methods. By 1971, he had developed a formal assessment apparatus called the Learning Style Inventory that scored and sorted his students into one of four categories: diverger, assimilator, converger, or accommodator. "As a result of our hereditary equipment, our particular past life experience, and the demands of our present environment," Kolb explained, "most people develop learning styles that emphasize some learning abilities over others."[5]

Drawing upon the work of the social psychologist Kurt Lewin, Kolb argued that students learn and process information in one of four ways: they either feel the new information through concrete experience, watch the information through reflective observation, think about the information through abstract conceptualization, or interact with the information through active experimentation. Crossing these learning preferences with one another, he established four main kinds of learners: divergers perceived new information concretely and process it reflectively; assimilators perceived new information abstractly and process it reflectively; convergers perceived new information abstractly and process it actively; and accommodators perceived new information concretely and process it actively. He assigned strengths to each one. According to Kolb, the diverger's strength lay in their "imaginative ability," the converger's in their "practical application of ideas," the assimilator's in their "ability to create theoretic models," and the accommodator's "in doing things, in carrying out plans and experiments and involving himself in new experiences."[6]

Kolb's learning style typology built on a broader learning theory he called "experiential learning" that synthesized how people perceive and process new information. In addition to the work of Lewin, Kolb was inspired by the pedagogy of John Dewey's and Jerome Bruner's work on cognitive processing, particularly Bruner's emphasis on the dialectic tension between abstract detachment and concrete involvement. Kolb emphasized that all learners engage in the acts of thinking, feeling, watching, and interacting as part of the learning cycle when they engage in experiential education, but individuals demonstrated strengths in particular areas and so an organization would run more effectively as these strengths were recognized and exploited.

With his background in organizational management, Kolb pursued the application of his typology to the business world. Because professional occupations required that people become lifelong learners, Kolb argued, employers ought to pay more attention to employee learning styles in the workplace. Thus, much like the Myers-Briggs Type Indicator, Kolb's learning style approach was not merely about improving students' classroom experience, but also about labeling, sorting, and aligning individuals with complementary tasks for better cooperation and productivity. "If the organization is thought of as a learning system," Kolb explained in 1976, echoing the structuralist thinking of the previous generation, "then each of the differentiated units that is charged with adapting to the challenges of one segment of the environment can be thought of as having a characteristic learning style that is best suited to meet those environmental demands." Accordingly, Kolb aligned corporate specializations with optimal learning styles. He identified workers in marketing as best having "an accommodative learning style—concrete and active," those in research as "assimilative . . . abstract and reflective, a style fitted to the world of knowledge and ideas," those in personal/labor relations as "divergers, concrete and reflective," those in engineering as "convergent . . . abstract and active, although they should be less abstract than the research group," and those in finance as "convergent . . . given their orientation towards the mathematical task of information-system design."[7] Although Kolb drew upon the postwar tradition of cognitive psychology, he nevertheless seemed to share behaviorists' quest for social engineering, sorting, prediction, and control. He seemed less concerned about reaching underserved students than he was about using the learning style inventory to forge and manage a harmonious organization.

Initially, Kolb did not intend to apply his theory to precollegiate children. However, in 1979, a former teacher working on her doctorate in education, Bernice McCarthy, reached out to Kolb with a plan to develop his framework for wider use. Working with Kolb, she developed the 4MAT system that was also based around four learning styles—divergers, assimilators, convergers, and accommodators. More significantly, she combined Kolb's learning styles with learning characteristics derived from Betty Edwards's recently published book, *Drawing on the Right Side of the Brain*. In this influential book, published in 1979, Edwards argued that schools had placed too much emphasis on analytic thought, at that time believed to be directed by the left side of the brain, but needed to place more emphasis on nonverbal and intuitive thought, directed by the right side of the brain.[8] Today this right brain/left brain theory has largely been debunked, but at the time it seemed plausible and appealed to those who were hoping to reintroduce creativity and arts to the curriculum, which had been marginalized during the Cold War quest for academic rigor via a renewed emphasis on math and science. Furthermore, the right brain/left brain theory provided even more evidence that students learned differently and that teachers ought to recognize and accommodate this fact. McCarthy followed up the publication of the 4MAT system with pedagogical manuals on lesson and unit planning, thus making the learning style available to a much wider educational audience.

Whereas Witkin's learning style theory emerged from his long-standing empirical studies of perception and personality and Riessman's theory emerged from his urgent efforts at improving the educational outcomes of inner-city youth, Kolb's learning style typology developed from his own pedagogical experiences in the college and graduate school classroom and his background in organization management. Yet, broadly speaking, Kolb's learning style theory was inspired by the work of Jerome Bruner, whose pioneering work on cognitive psychology highlighted the importance of process—not just the inputs and outputs—to learning. In this sense, Kolb shared an antagonism to behavioral psychology with Gordon Allport, Frank Riessman, and Witkin because behaviorists treated all minds as more or less the same. Learning style advocates, on the other hand, recognized and celebrated individual differences, an understanding that accorded well with the rights revolutions of the 1960s and '70s that spawned feminism and ethnic studies. Although Kolb was not necessarily a reformer like Riessman, he nevertheless anticipated where education and American culture was headed, and his learning style inventory sought to prepare students of all ages for a diversifying workplace and society.

So did Anthony Gregorc, who independently designed his own popular learning style typology a few years after Kolb. A 1972 an article that appeared in *Psychology Today* caught the eye of Gregorc, who was then assistant superintendent of schools in Skokie, Illinois. The article was called "Four Types of Personalities and Four Ways of Perceiving Time" by Harriet Mann, Miriam Siegler, and Humphrey Osmond. Drawing upon Jung and based on the authors' empirical study of time perception among adults, Mann and her coauthors suggested that people could be sorted into four types of personalities: the feeling, thinking, sensing, and intuitive types. For the feeling type, time was circular, and the emotional past was highly important. For the thinking type, time flowed from the historical past and so continuity and consistency were important. For the sensation type, time was present and so immediate action was needed, and for the intuitive type, the future mattered and what will happen was more significant than what was happening.[9]

At the time, Gregorc was investigating why in-service training seemed to impact the practice of some teachers but not others. When he stumbled upon the article on personality types, he incorporated it into his phenomenological thinking on the experience of working with teachers. "Before we can help teachers and administrators grow professionally, we must consider how they relate to the world, what fits their styles, and what types of behaviors feel correct to them," he wrote in 1975. "This will enable us to select topics and develop approaches that will have personal impact upon them."[10] He relabeled Mann's types as the romantic, the logician, the sensationalist, and the dreamer. Each personality type, Gregorc argued, held different views of reality, knowledge, and teaching, and needed to be accounted for, if in-service teacher training was to be effective. Based on extensive observation and interviews with educators, Gregorc confirmed his hypothesis that "mind sets rise from deeper driving forces" and that "individuals are predisposed to relate best to certain conditions for personal growth and development."[11]

A few years later, then an associate professor of secondary education at the University of Connecticut in Storrs, Gregorc shifted his attention from professional development to teaching and learning in general. His interviews with more than a hundred adults and high school students revealed that "individuals learn with ease when the environment demands, and expectations align with their particular systems of thought."[12] Gregorc abandoned his earlier romantic/logician/sensationalist/dreamer scheme and developed a learning style typology based on four "distinct learning preference patterns or modes": concrete sequential, abstract sequential, abstract random, and concrete random. Concrete sequential learners were those who had a "finely tuned ability to derive information through direct hands-on experiences" and preferred order and logical sequence when learning. Abstract sequential learners were those who had "excellent decoding abilities in the areas of written, verbal, and image symbols" and preferred sequential and rational presentation when learning. Abstract random learners were those who had the "extraordinary ability to sense and interpret 'vibrations,'" and preferred learning in an unstructured manner. Concrete random learners were those who had "an experimental mental attitude and accompanying behavior" and preferred a trial-and-error approach to learning.[13]

Gregorc had finalized his mind styles inventory by the late 1970s, although his Style Delineator would not be published for widespread use until 1982. The Style Delineator asked students to choose two from a set of four terms that best described them. For example, one set included the terms *imaginative/investigative/realistic/analytic*, and another set included the terms *reader/people person/problem solver/planner*. The simple assessment included fourteen sets of these words and a scoring guide at the bottom to determine the participant's mind style type. In the 1970s, Gregorc was active in the NASSP, a group that showed early interest in the learning style idea, before breaking off and forming his own professional development company in the early 1980s. A self-described "educator, researcher, practicing phenomenologist and Western Shaman," Gregorc later spread his mind style theory through fee-based consulting and lecturing.[14] Beyond the initial studies he used to create his Style Delineator, Gregorc never conducted any additional empirical studies to substantiate or support his typology. Nevertheless, due to the simplicity of his assessment tool and its distant connection to the well-known personality categories of Jung and Myers and Briggs, Gregor's learning style typology would continue to gain popularity in subsequent decades.

Rita Dunn and the LSI

By the 1960s, the civil rights and counterculture movements not only encouraged greater educational attention to students of color, but it also inspired educators to rethink many of the basic assumptions of schooling. Particularly, many educators pushed back against the educational bureaucracy that failed to engage students with its one-size-fits-all curriculum or to build on students' innate curiosity. No book depicted the potential of student freedom more than A. S. Neill's *Summerhill*, published in 1960. The popular book described the experimental school Neil had established in England in 1927 that rejected "all discipline, all direction, all suggestion, all moral authority."[15] Furthermore, firsthand accounts of the challenges of teaching inner-city students of color by Herbert Kohl, James Herndon, and Jonathan Kozol published in the late 1960s further endorsed radical new approaches to teaching that freed it from the bureaucratic structures that reinforced racism and curricular irrelevance.[16] To this end, in 1970, Charles Silberman published an extensive study funded by the Carnegie Corporation of New York titled *Crisis in the Classroom: The Remaking of American Education*. Based on years of research, Silberman affirmed empirically that American classrooms had been overrun by bureaucratic structures, an irrelevant curriculum, and shallow, tedious instruction. Looking to the student-centered reforms in the English primary schools for inspiration, Silberman endorsed an "open" curriculum in which students voluntarily engaged in individualized, relevant, meaningful inquiries. As a result, innovative educators pursued free, alternative, and open schools that sought to capitalize on students' innate curiosity and offer them more freedom to pursue their own interests. "The open classroom appears to be generating widespread enthusiasm," one professor of education observed in 1974. "It is rooted in a substantial body of theory about the nature of children and the nature of learning."[17] By the early 1980s, there were more than ten thousand alternative schools in the US, and 80 percent of the nation's largest school districts offered an alternative school option.[18]

Rita Dunn's interest in learning styles emerged from her work in open and alternative education. Dunn was a professor of education at St. John's University in Queens (NY) who specialized in individualized instruction. Her interest in this topic began in 1967, when she directed a new graduate program in New York aimed at developing effective teachers for "educationally disadvantaged students." Dunn and the candidates experimented with dozens of nontraditional teaching methods—such as games, simulations, and small group instruction—affiliated with the open-school concept. During this experiment, Dunn was struck by the fact that "selected methods appeared to be extremely effective with some youngsters but failed to produce anything other than minor gains with others." To address this concern, Dunn reviewed the literature about how students learned differently and identified eighteen areas in which students could potentially diverge from one another in learning patterns. Based on this research, Dunn and her collaborators published the

Learning Style Inventory in 1975, which they declared was the "first comprehensive approach to the assessment of an individual's learning style in grades 3 through 9."[19] The learning style typology was codesigned by Dunn; her husband, Kenneth Dunn, who was principal at a school on Long Island, New York; and Gary E. Price, a professor of counseling at the University of Kansas.

Unlike the typologies of Gregorc, Kolb, and Witkin, Dunn's LSI did not reduce student learning styles to a mere two or four types. Instead, Dunn's LSI was based on a hundred questions in eighteen areas in the domains of environment, emotionality, sociological, and physical needs that she had identified in her literature review. Admitting that the "questions in the instrument" were "highly subjective and relative," Dunn and her coauthors further admitted that their inventory merely assessed how "students prefer to learn, not the skills they use."[20] Thus, Dunn removed her LSI from the burden of testing validity because she was not necessarily making any ontological claims about the existence of learning styles or the ability of the LSI to identify them with precision. Rather, by using the term learning *preference* instead of learning *style* or *type*, she acknowledged that students were the ones deciding what worked best for themselves. And though the LSI was multifaceted, the Dunns suggested that the VAK learning style typology was at the center of it, at least in terms of how students absorbed and processed new information: "Some people tend to remember when they have been exposed to when they are introduced to the material through their auditory (hearing) perception. Others tend to retain most easily when they have seen the information (visual) . . . while a smaller segment of the population appears to absorb or retain most easily when they are involved in kinesthetic learning." The typology also included a fourth sensory channel, tactile, for students who "must be taught tactually (through their sense of touch)."[21]

To support this VAKT typology, the Dunns cited several studies dating back to the early twentieth century that studied the efficacy of different learning channels. However, most of the studies assessed only the visual and auditory channels, and many of these studies found that learning through the visual channel was superior to learning through the auditory one. Thus, the research the Dunns presented was far from an airtight justification for the VAKT typology—these studies recommended a mix of teaching methods or greater emphasis on the use of visuals with *all* students, not just those identified as visual or auditory learners. In addition to this research, the Dunns cited Witkin's *Psychological Differentiation* to support the idea that students learned differently; but the researchers seemed to be unaware of Fernald's kinesthetic method or Riessman's articles on the VAK learning style.

The LSI assessed students' learning style through a questionnaire that asked students to answer "true" or "false" to a series of statements related to environmental stimuli, emotional stimuli, and physical needs. Under "Perceptual Preferences," students were asked to agree or disagree with a series of statements such as: "If I learn something new, I like to learn about it by: a) reading a book b) hearing a record c) hearing a tape d) seeing a filmstrip e) seeing and hearing a movie." Another set of questions asked, "The things I remember best are things: a) my teacher tells me b) someone other than my teacher tells me c) someone shows me d) I learned on trips." Teachers were asked to add up the scores from the four sections to determine the students' learning style profile so that learning activities could be catered their strength. Using the spatial resources of the open classroom, teachers accommodated the specific preferences of each student. The Dunns had implemented learning style–based activities in several area schools, and their 1975 book *Educator's Self-Teaching Guide to Individualized Instruction* included dozens of photographs taken by Kenneth Dunn of students studying in different contexts, areas, and circumstances reflective of the open classroom concept. Despite Rita Dunn's experiences teaching disadvantaged students of color, all the students in the photographs in the *Educator's Self-Teaching Guide* are White.[22]

A 1983 profile in the parenting magazine *Redbook* featured the work of the Dunns at PS 200 in Queens. The school, the journalist related, was housed in a "transient community" that was "working class, comfortable, underprivileged" and included children with names such as "Wei-Jen, Gregaulf, Rajesh, Vadim, Toniqua, and Erwin." The school's principal implemented the Dunns' LSI and their learning style–based curriculum and "open-classroom" concept with great success. The curriculum at PS 200 catered to the temporal, mobility, hemispheric, and social learning preferences of these students, but, according to the journalist, "perceptual strengths" were "probably most important for all" because "some of us learn best visually, some aurally, some tactually—by feeling—some kinesthetically—through whole body activity and real experiences." Although the journalist presented no evidence of improved learning, the students she observed were all engaged and on task as they moved around the room. Highly impressed by what she saw, she encouraged parents to "challenge any facile diagnosis of learning disability or any remedial work that isn't working and find out how the school superintendent and board of education are assimilating new ideas."[23]

Advocates suggested that a conflict of learning styles was at the heart of what was inhibiting the education of students with learning disabilities in the first place. "The 'learning-disabled' may not be disabled, but only unable to align to the teacher's style or environment," Gregorc suggested in 1981, adding more momentum to the student-teacher misalignment theory first introduced by Riessman, but applying it to students with disabilities instead of low-income students or students of color.[24] The *Redbook* feature also highlighted the "astonishing" success of learning style–based instruction for students with learning disabilities. Kenneth Dunn related two examples of how their program helped students with disabilities. In one instance, a struggling student was allowed to wear headphones so he could better concentrate on his schoolwork; in another instance, a dyslexic student who was reversing his letters used water to trace his letters on the chalkboard correctly. As Dunn explained: "Touching, feeling, and doing was what that youngster needed to start him learning."[25] The increasing focus on sensory learning among special educators made the VAKT learning style typology seem plausible, despite the lack of evidence supporting the idea. Overall, the mandate to integrate students with special needs into American classrooms provided additional demand for the learning style idea, as teachers were forced to accommodate these new students in their mainstream classrooms. Dunn even went so far as to suggest that schools could be legally liable if they did not provide a differentiated curriculum for struggling students because school districts in California and New Jersey were currently being sued for educational malpractice for issuing diplomas to students who were barely literate.[26]

Over the next three decades, Rita Dunn worked harder than anyone to spread the VAKT-based learning style idea. She did so in four ways. First, she forged relationships with influential organizations and tapped into existing practitioner networks. Second, she adapted her approach to meet the shifting concerns of teachers, administrators, and schools. Third, she conducted and supervised empirical research in schools documenting the positive effects of her learning style approach. Finally, she defended her LSI against critics and relentlessly pushed the VAKT-oriented learning style typology to meet the rising popularity of that version of the idea.

In 1979, Dunn founded the Center for the Study of Learning and Teaching Styles at St. John's University, began issuing a newsletter on behalf of the center, and cofounded the International Learning Styles Network (ILSN). These efforts benefited from their early affiliation with the National Association of Secondary School Principals (NASSP), a relationship that remained strong until its executive director, the learning style enthusiast Scott Thomson, retired in 1990. Between 1979 and 2010, Dunn supervised dozens of doctoral dissertations at St. John's on learning styles, authored or coauthored hundreds of articles on the topic, and published more than a dozen textbooks related to the learning style idea. By the turn of the twenty-first century, educators had implemented her LSI in Bermuda, Brazil, Canada, Czech Republic, Germany, Honduras, Hungary, Korea, Malaysia, Philippines, Taiwan, and schools in more than thirty US states were part of the learning style network. She helped establish satellite learning style centers at George Mason University in Virginia, University of South Carolina at Aiken, State University of New York at Buffalo, and Tarleton State University in Texas, where additional dissertations were completed using her LSI. Starting in 1993, Dunn began issuing official certifications to "Learning Style Trainers," a credential awarded to eighty educators. She also developed or codeveloped additional learning style inventories specifically for secondary students and reading instruction. Throughout her career, Dunn kept a close watch on how her learning style inventory was being used, and she did her best to ensure that it was being implemented faithfully.[27]

In addition to collaboration with the NASPP, Dunn's learning style advocacy appeared in leading practitioner journals such as the *Phi Delta Kappan* and *Educational Leadership*, the flagship journal of the Association for Supervision and Curriculum Development (ASCD). Although not as rigorous as the journals of the American Educational Research Association (AERA), these journals were nevertheless considered high impact due to their selectivity, the esteem in which they were held by practitioners, and their influence on classroom practice. Dunn's articles in the *Phi Delta Kappan* and *Educational Leadership* often appeared alongside those of learning style skeptics, which allowed these journals to appear neutral, even though the mere inclusion of the learning style idea provided the idea with legitimacy. In general, after the 1980s, the learning style idea continued to be discussed in the high-impact practitioner journals; however, it rarely appeared in the most rigorous peer-reviewed journals in education, such as those of the AERA. Dunn's steady appearances in these journals nevertheless helped push the learning style idea into the educational mainstream. Whereas Dunn was the first educator to incorporate the VAK model into her learning style assessment, it was only one part of a broader eighteen-category scheme. The first learning style assessment based solely and entirely on the VAK model was the Swassing–Barbe Modality Index (SBMI), introduced in 1979.

The Diagnostic/Prescriptive Approach

Raymond Swassing was an associate professor of education at the Ohio State University, and Walter Barbe was an adjunct professor and educational consultant. Together, with Michael Milone Jr., they wrote *Teaching through Modality Strengths: Concepts and Practices* (1979). This book was the first to declare unequivocally that *all* students had a modality strength in either visual, auditory, or kinesthetic learning, and that *all* subjects, not just language arts/literacy, would benefit from a learning style approach: "The three modalities that have the greatest utility in the classroom are the visual, auditory, and kinesthetic. An individual's dominant modality is that channel through which information is processed most efficiently." Barbe and Swassing recognized the pioneering work of Dunn, but they dismissed her LSI because "personal preference is not very reliable, since most individuals are not well-trained observers of their own behavior."[28] That is, they did not think students were conscientious enough to identify their own learning style accurately through a self-administered survey; students needed a trained adult and a valid assessment instrument to identify their learning style for them. In another effort to distinguish their Swassing–Barbe Modality Index (SMBI) from Dunn's LSI, Barbe and Swassing deliberately employed the term *modality strength* instead of *modality preference*. They accompanied their introduction with discussions of the SBMI's reliability and validity with an extensive literature review and the results of a pilot study conducted on six hundred students in a California school district. They had found that roughly 30 percent of students learned best through visual methods, 30 percent learned best through mixed modalities, 25 percent were "auditory," and "the remaining 15 percent [were] kinesthetic."[29] This generally aligned with what Dunn had reported in her research.

In addition to dismissing Dunn's LSI, Barbe and Swassing also criticized Kirk and McCarthy's Illinois Test of Psycholinguistic Abilities and Mills's Learning Methods Test for taking too long to administer to be of any use for teachers. The SBMI, in contrast, required just twenty minutes per pupil. Thus they asserted that their SBMI was simple enough to be administered by a teacher, but rigorous enough to claim scientific accuracy and precision.[30] Administration of the SBMI involved presenting the student with a sequence of shapes and then asking them to reproduce the sequence after seeing it (visual), being told the sequence (auditory), and then feeling the shapes with their eyes closed (kinesthetic). Based on their performance in each modality, the student was assigned a percentage score, and their modality strength was identified. A score-conversion chart was provided in the appendix of the book to help teachers translate the scores into percentages.

The SBMI was innovative in several ways. First, it did not embed the VAK learning style typology into a broader scheme, such as Dunn's eighteen categories, nor did it include the VAK typology as part of a more complicated theory, such as David Kolb's theory of experiential learning or Dunn's individualized instruction. Rather, the VAK typology *was* the entire educational scheme, and it applied to all learners in all domains of learning. "Teaching to modality strengths is a readily understandable concept," the authors noted. "All it entails is that teachers present a lesson in such a way that students can apply their learning strengths to understanding the material." Second, Barbe and Swassing emphasized that educators should be teaching entirely to students' learning strengths, not their deficiencies. Although the idea of teaching to a student's strongest learning channel had been suggested for decades, prior scholars had emphasized the importance of developing the weaker channels as well, or at least using one channel to supplement weaknesses in the others. Barbe and Swassing abandoned this idea altogether. They argued that students should be taught exclusively through their modality strength and that teaching to the weaker modalities might even be counterproductive. Teachers should not teach the entire class through "a multi-sensory approach," they admonished, because such an approach would "be distracting at best, and at worst will actually inhibit learning."[31] Third, the SBMI was designed to be teacher administered. Barbe and Swassing designed the teacher-directed assessment to be more valid than student-centered assessments, and also to be less time consuming than previous VAK-oriented assessment tools. Most significantly, the VAK typology of Barbe and Swassing applied to the teaching and learning of all subjects. Their book included teaching examples of modality-based methods in reading, handwriting, arithmetic, spelling, basic skills, and art. At this point, what little research existed to support the idea of VAK learning modalities was exclusively in the domain of literacy, and most of it was focused on remedial education for students with learning disabilities. So Barbe and Swassing's jump from remedial instruction in literacy to all subject areas was in no way supported by the literature. However, lack of evidence did not stop them from declaring the efficacy of teaching all subjects through modality strengths. Finally, the SMBI initiated the practice of labeling students as either visual, auditory, or kinesthetic learners. Because this instrument allegedly identified a student's biologically determined sensory strength, this strength became a permanent part of the student's identity in the eyes of the teacher.

With multiple learning style instruments and approaches available, many teachers and administrators began to adopt and apply the idea. David Cavanaugh, the principal at Worthington High School, first came across Dunn's Learning Style Inventory in a 1974 article by Dunn in the *Phi Delta Kappan*. After attending a three-day workshop on learning styles, he decided to pilot the LSI in his Ohio school to provide a "reliable and valid diagnostic tool" for students. In 1978, Cavanaugh asked his teachers for volunteers to try the learning style–based pedagogy, which he supported with monthly meetings and official LSI teaching manuals. He even agreed to teach a social studies class himself so he could fully participate in the experiment. After he assessed his volunteer teachers using the LSI to determine their own learning styles, he had them administer the LSI to their students so they could align them with the learning style–appropriate activities through learning contracts. The results were so positive that he expanded the approach to other teachers and students. By the end of the decade, Cavanaugh would become one of the most enthusiastic advocates in the nation for the learning style approach. "Ours is the first schoolwide secondary program to use a diagnostic/prescriptive education by means of learning style identification," Cavanaugh boasted in 1981, "and, to date, we have every reason to believe that we have made a breakthrough in high school instruction."[32]

In addition to being featured in the *US News and World Report* article quoted at the beginning of this chapter, Cavanaugh's work in Worthington was included in an article in learning styles for the *New York Times*. "Most American schools organize their teaching around books, encourage silence, and look askance at the thought of a student dipping into his lunch box while struggling with the multiplication tables," the journalist explained, "But many children, like many adults, retain more of what they hear than what they see and seem to do best in the presence of a record player and a cookie jar." According to the article, "several hundred districts across the country" had begun to offer different learning options to students, although it was unclear how closely these experiments were tied to the learning style assessment tools as opposed to merely including student choice in accordance with the open-classroom educational model. Besides Cavanaugh's, the article included the testimony of just two other local educators who implemented a learning style approach: a principal from PS 220 in Queens and a dean from Baldwin High School on Long Island. Both were near Dunn's St. John's University in New York.

Cavanaugh not only expressed his enthusiasm for the learning style idea in these articles, but he also accused traditional educators as engaging in educational malpractice, and he cast the learning style approach as an educational breakthrough. The *Redbook* article related to parents that the learning style idea was a "pioneering concept that may be the most important thing you'll ever know about your child's education, one that will affect anything and everything he learns for the rest of his life."[33] But what exactly was the state of the science behind the learning style idea in the early 1980s? Did the research really support the learning style idea? Did teaching through a diagnostic/prescriptive approach based on learning styles really lead to increased learning? Two important studies provided divergent answers to this question.

Early Critiques of Learning Styles

Since the origins of the VAK typology in the early twentieth century, researchers continued to explore the efficacy of teaching to students' learning styles. Whereas early studies were hopeful and suggestive, later studies were more skeptical. The first major literature review on the VAK learning style was published in 1978 by Sara Tarver and Margaret Dawson; the authors reviewed ninety studies on the role of VAK modality strength in learning how to read. They provocatively concluded, "[The] validity of the modality strength concept finds strikingly little support; thus practical wisdom [on the existence of learning styles] is not supported by research data." According to their review of the literature on the VAK-based learning style methods in reading, only five of the ninety studies demonstrated increased learning by teaching to the student's learning style strength. "In summary," the authors concluded, "the evidence indicates conclusively that modality preference and method of teaching reading do not interact significantly when we are concerned with actual teaching of reading and measures of reading achievement rather than listening tasks and measures of recall or recognition."[34] In other words, modality preferences showed some effectiveness when it came to recognizing and memorizing words, but this did not translate into increased overall literacy skills. Thus, for most students, reading could not be improved by using teaching methods catered to their learning style. The authors suggested that teachers and researchers invert the learning style model by focusing more on the visual, auditory, and kinesthetic demands of the learning task, rather than identifying the learning style of the student and then trying to align teaching methods to it.

A second significant paper was presented by Lynn Curry of Dalhousie University (Nova Scotia, Canada) at the annual meeting of the AERA in 1983. Although the paper was never published, it was deposited in the Education Resources Information Center (ERIC) database, where it would become one of the most cited studies in the history of the learning style idea. As a professor of medical education, Curry approached the learning style idea from the opposite end of the spectrum than Tarver and Dawson—that of adult learners in the professions. Unlike Tarver and Dawson, Curry did not set out to prove or disprove the existence of learning styles outright, nor did she seek to assess the efficacy of aligning instructional methods to the learning styles of students. In fact, she admitted that "learning style researchers [had] not yet unequivocally established the reality or utility of this concept." Rather, with her study, Curry hoped to impose some order on the "bewildering confusion of definitions surrounding learning style conceptualization." She further hoped to synthesize the twenty-one learning style typologies she had identified into a single conceptual model to make the learning style theory less cumbersome. Accordingly, her list included the VAK-oriented typology of Dunn and the non-VAK-oriented typologies of Gregorc, Kolb, and Witkin, in addition to many others. "Studies in learning styles initially developed as a result of interest in individual differences, . . . [and] enjoyed a continuing popularity during the early 1970s," Curry stated. However, she lamented, "Society and the profession of psychology have become more interested in between-group differences, sexual differences and social class differences." She found this development to be discouraging because it "left the whole field of investigation fragmented and incomplete."[35]

Curry was correct to point out that the proponents of the different learning style typologies made no attempt to collaborate or communicate with one another. In fact, they seemed to be operating on completely different planets. Dunn and Kolb incorporated newer learning theories and concerns such as special education, right brain/left brain, and (later) the theory of multiple intelligences into their typologies. However, few beyond Curry were attempting to reconcile the multiple learning theories with one another. To address this, Curry developed a three-level conceptual model that included instructional-format preference, information processing, and cognitive personality style, which she presented through the visual of three-tiered onion. The instructional-format layer included the VAK-oriented learning preferences of Dunn and others, the information-processing layer included the work of Kolb and others, and the cognitive personality level of the onion included the work of Myers, Briggs, and Witkin. "The constructs at inner layers will be more stable than those at the outer layers," Curry noted. She validated this observation by examining the available data on test/retest correlations. She cautiously asserted the plausibility of her model and suggested that others find additional data to further assess and validate it.[36] Despite these cautions, Curry's framework was interpreted by many as an overall validation of the learning style idea at a moment when the idea was both becoming more popular and undergoing greater scrutiny.

In fact, even those sympathetic to the learning style idea began to express doubts about the instruments being used to diagnose them. In 1981, Leonard Davidman of California Polytechnic State University attacked Dunn's VAK-oriented learning style instrument for its claims of scientific precision. Although Davidman was open to the idea that students may have learning styles, he was disturbed by the inconsistences among the different typologies and their assessment instruments. He specifically objected to Dunn's LSI because it assumed that "human beings possess certain consistent, enduring traits such as IQ or learning style that are difficult to change significantly," whereas other typologies approached learning styles as more malleable and dynamic. He objected to Dunn's assertion that young children could accurately identify their own learning style, and he found many of the questions on the LSI as "open to interpretation" because there were "simply too many ways students can misinterpret, or interpret inventively, questionnaires that seem very clear to adults." Finally, he was troubled by the entire philosophical premise of individualized instruction, which, he insisted, "undermine[d] the greater vision of public education as a vehicle for creating enlightened citizens" because learning style–based instruction prioritized the needs of the individual over the broader needs of the community and group.[37] Barbe and Milone also critiqued Dunn's LSI for asserting that learning styles were fixed and that students could accurately identify their own learning strengths.[38]

Similarly, a brief 1980 entitled "Learning Style Theory: Less Than Meets the Eye," two professors at New York University attacked Kolb's theory and questioned its use in management education. After reexamining Kolb's own data, the critics found that factor analysis offered "weak support for the theory," therefore "the instrument [was] invalid and little empirical evidence currently support[ed] this theory of learning styles."[39] In a lengthy response, Kolb admitted that his learning style assessment was based on self-reporting and that it was not designed to meet the bar of "widely shared doctrine of psychological testing—namely that above all any test must meet statistical criteria of independence and stability." His theory of experiential learning, Kolb rebutted, was specially designed to include the subjectivity of individual learners' preferences as well as "situational variability in response to environmental demands."[40] The ignoring of subjectivity and situational variability were both common critiques of standardized testing in general, and so Kolb's response likely met a sympathetic audience on those points. Nevertheless, his response was not entirely convincing, because if he did not expect his theory to hold up to scientific and statistical verification, then why did he even include data on construct validity in the first place? Kolb and his followers never fully answered this question.

Ultimately, during the 1970s and '80s, the research base that learning style advocates hoped would provide unconditional support for the validity of their methods did not emerge. To the contrary, the recent studies cast doubt on the validity of the learning style idea, and the further proliferation of typologies in the '70s and '80s only added more theoretical and conceptual confusion to the field. There was an irony to the proliferation of learning style typologies. On the one hand, the many independently constructed models provided proof to many that students differed in dozens of significant ways that traditional schooling failed to recognize (e.g., brain hemisphere, learning style, disability status, race); on the other hand, the failure of educators and psychologists to coalesce around one or two learning style models made the validity of each model seem suspect. How could all these typologies be valid?

*

Despite the significant theoretical and empirical problems with the learning style idea, it continued to gain momentum during the 1980s through national coverage in the *New York Times*, *Redbook*, and *US News and World Report*, and more teachers began to adopt the approach. Dunn and Kolb not only spread their learning style programs through textbooks and professional development workshops for classroom teachers and administrators, but they also encouraged graduate students to write their dissertations on the impact of their learning style typologies.[41] Barbe and Swassing, Dunn, and Kolb seemed eager to engage in statistical affirmation of their instruments to assert the scientific rigor of their approaches. However, when peers challenged their statistical validations, they backed off some of their scientific claims, perhaps because they knew that practitioners were not going to be dissuaded by these esoteric statistical critiques anyway. Whereas Witkin was not only willing but eager to engage with peer-reviewed journals and rigorous triangulation to affirm his cognitive styles theory, Barbe and Swassing, Dunn, Gregorc, and Kolb developed their learning style theories relatively quickly and without peer review and experimental design. In fact, these learning style advocates largely pitched their theories directly to teachers and administrators, thereby mostly circumventing the peer-review process. At this point, the reader might ask: If the research behind the learning style idea was so problematic and unpersuasive, why did teachers and administrators adopt it so quickly and enthusiastically?

The historian Jack Schneider offers an answer this question in his book *From the Ivory Tower to the Schoolhouse: How Scholarship Becomes Common Knowledge in Education* (2014).[42] In his study, Schneider explored several educational ideas that successfully moved from educational theory to educational practice, such as the project method and Bloom's Taxonomy of Educational Objectives, and he contrasted these with those that did not catch on, such as Robert Sternberg's triarchic theory of intelligence. Based on his analysis of successful educational ideas, Schneider identified four characteristics of educational research that was widely adopted by practitioners: perceived significance, philosophical compatibility, occupational realism, and transportability. The learning style idea—and particularly the VAK-oriented version of it—had these four characteristics. It had perceived significance because it claimed to explain why some students failed and others succeeded when faced with the same teaching experiences. The learning style theory spread through American classrooms during a time in which many White teachers engaged students of color and students with disabilities for the very first time. The idea not only provided a plausible explanation for the achievement gap in American schools among these student populations, but it also provided an achievable solution for how to better teach them.

The learning style idea also had philosophical compatibility because it aligned with the long-standing preference for student-centered, hands-on learning first introduced during the nineteenth century and the progressive education movement, and then reinforced by the more recent initiatives for free and open education that emerged during the 1960s and '70s. Teachers who were already employing student-centered activities to engage their students were the most likely to adopt the learning style theory, because these teachers only had to make minor adjustments to their teaching to do so. Furthermore, learning style assessment instruments were designed to be teacher friendly, intuitive, and (allegedly) scientific. By recognizing student voice, contextualized variations, and local scoring, the learning style inventories stood in contrast to the cold, distant rigidity of norm-referenced standardized tests, which were already under attack. In further contrast to standardized tests, the learning style assessments classified rather than ranked students, and they also emphasized student differences and strengths instead of their similarities and weaknesses. For these reasons, the learning style idea matched the anti-establishment, anti-bureaucracy, free-education zeitgeist. It represented a critique of the one-size-fits-all approach to schooling that Cavanaugh dismissed as "educational malpractice."[43]

The learning style idea had occupational realism because it confirmed many things that progressive minded teachers had learned through the wisdom of their practice: students learned differently, lecture- and textbook-based instruction was not effective for many students, diversifying instruction better engaged students' attention, approaching the content from a number of different angles helped students better understand the material, and developments in cognitive theory required a new, nonbehaviorist approach to teaching. "We've always done [learning style–based teaching] but never labeled it," one teacher said to the *Chicago Tribune* in 1989. "I have always tried to put enough variety in my lesson to address all modalities."[44] A close reading of the literature on learning styles reveals a split over whether a teacher ought to teach across all the learning styles (e.g., visual, auditory, kinesthetic, mixed) during a single lesson, or whether teachers ought to plan differentiated lessons and activities catered to students' preferred modality. The former—teaching to all the learning styles across a single lesson—required far less time and effort from a teacher than the latter—planning multiple lessons aligned to students' modality strengths—and so most teachers likely implemented the former by simply including more visuals and hands-on activities into their preexisting lessons. In fact, this is the main way teachers implement the VAK-based version of the theory today (e.g., "This picture is for my visual learners out there"). Furthermore, learning style–based instruction in no way disrupted what the historians David Tyack and Larry Cuban call the "grammar of schooling"—a set of familiar, time-proven practices such as "age-grading of students, the division of knowledge into separate subjects, and the self-contained classroom with one teacher."[45] Learning styles could be integrated by individual teachers without disrupting the day-to-day operations of the school or interfering with the decisions of other teachers. Thus, one teacher could fully embrace the learning style idea while the teacher across the hall could completely ignore it, without any direct consequence to either.

Finally, the learning style idea had transportability because it could be implemented easily across subject areas, grades, and age groups. As demonstrated in this chapter, the origins of the VAK-based learning style typology emerged solely from the research on the recall of words in remedial instruction in reading, and this research in no way supported the application of the theory to other subject areas beyond literacy. Yet the simplistic and intuitive nature of the learning style theory allowed it to move freely through the practitioner-based networks because, as Schneider has explained, an educational idea "made of five simple elements . . . is far more likely to move across settings than one made up of fifty."[46] The simplistic and intuitive nature of the learning style idea not only explains why it continued to spread even as the research base supporting the idea became problematic, but it also explains why the VAK-based typology became more popular than Kolb's more complicated experiential learning approach and Witkin's more rigorous field dependent/independent cognitive style approach. The VAK typology was and continues to be most transportable version of the theory. Nevertheless, the next chapter explores the discourse in which Witkin's learning style typology did make its biggest impact—the rise and fall of the idea that Black and Latine students have their own learning style.

3

The Rise and Fall of the Black Learning Style Idea

Frank Riessman was not only the first educator to suggest that teachers could and should align individual students with VAK-based labels, such as visual, auditory, and physical, but he was also the first to introduce a far more dangerous idea: that entire groups of students, such as low-income Black and Latine children, could be aligned with the "physical style of learning" that required hands-on engagement and immediate utility. As explained in chapter 1, prior to Riessman, some researchers had already aligned the motor, kinesthetic, or physical style of learning with students of low IQ. So when Riessman aligned Black and Latine students with the "physical learner" label, he reinforced long-standing stereotypes about the intellectual potential (or lack thereof) of students of color. Riessman meant well, and he later qualified and corrected his ideas. Nevertheless, he offered up a simplistic solution to a complicated issue of cultural conflict in the classroom. During the 1970s and '80s, Black and Latine scholars began to explore the issue of cultural conflict and learning styles themselves.[1] However, they consistently steered clear of the VAK learning style model and "physical style of learning" stereotype suggested by Riessman and others, and instead drew upon the field dependent/independent typology of Witkin to suggest that Black and Latine students learned in qualitatively different ways than how their White teachers taught and administered schools.

To this end, in 1987, the New York State Board of Regents distributed a controversial pamphlet to fifteen thousand educators across the state offering suggestions on how to increase the graduation rates of Black and Latine students. The publication asserted that the high dropout rate of Black children could be attributed in part to the failure of teachers and schools to engage the learning style of these students, which, according to the pamphlet, consisted of "inferential reasoning, rather than deductive or inductive reasoning" and a "tendency to approximate space, number and time, instead of aiming for complete accuracy." To support the Black learning style idea, the pamphlet cited the research of the education professors Asa Hilliard III and Janice Hale. For many who had not been following the emergence of the learning style idea, the suggestion that Black students learned differently from White students was outrageous and offensive. Opponents included the world-renowned Black psychologist Kenneth Clark, who said, "I don't know why the Regents would be part of this idiocy. . . . If [Black] kids are respected and taught, they will learn."[2] In response, the Board of Regents convened a panel of experts to debate whether or not there really was a Black learning style that differed from the learning style of White students, and they issued a nuanced and lengthy report the following year that neither endorsed nor denounced the idea. Although the Board of Regents controversy made the debate over the Black learning style idea conspicuous to politicians and to the public, the idea had been in gestation since the 1960s. This chapter traces the rise and fall of this controversy.

Race and IQ Testing

Two of the most respected postwar studies of race, Gunnar Myrdal's *An American Dilemma* (1944) and Gordon Allport's *The Nature of Prejudice* (1954), prescribed comprehensive approaches to combating racism in the United States that included some form of economic and social reform to improve the circumstances of Black citizens, in addition to eliminating legal segregation and reducing individual prejudice.[3] However, most postwar liberal reformers continued to view racism as a matter of individual personality that could best be remedied through educational interventions and legal reform.[4] Furthermore, some social scientists in the 1950s documented how racism and segregation had damaged Black students' self-esteem.[5] The most noted studies were by Kenneth and Mamie Clark, whose research had demonstrated that Black children preferred to play with White dolls over Black dolls. Based on these findings, the Clarks concluded: "The Negro child accepts as early as six, seven or eight the negative stereotypes about his own group."[6] Kenneth Clark testified during the landmark *Brown v. Board of Education* trial, and Chief Justice Earl Warren cited his work as part of the pivotal 1954 Supreme Court decision that found racial segregation to be unconstitutional. By the 1960s, civil rights leaders, Black Power advocates, and New Left scholars began to attack this individualist approach to racism that justified the *Brown* decision. They searched for alternative solutions to explaining and combating racism that did not begin the with the assumption that Black culture was deficient and that the Black psyche was damaged.

Riessman's attempt to improve the achievement of Black students through pedagogical reforms was imbued with a sense of optimism and urgency that characterized the community-organizing impulses of the New Left in the early 1960s. By the end of the decade, it was clear that many of the educational interventions such as Head Start had failed to close the achievement gap between White students and students of color. Many White policymakers continued to place the onus of failure on Black students, but they disagreed about whether the cause was environmental or hereditary. In other words, they continued to assert that Black student failure was somehow caused by student deficiencies, but they debated whether these deficiencies were innate or learned.

Controversial reports such as Daniel Patrick Moynihan's *The Negro Family*, issued in 1965, and James Coleman's *Equality of Educational Opportunity*, issued the next year, provided more deficit-based evidence that the learned cultural traits of people of color may be the biggest impediment to their success in school, and that their impoverished condition was, in part, the fault of their own cultural attributes. The Moynihan report infamously described the poor Black experience as "a tangle of pathology," and the Coleman report demonstrated statistically that family background, not per-pupil expenditure, was the biggest determinate of success in school, regardless of race.[7] This undermined the efforts of educational reformers who, in the early 1960s, hoped that increased funding for inner-city minoritized youth would help close the achievement gap between Black and White students. Concurrently, neohereditarian scholars such as Arthur Jensen and Richard Herrnstein continued to explore racist explanations for the failure of Black students by arguing that Black people had lower IQs, and that educational interventions could do little to overcome this fact. It was in this context of debates over social policy and critiques of the cultural-deficit approaches to Black students that Riessman's learning style idea took on new relevance in the late 1960s as an alternative to hereditary/innate/damaged psyche explanations for disparities in school achievement among racial groups. Riessman's learning style thesis suggested that the low achievement of Black students was due more to a mismatch between the instruction of White middle-class teachers and the learning style of urban Black students than it was to innate deficiencies in intelligence and/or cognitive potential.

Advocates for the idea that there may be a Black or Latine learning style almost always housed their discussion in a critique of the alleged objectivity of norm-referenced standardized tests that had consistently rated students of color lower than their White peers. The Black learning style idea emerged out of alternative ways of assessing student strengths that went beyond mass-produced, norm-referenced standardized testing. Since minoritized students consistently scored lower than their White peers on standardized assessments, critics attacked the so-called objectivity of these tests as misguided at best or, at worst, as racist and/or culturally biased attempts to systemically deprive minoritized students of a quality education.

Aware of the racist history of intelligence testing, Riessman attacked the continued use of standardized testing in his book *The Inner-City Child*. In a chapter on "The Hidden IQ," Riessman cited several recent research studies demonstrating that IQ scores of Black students could be raised over time with quality interventions, and that IQ tests were culturally biased against inner-city children. "If IQ test scores among Blacks and others can be raised through various devices including coaching, training, changing testers, changing the testing environment, [and] rewording the language of the test," Riessman wrote, "then the immutability and power of the IQ test score is questionable."[8] He proposed catering to the Black learning style idea as an alternative to pouring more money into ineffective social programs such as Head Start, which, even he admitted, was unlikely to solve the problem of struggling Black students.

Herman Witkin also recognized the limitations of IQ testing and how these tests disadvantaged certain students who may have strengths in other areas. He and his coauthors stated how his field dependent/independent typology addressed the "need for a more comprehensive and complex view of intellectual functioning than IQ [provided]."[9] He worried that IQ tests placed too much emphasis on verbal ability and that as a result, too many students were being classified as "retarded" at a young age who may have been able to demonstrate more potential and ability in other cognitive areas. Witkin did not directly address race as factor in the article, nor did he suggest that IQ tests were racially or socioeconomically biased against Black students. In fact, as Witkin explained, his previous studies on cognitive styles had demonstrated that "socieconomic status did not relate to field dependence" and field independence could "develop even under conditions of cultural deprivation." However, in another article published the following year on the cross-cultural application of his cognitive style approach, Witkin inched slightly closer to affirming Riessman's cultural clash thesis: "In cultures such as the American one great emphasis is placed on verbal skills . . . to the relative disregard of other cognitive abilities."[10] This was far from an endorsement of the idea that there may be a Black learning style, but it did provide evidence for the fact that both school structures and standardized testing had biases that may be affecting how Black students performed. Subsequent researchers would further develop the idea that American schools and standardized assessments reflected certain values that were incompatible with how students of color learned and expressed their knowledge. In other words, scholars further explored the idea that there was a cultural mismatch between American schools and its Black and Latine students.

The Stylistic Mismatch Theory

Despite Witkin's hesitancy to apply his theory of cognitive styles to race or cultural conflict, many others were more than willing to apply his typology toward this goal. A major affirmation to the cultural mismatch theory appeared in 1969 when Rosalie Cohen, an anthropologist at the University of Pittsburgh, published a groundbreaking study in *American Anthropologist* on the mismatch between disadvantaged students and the culture of most American schools. Cohen argued that many disadvantaged students tended to have a "relational cognitive style" that approached knowledge and problems holistically, but most school settings and intelligence tests exclusively valued an "analytic cognitive style" that broke knowledge and problems into discrete steps and parts. Cohen's typology aligned somewhat with Witkin's field dependent/independent typology, but unlike Witkin, whose conclusions relied on data from his cognitive assessments such as the embedded-figures test and the rod-and-frame test, Cohen developed her scheme through half a decade of observation of low-income students inside and outside school settings. "Once one has become aware of the stringent analytic requirements for performance in school," Cohen noted, "it is no longer appropriate to speak of 'deprivation,' 'culture difference,' and 'cultural conflict' as synonymous." As Cohen explained, cultural deprivation and cultural difference applied to misalignments in the vocabulary and content knowledge between the child and the curriculum, but cultural conflict involved a "conflicting style of conceptual organization." Although cultural deprivation and cultural difference could be remedied through curriculum revision and individualized intervention, cultural conflict was "an educational problem of some magnitude" because recognizing it involved the complete "abandonment of assumptions that there is a single method of knowing."[11] Cohen did not explore the racial repercussions of her mismatch theory, but she seemed to imply that the epistemological incompatibility between certain students and schools was a more challenging issue than either class or racial conflict because the long-standing analytic expectations and structures of schooling were much harder to reform than the curriculum.

A similar study by Stephen Baratz and Joan Baratz published in *Harvard Educational Review* attacked the ethnocentric assumptions of the Head Start program because it approached Black students through a cultural-deficit lens of "altering the child's home environment, improving his language and cognitive skills and most particularly with changing the patterns of child rearing within the Negro home." The deficit outlook did not understand "Negro behavior as it is, but rather as it deviates from the normative system defied by the white middle class," and dismissed Black culture as "sick, pathological, deviant, or underdeveloped." To refute the deficit approach to Black culture, Baratz and Baratz pointed to research on the consistency of urban Black language and cultural continuities in child rearing carried over from Africa—such as "more body contact," collective parenting practices, and more frequent human interaction during learning—to demonstrate that cultural difference, not deficiency, was the root cause of Black students struggles in school. "The behavior of Negroes is not pathological," Baratz and Baratz wrote, "but can be explained within a coherent, structured, distinct, American-Negro culture which represents a synthesis of African culture in contact with American European culture." Furthermore, they argued that the way that many low-income Black students were taught at home clashed with how learning took place in school. White and Black students who were raised in a middle-class home "perform better in a testing situation—and subsequently in school situation—which requires mainstream behaviors and heuristic styles than do lower class children, who have learned something else." Although the researchers did not explicitly endorse the idea of a Black learning style, they did invite further research in how Black "maternal teaching styles" can be "used to help the child function better in interactions with the mainstream culture." The struggles of Black children, they concluded, were not caused by the "inappropriate educational goals" but rather "inadequate means for meeting these goals."[12]

Another endorsement of the cultural mismatch theory came from the anthropologist Edward T. Hall. Hall had studied under Ralph Linton at Columbia University, whose own entry into the postwar genre of personality studies included *The Cultural Background of Personality*, published in 1945. After graduating with his PhD in 1942, Hall conducted fieldwork on Indigenous cultures. In the 1950s, Hall worked for the US State Department training American workers to understand the unspoken cultural cues of foreign countries. In his books *The Silent Language*, published in 1959, and *The Hidden Dimension*, published in 1966, Hall studied the unspoken language of gestures and nonverbal cues of different cultures. He concluded that some cultures communicate in sophisticated ways through nonverbal cues and spatial recognitions that are missed and/or ignored by middle-class, White culture, which tended to be highly verbal. "People from different cultures not only speak different languages," Hall wrote, "but, what is possibly more important, they inhabit different sensory worlds."[13] Hall included examples of how urban dwellers had drawn upon different spatial cues than those living in suburban and rural areas, suggesting that urban youth had different cognitive/cultural approaches to their lives.

By the late 1960s, Hall began to explore the educational implications of his finding. In a pair of articles in education journals, Hall applied some of his findings to cross-cultural interactions that took place in American classrooms. He was convinced that Black students had a different cultural orientation that affected the way that they learned. "When I started studying black-white encounters in America in detail, I wasn't sure that black culture was significantly different from the dominant white culture on the point of listening behavior," Hall admitted in 1969. "My research ultimately revealed that actually there does exist in black culture a series of responses governing the eyes, the hands, orientation of the body, position of the body and tone of voice . . . [which] are frequently misread by whites and vice versa."[14] He discussed eye contact (or lack thereof) as being interpreted differently in diverse cultures, and how this and other behavioral assumptions led to cultural conflicts between White teachers and their Black students. He pointed out, for example, how White parents expect their children to internalize discipline through self-control, but Black parents do not necessarily expect this internalization because "any responsible adult in the immediate vicinity is expected to correct a black child." In another example, he related how "Mexican American" children were taught not to stand out or draw attention to themselves—a behavior many White teachers interpreted as "lack of interest or lack of motivation."[15] Hall implored educators to overcome their deficit approach to teaching so that the unique cultures of Black and Mexican American students could be appreciated and understood as different instead of pathological or disrespectful.

Although Hall focused on specific interactions, not learning, others speculated on how a teacher's or school's lack of cultural understanding could inhibit the academic success of students who were not from the dominant White culture. Practitioner-based articles published in the 1970s cited Riessman and Cohen as justification for the idea that a Black or culturally disadvantaged learning style could be identified and addressed, particularly in the development of literacy.[16] George Cureton, an education professor at Medgar Evers College of the City University of New York, asked provocatively in 1978, "Is there a black learning style, a learning style especially suited to innercity [*sic*] students?" He answered himself: "I believe there is."[17] More significantly, Manuel Ramírez III, a professor at University of California–Riverside, used a Witkin-inspired test to assess 596 Mexican American and 571 White children in 1973. He found that Mexican American students tended to be more field dependent, whereas White children tended to be more field independent, but American schools tended to value field independence, giving White students a cognitive advantage. "I am hypothesizing that the primary reason for the failure of educational institutions to fulfill the needs of the majority of Mexican Americans," Ramírez proposed, "is that they are not sensitive to the cognitive styles of these people." The following year, Ramírez employed the portable version of Witkin's rod-and-frame test to assess 180 Black, White, and Mexican American subjects at a Catholic school in Houston, Texas. The findings confirmed his hypothesis: Mexican American and Black students were more field dependent, whereas White students were more field independent. "The data obtained in this study indicate that the cognitive style of most educational institutions is not consonant with that of most Mexican-American and Black children," Ramírez concluded. "This lack of consonance may be contributing to the failure which members of these groups experience in school." Ramírez postulated that the reason Mexican American and Black students tended to be more field dependent—or "field sensitive," as he called it—was because they placed more value on the thoughts and relationships of their family, whereas White students valued independence and initiative.[18] Similar international studies using Witkin's embedded-figures and rod-and-frame tests found cognitive/cultural divergences between different racial and cultural groups, such as between the Temne and the Mende peoples in Sierra Leone, Africa, between the Temne and the Inuit in Alaska, between assimilated and unassimilated Jews in France, and between Orthodox Jews and Anglo-Americans in the US.

Despite this growing momentum for the idea of race- and ethnicity-based learning styles, it was still a marginal idea up until the 1980s. However, this would soon change. The most significant and influential study making the case that Black students learned differently than White students was a 140-page white paper authored by Asa G. Hilliard III, the dean of the College of Education at San Francisco State University, published in 1976.

Afro-American Behavioral Style

Hilliard was born in Texas, but he received his bachelor's (1955), master's (1961), and doctorate in educational counseling (1963) from the University of Denver in Colorado. Hilliard's father and grandfather had been school principals, and so he followed in their footsteps by entering educational administration at San Francisco State University, first as department chairman and then as dean. He had close ties with Africa, where he served as a consultant for the Peace Corps and as superintendent of schools in Monrovia, Liberia. He was also a founding member of the Association for the Study of Classical African Civilizations. Thus, in addition to being an educational leader, Hilliard was a key figure in the Afrocentric curriculum movement that emerged out of the civil rights and Black Power movements of the 1960s.

In 1974, the California State Department of Education awarded a grant to Hilliard to explore better ways than IQ tests to identify "gifted minority students." As Hilliard began to review the literature, he identified a problem "when it came to the assessment of different cultural populations which could not be solved simply by changing from a standard IQ test to a standard check list or observational scheme for looking at children of color." The research demonstrated that the cultural context of the testing affected the student's score as much as the contents of the test itself. Because the cultural context of the tests aligned with the behavioral style of middle-class White America, the context and style of IQ tests put minority students at a disadvantage. Drawing upon the work of Witkin and of Cohen, as well as his own personal experiences as a Black man and his expertise in Black history, Hilliard used the Black cultural experience as an example of how understanding the "Afro-American" background could be used to better assess gifted Black students that moved beyond standardized testing. Although he focused on Black people, he hoped that "the general approach" he outlined in the report could be used as a model to be "applied to any cultural group."[19]

Hilliard and his team of consultants assumed from the outset that any "assessment of human behavior" could be understood only "by the explication of the specific manifestations of behavior within in that cultural context."[20] Drawing upon research in history, psychology, anthropology, and education, Hilliard proposed that all individuals could be aligned with one of two major behavioral styles: an "atomistic-objective style" or a "synthetic-personal style." Individuals with an atomistic-objective style approached a learning experience by breaking it down into "components which can be understood" by feeling "himself or herself to be separate from the phenomenon being observed," and valuing "permanence, regularity, predictability, uniformity, and environmental control." Individuals with a synthetic-personal style, on the other hand, approached experience by perceiving themselves as "an integral part of the phenomena which are being observed" and valued "divergent experimentation, expression, improvisation, and harmonious interaction with the environment." As he explained, these behavioral styles aligned roughly with Witkin's field-independent and field-dependent cognitive styles and with Cohen's analytic and relational cognitive styles, respectively. "It should be obvious that a stylistic bias is inherent in most standardized tests of achievement," Hilliard commented. "In fact, it is the very standardization which tends to favor analytic . . . or atomistic-objective style users." For this reason, Black students, who tended to have a synthetic-relational behavioral style, were scoring lower on norm-referenced standardized tests because these tests reflected an atomistic-objective behavioral style of White, middle-class culture. The preoccupation with particulars, Hilliard argued, not only permeated schools, but was "the predominant pattern for mainstream America" that missed the "sense of the whole" that Black people tended to appreciate due to their synthetic-personal style of behavior.[21]

Hilliard demonstrated how the synthetic-relational behavioral style of Black culture could be seen in the Black approach not only to education, but also in the Black approach to language, religion, music, and humor, and he provided many examples of how the Black cultural style manifested itself in these areas. Whereas a decade earlier Harrington, Moynihan, and Riessman had notoriously listed a set of negative traits that allegedly characterized culturally deprived Black students, Hilliard concluded his study of the Black behavioral style by listing a set of positive attributes of Black culture that should be appreciated: "Afro-American people tend to prefer a focus on people and their activities rather than things[;] Afro-American people tend to lean towards altruism, a concern for one's fellow man." Regarding the Black approach to learning, Hilliard explained in a section later quoted by the New York Board of Regents pamphlet, Afro-American people tended to prefer "inferential reasoning to deductive or inductive," had an "impatience with unnecessary specifics," and tended "not to be 'word' dependent." Since these traits could not be tested on IQ tests, Hilliard concluded that mass-produced norm-referenced standardized tests could "function only by doing violence to the truth."[22] Hilliard made suggestions for more holistic ways to identify gifted Black students and included some examples that had been piloted in San Francisco.

The clarity, length, and analytic sophistication of Hilliard's study made its publication in 1976 a pivotal moment in the history of the Black learning style idea and cultural mismatch theory. However, what this 140-page report did *not* say was as important as what it did say. First, Hilliard described Black culture without any reference to cultural, social, or economic depravity or deprivation whatsoever. In stark contrast to the work of Moynihan and Riessman, the Afro-American experience he depicted was far more of a celebration than a lament. Hilliard depicted the synthetic-relational behavioral approach of Black people so positively that the atomistic-objective style of White people came off as cold, lifeless, and dull in contrast. Second, Hilliard made no mention of the VAK learning style model. It is unclear whether he ignored the work of other learning style theorists on purpose or whether he was simply unaware of them. Either way, he did not entertain the idea, suggested by Riessman and others, that Black students were inclined to be "kinesthetic," "motor," or "physical" learners. On the contrary, Hilliard argued that art, language, and music were central to the Black experience, thus underscoring the role of the visual and auditory channels to the Black experience and Black student learning. Finally, Hilliard was careful to call his classification system "behavioral" and/or "cultural" styles, not "learning" styles. In fact, he completely avoided using the term *Black learning style*. In his emphasis on behavior and culture, he was sure to underscore the importance of environment and interaction on learning and was careful not to classify what was inside the heads of students. By using contingent language such as *tend to* and *may*, he avoided labeling the entire race with a particular style in absolutist terms.

However, a few years later, his peer and collaborator Janice Hale would further develop that idea that there was, in fact, a Black learning style. Hale, a professor of early childhood education at Cleveland State University, published *Black Children: Their Roots, Culture, and Learning Styles* in 1982. Hale had been a consultant on Hilliard's study. Her book opened with a foreword by Hilliard in which he confirmed that "abundance data show that culture patterns influence the way information is perceived, organized, processed, and utilized." Drawing upon some of the same research as Hilliard (especially Cohen), Hale's book made a compelling case for cultural clash being at the heart of Black students' struggles in school. However, she extended this previous work of Cohen and Hilliard, and Edward Hall by arguing that Black American culture, particularly its child-rearing practices, were cultural retentions from their historical roots in West Africa: "If the cultural orientation of the Afro-American home and community is different from that of the public schools, [then] educators need to understand this orientation and its relationship to the school performance of Black children." Hale noted that Black children had "distinctive learning and expressive styles," and she predicted that "improvement in school performance would occur" if the curriculum and environment aligned better with the "particular learning styles and cultural background of the students." Whereas Hilliard had limited his discussion to assessment practices, Hale extended the cultural mismatch theory to the entire curriculum and school experience.

Clearly, Hale was more comfortable using the term *learning style* than Hilliard was, and she was also more specific in issuing pedagogical recommendations. For example, she suggested that teachers of Black children needed to be sensitive to students' nonverbal cues, allow more time for students to talk, employ small-group learning, and incorporate more movement, games, and music into lessons. Teachers, she continued, needed to include "an accurate historical and political analysis of the situation of Black people in America and the world."[23] She even commended the creation of alternative Black-only schools and recommended that Black students be taught by Black teachers. When this book was published, Hale was directing a Black preschool outside Cleveland in which students were placed in groups named after African tribes, taught by multiple teachers, and allowed space to move and roam. Furthermore, she replaced American holidays such as Thanksgiving and Independence Day with celebrations of the Emancipation Proclamation and Family Day. As Hale told a reporter, "We don't dress Black children up in Pilgrim hats and tell them those were their ancestors."[24] Hale's school and the recommendations made in *Black Children* supported the emerging Afrocentric curriculum model that contradicted the integrationist impulses of the previous generation of Black educators, such as the psychologist Kenneth Clark.

Both Hilliard and Hale synthesized dozens of studies in history, psychology, anthropology, and education to support their cultural clash thesis. Both drew heavily upon the cognitive style typologies of Witkin and Cohen, and the cultural mismatch theories of Baratz and Baratz and Hall. However, neither Hilliard nor Hale recommended that individual Black students be assessed for whether they actually had a Black learning style. In other words, both scholars were interested in creating a cultural context and employing teaching methods that that were more inviting to Black students, but they were not interested in constructing a learning style assessment instrument or inventory, such as those created by Witkin, Gregorc, Kolb, Dunn, or Barbe and Swassing. Thus, they framed the term *learning style* as something that was culturally acquired as part of a group, not as an individual cognitive or modality strength. Hilliard later explained: "I fully recognized that efforts to attribute precise cultural identities to individuals are certain to be fraught with error. Thus, I focused on central tendencies within groups."[25]

Since Witkin passed away in 1979, the influential psychologist never got to weigh in on whether he thought aligning entire races with one cognitive style was a valid application of his typology. As mentioned in chapter 1, a 1970 study by Max Rennels employing Witkin's typology found that aligning specific analytic or synthetic methods with students identified with having those learning styles was not effective for the twenty-six disadvantaged Black eighth-grade students in the study. To the contrary, Rennels's study demonstrated the overall "superiority of analytic method over the synthetic method" for all the Black students.[26] Another study, with eighteen Black and eighteen White college students, also found that race had no impact on whether an individual was field dependent or independent, and an additional study with Black and Italian Americans found there was "no primary causal relationship between field dependency and ethnicity."[27] However, these researchers pointed to previous studies showing a more pronounced racial divergence for younger students. So, by the early 1980s, the empirical research seemed to confirm that there was a racial basis for whether one was more likely to be field dependent or field independent, but that this distinction became less significant as students grew older, and perhaps disappeared altogether by the time they reached young adulthood.

What about the VAK model? Did the other learning style typologies recognize racial differences among students with visual, auditory, and kinesthetic learning styles? The VAK-based pilot study conducted by Walter Barbe and Raymond Swassing in the unnamed Southern California school district in their book *Teaching through Modality Strengths* included Black and Latine students in the sample. As the authors explained, the "proportion of white to black students approximated the national ratio," but 30 percent of the six hundred students in the sample were Hispanic. Despite their concern that "this large number of Hispanic students would bias the results," Barbe and Swassing noted that there was "no discrepancy in the scores of these students."[28] Rita Dunn repeatedly reported on the ability of her VAK-oriented Learning Style Inventory to raise the achievement of struggling students, many of whom were Black and Latine. However, she seemed unsure about whether specific learning styles aligned with different racial or ethnic groups. In the 1970s, she aligned economically disadvantaged students with the kinesthetic learning style, but in a coauthored article published in 1990, she suggested that "Euro-Americans may be more analytic than Afro-Americans." However, that same year, when Dunn and coauthor Shirley Griggs reviewed the literature on race and learning styles, they concluded that "individual rather than group characteristics must be addressed when providing instruction—regardless of cultural and racial background."[29] Thus, the VAK typology appeared to be race neutral; or, at least, race was less significant than the learning style of the individual. This contradicted Dunn's earlier assertion that disadvantaged children tended to be kinesthetic learners (see chapter 5), and it also clashed with learning style research that drew upon Witkin's work that demonstrated learning style differences among racial and ethnic groups.

By the 1980s, there appeared to be a growing consensus that culture—or more importantly, cultural interaction and cultural context—mattered more than individual learning style differences when it came to teaching Black students. A 1982 article by Barbara Shade in the prestigious journal *Review of Educational Research* considered the question of whether "Afro-American cognitive style" was "a variable in school success." Shade concluded that, although the research could not definitively establish a causal link between culture and learning, the idea that a Black student learning style clashed with school culture was certainly plausible and even likely. Shade explained how "successful functioning within the current school context required the cognitive strategies that are described as sequential, analytic and object-oriented." However, the "world view of Afro-Americans" reflected "strategies designed to foster survival and therefore [tended] to be rather universalistic, intuitive, and, more than that, very person-oriented." Based on these two findings, she "postulated that an enhanced ability in social cognition may work to the detriment of individuals within an object-oriented setting such as the school."[30] In other words, American schools had a culture that was structured, individualistic, and depersonalized, but Black students came from a culture that valued the opposite attributes.

This thesis, however, Shade added, required "strong and methodologically rigid empirical studies" to validate it with certainty. However, before the cultural mismatch thesis could be empirically proven or disproven, the work of Hilliard and of Hale was quoted as evidence that there was a Black learning style in the controversial New York Board of Regents pamphlet.

The Black Learning Style Controversy

By the late 1980s, the idea that Black and White students learned differently had become accepted by many educational scholars, and there was substantial research in some of the top journals in the field of education, such as the *Harvard Educational Review* and *Review of Educational Research*, to support the idea. However, the concept proved to be more controversial among politicians and the older generation of educators who had fought hard for inclusive, colorblind schools and were hesitant to abandon this paradigm by explicitly taking race into account. This split was demonstrated by the controversy that erupted over the booklet issued by the New York State Board of Regents in 1987 stating that "children's racial, ethnic, and emotional backgrounds and cultures influence the manner in which they learn concepts and process information."[31]

The backlash to the pamphlet was immediate and cut across racial lines. Cynthia Jenkins, a Black assemblywomen from Queens, rejected the idea that Black students learned differently, and she demanded that the booklet be recalled. "God didn't give brains on the basis of color," she noted, "What are you going to tell teachers that have Asian, Black, White and Hispanic kids—that they are going to have four different lesson plans?" Another critic, Louis

Grumet, executive director of New York State School Boards Association, asserted that recognizing a Black learning style "leads to stereotyping of the worst degree. It's a very short step to separate classes, which goes back to the 1954 court case—Brown v. the Board of Education. I just can't believe this discussion is being held in New York State in 1988." Many professors of education were also skeptical of the idea but were more measured in their responses. Robert Koff, dean of education at the State University of New York at Albany, did not deny that there were cultural differences between White teachers and their Black and Latine urban students, but he did not believe that these differences were great enough to warrant specific lesson plans for specific cultural groups. As he explained, things like providing quality pre-K instruction, recruiting more Black and Latine teachers, and general improvements to pedagogy were likely to make a bigger difference "in the long run than style . . . primarily because we talk about style, we don't know what its practical applications are." Kenneth Clark was so appalled by the suggestion that there might be a Black learning style that he refused to participate in the panel of experts selected to review the pamphlet.[32]

Described as "the quintessential integrationist" by one historian, Clark's research was cited by Supreme Court Justice Earl Warren in the pivotal *Brown v. Board of Education* decision of 1954 that overturned *Plessy v. Ferguson* and declared racial segregation to be unconstitutional.[33] Based on interviews of Black children discussing White and Black dolls, Clark found that the Black children preferred the White dolls, which Clark interpreted as "a consequence of being almost universally regarded as inferior."[34] He argued that the only remedy for overcoming this sense of inferiority was to intermingle with White students in American schools. Due to his role in the *Brown* case, Clark was the most famous Black psychologist in the nation. The battle of racial integration was long, bitter, and still ongoing when the Black learning style idea emerged in the 1970s.[35] In the midst of this debate, Clark published the book *Dark Ghetto* in 1975, in which he reiterated his support for racial integration. Clark was circumspect about the reality of education in urban areas, which, due to residential segregation, consisted almost entirely of students of color. Yet even under these circumstances, Clark insisted, Black students could still get a good education if teachers pushed them harder, and he agreed with Riessman, Hilliard, and Hale that having high expectations for Black students was critical to their success. However, Clark dismissed the Black learning style idea because its advocates suggested that "children from working class cultures . . . need not only a different approach to the educational process, but a different type of education from that provided for children from middle-class families." The thinking behind the Black learning style idea, Clark wrote, had "led to a great deal of confusion, misunderstanding, and injustice." Clark concluded that the biggest issue facing Black students was not the style of teaching being used, it was the dismissive attitude of White teachers toward Black students: "To assume that Negro children are inherently inferior or that environmental inferiority is responsible for poor school performance is educationally irrelevant—and even false." All Black students really needed to succeed, he pointed out, were "competent teachers who have confidence in children to achieve."[36] To Clark, the Black learning style idea was yet another environmental explanation used to deny a rigorous academic curriculum to Black students. For this reason, he opposed it.

Others were less disturbed than Clark by the idea that culture played into learning, but nevertheless agreed that the Black learning style idea was dangerous. "Race and ethnicity are only small part of the learning picture," said Ira Blake of Teachers College, Columbia University. "All children learn in the same manner, but they individually bring patterns to the learning process that are continually influenced by different factors in the environment." Even Leon Moore, director of an all-Black private school in Newark, New Jersey, rejected the notion that "children, be they black or white, learn differently." Moore supported the idea of an Afrocentric curriculum as a tool for engaging and exciting his Black students, but he balked at the idea that race had anything to do with how they absorbed and processed new information. He stated, "Every child may not be capable of achieving the same academic level but we as educators are supposed to get the highest level of achievement out of every one of them." There was no indication that any of these critics had read the research of Baratz and Baratz, Shade, Hilliard, or Hale, nor were they familiar with the cognitive theories of Witkin and Cohen. But, when confronted by a journalist with the idea of a Black learning style, most reacted with skepticism or outrage.[37]

To address the controversy over the pamphlet, the New York Board of Regents appointed a Black psychologist, Edmund W. Gordon of Yale University, to chair a panel to study the literature on learning styles. Gordon's panel issued their final report in 1988 along with a set of position papers by Hilliard, Dunn, and others. According to Hale, "No meaningful effort was made to solicit [her] participation," and the panel was appointed solely to "extract the passage [on the Black learning style] from the handbook, not examine the dropout rate and reduce it."[38] Despite this alleged predetermined antagonism toward the Black learning style idea, the panel stood by the general recommendations made in the pamphlet but admitted that the authors of the pamphlet should have done a better job of explaining that learning style differences across racial and ethnic groups should not be applied to individual students from each group. The pamphlet also should have done a better job of distinguishing learning styles from cognitive/behavioral styles; the latter terms would have been more appropriate and less controversial. Even though Gordon and his coauthors confirmed that the research supported the idea of learning preferences in general, their review of the literature on the Black and Latine learning style idea revealed a greater degree of skepticism: "To-date most of the literature on cultural styles generated from research on the African-American and Latino-American cultures has been inconclusive and conclusions are speculative." Gordon also recognized that the "wisdom of practice" and "intuitive support for the paradigm" provided additional momentum for the learning style idea, even though there was "little support in the accumulated studies of efforts at matching learner traits and instructional practices."[39]

In the face of the growing controversy around the Black learning style idea, Hilliard and Hale defended the approach. Hale pointed to the more than two hundred independent Black schools around the country and their ability to achieve better test scores for Black students than integrated and White-majority schools. She also pointed to the basketball star Michael Jordon and the comedian Eddie Murphy as examples of Black citizens who had made "distinct contributions to American culture but would have been a kindergarten teacher's worse nightmare" because their behavior would not have conformed to White standards of school. Hilliard, who had moved to Georgia State University as an endowed professor of urban education, recognized the underlying fear among skeptics of the Black learning style idea: "Everybody gets frightened if you acknowledge style, because they think they know what follows, after you acknowledge it. They think that what you mean is that you're not going to teach the black kid to count. You're not going to teach him English." He assured his critics that this was nonsense, and implored educators to "treat the stylistic mismatch between some students and schools as a student deficiency or problem requiring the student to change."[40]

Hilliard addressed the controversy more fully in a 1992 essay for the *Journal of Negro Education*. Although he still supported the idea that there was a Black cultural and behavioral style, he was less certain than Hale was that there were clear pedagogical implications for this. The main takeaway of his research, he explained, was that Black students should not be dismissed simply because they did not score highly on standardized assessments. "It is not the learning style of the child that prevents the child from learning," Hilliard asserted, "it is the perception by the teacher of the child's style as a sign of incapacity that causes the teacher to reduce the quality of instruction offered." Hilliard pointed the willingness of the business community to recognize different cultural styles and suggested that educators lagged the corporate world in that respect. Ultimately, Hilliard leveraged his Black behavioral style idea into a critique of the entire American educational system. "Unfortunately, educationalists tend to treat the stylistic mismatch between some students and schools as a student deficiency, that is, as a problem that requires students to change," he wrote. "As a result, . . . we fail to see that the traditional school style has severe limitations."[41]

Around the time of the New York Board of Regents controversy, two leading Black educators, James A. Banks and James A. Anderson, independently weighed in on the Black learning style debate. In an article for the *Journal of Negro Education*, Banks framed his discussion of the Black learning style idea around a controversial question that emerged in the wake of the publication of William J. Wilson's *The Declining Significance of Race* (1978). Banks asked: Which was a more significant variable in school success, class or race? He concluded that, despite the evidence in Wilson's book, race was still a more significant factor than class. In his review, he included a section on cognitive styles in which he reviewed the work of Witkin, Cohen, Ramírez, Hale, and Hilliard. "Collectively the studies reviewed in this article provide more support for the cultural difference than the social-class hypothesis," Banks noted. "They indicate that ethnicity continues to have a significant influence on the learning behavior and styles of Afro-American and Mexican American students, even when these students are middle class." Although there was much more research to be done, Banks nevertheless speculated on why race may be more of a factor than class. Although most middle-class White families lived in middle-class communities and had middle-class family and friends, Banks explained, this was not the case for many middle-class Black families, who still had ties to family and friends living in lower-class areas and circumstances. "The middle-class Black family is often a first-generation middle-class family that exists within an extended family and community network that have definitive group expectations for it and strongly influence its behavior and options," Banks hypothesized. He suggested that researchers examine "generational middle-class status" to further study this phenomenon. Finally, in a section in "Implications for Practice," Banks suggested that, because "Afro-American and Mexican American students tend to be more field sensitive in their learning styles than are mainstream Anglo-American students," teachers should motivate students of color with "curriculum content that is presented in a humanized or story format," and he implored teachers to "vary their teaching styles so as to appeal to a diverse student population."[42] This would serve as a foundational understanding of multicultural education, and, over the next two decades, Banks would be its most influential and popular theorist.

Anderson provided a more extensive review of the literature of culture-based learning styles and likewise endorsed the idea. Drawing upon the research of Cohen, Witkin, and Ramírez, and many others, Anderson presented five tables of characteristics that he attributed to Western and non-Western worldviews. Westerners, for example, tended to "emphasize individual competition," "perceive elements as discrete from their background," "use hierarchical modes of classification" and prefer "theoretical statements." Non-Westerners tended to "emphasize group cooperation," "perceive elements as part of a total picture," "use relational and institutional classification," and prefer "visual" forms of representation. According to Anderson, the Western group included "Euro-Americans (primarily males)" and "minorities with a high degree of acculturation," and the non-Western group included American Indians, Mexican Americans, African Americans, Vietnamese Americans, Puerto Rican Americans, Chinese Americans, Japanese Americans, and "many Euro-American females." Published in the *Journal of Teacher Education*, Anderson's article was directed at the teachers of teachers, and he implored them to recognize the role of cultural conflict in the classroom and to do a better job of preparing teachers to accommodate the different world views, language patterns, and cognitive styles of the diversifying student population. "A different set of understandings about the way diverse populations communicate, behave, and think needs to be developed by educators," Anderson wrote. "Until this occurs, education will continue to stagnate in the dark ages and educators will provide lip service rather than action to the egalitarian values associated with pluralism and multi-culturalism."[43] Neither Banks nor Anderson could have been aware of that fact that 1988 marked the peak year of racial integration in American schools. This year was also the time in which the achievement gap between White and Black students would be at its narrowest point. In the decades that followed, residential segregation and the defunding of many social and remedial programs for low-income students would slowly reverse these hard-fought gains and the achievement gap between White and Black students would once again widen.[44]

What emerged from the controversy over the Black learning style idea was a growing recognition that, as the American school population continued to diversify, the American classroom was becoming a major location for cultural interaction. All ethnic and cultural groups had certain behaviors that could be misinterpreted by teachers, and educators could no longer expect all their students to assimilate seamlessly into the presiding White culture of the school. In other words, the Black learning style did not disappear so much as it served as a foundation for additional inquiries into the ways that race, culture, and ethnicity affect classroom interactions. Research into the role of race and ethnicity would continue to develop; however, it would largely do so independently of the Black learning style idea. Aware of the potential dangers of the Black learning style idea, but not wanting to dismiss the role of race and culture in learning outright, Banks warned teachers explicitly to be careful not to automatically align individual Black students with a Black learning style. "The teacher cannot assume that every Mexican American student is field dependent and that every Anglo student is field independent," Banks admonished. "These kinds of assumptions result in new stereotypes and problems."[45]

A Dangerous Idea?

Both Hilliard and Banks endorsed the general idea that culture and cultural interaction mattered a great deal in the classroom, but both worried that teachers would misapply the Black learning style idea to individual Black students when, in fact, the validity of the idea was linked to mean differences across groups. They were not the only scholars worried about the misapplication of the Black learning style idea. In fact, one of its earliest proponents, Manuel Ramírez III, issued a series of qualifications and caveats to his suggested cognitive style framework in 1981.

During the early 1970s, Ramírez's research on field dependency/independency among White, Black, and Mexican American students were some of the most commonly cited studies in support of the ethnic cognitive style and cultural mismatch ideas. Yet by the 1980s, Ramírez lamented how the idea had been "oversimplified and misunderstood or misinterpreted . . . to stereotype minority students or to further label them rather than to identify individual differences that are educationally meaningful." Ramírez and his coauthor not only worried that his research may have had "a negative effect" on schools because of "common problems associated with looking at mean differences," but he also admitted that his own pioneering studies had ignored "situational aspects that may [have] contribute[d] significantly . . . in educational practice." Accordingly, he recommended using classroom observations and the use of a checklist to determine students' individual learning style instead of employing Witkin's decontextualized frame-and-rod test, as he had done in his initial studies. Furthermore, Ramírez suggested that teachers needed to expose students to teaching methods that both aligned and clashed with their preferred cognitive style to "gradually introduce the child to learning in new ways."[46] Ramírez's suggestion contradicted the approaches of Dunn and of Barbe and Swassing, who argued that students ought to learn solely through their identified learning style. Thus, Ramírez—one of the earliest, most enthusiastic, and most cited proponents of the ethnic learning style idea—still subscribed to the ethnic learning style approach, but with a long list of caveats, qualifiers, and warnings that likely made the idea too complicated for many teachers to implement properly.

In 1993, Craig Frisby, a Black psychologist at the University of Florida, published a direct attack on the "myth" of the Black learning style in the journal *School Psychology Review*. He argued that "no compelling support exists for the notion that blacks learn in fundamentally different ways than whites." Not only did Frisby reject race- and ethnicity-based learning styles—and, in fact, learning styles in general—but he resented how the issue had become politicized. According to Frisby, Black learning style proponents had "adopted [liberationist] ideology and reinterpreted it as a conflict between eager, exuberant black learners and oppressive, spirit-crushing 'European' education systems . . . [with a] pungent tone of accusatory moral indignation."[47] Frisby's exaggerated and dismissive characterization of the literature on the Black learners did not go unchallenged. In fact, Hale wrote a direct rebuttal: "Clearly this distorted analysis and dismissal of African-American culture stems from Frisby's self-professed lack of understanding of deep structure African-American culture. It seems to me that he would benefit from deepening his own understanding of African culture before attempting to criticize this knowledge base."[48]

A more conflicted evaluation of the Black learning style idea was published in 1995 by Jacqueline Jordan Irvine and Darlene Eleanor York. In a chapter in the *Handbook of Research on Multicultural Education*, the authors reviewed the most recent research on learning styles and ethnicity-based cognitive styles and found the research base to be unconvincing. Regarding learning styles in general, the authors concluded that "despite the continuing popularity of the instruments, the surrounding research has not fully supported the underlying idea of learning styles." They also found the idea of race- and ethnicity-specific learning styles to be equally problematic: "The research on learning styles using culturally diverse students fails to support the premise that members of a given cultural group exhibit a distinctive style." Despite their skepticism of the Black learning style idea, the authors still recognized several positive outcomes of the popular theory that aligned with the broader goals of multicultural education. First, the racial and ethnic learning style idea emphasized the cultural context of teaching, which they accepted as a central component of multicultural education. Second, it recognized the "importance of affect in teaching culturally diverse students." Third, "it rightly place[d] responsibility for student learning with teachers, instead of ascribing blame to students and their parents."[49] Whether this was a qualified endorsement and or a qualified dismissal of the Black learning style idea, it demonstrated that the early promise surrounding the controversial idea had not come to fruition. In general, the Black learning style idea was losing momentum by the 1990s. In fact, this uncertainty over the ethnic learning style idea was demonstrated in the work of the leading advocates for culturally responsive and culturally relevant pedagogy, such as Geneva Gay, Sonia Nieto, and Gloria Ladson-Billings.

Culturally responsive pedagogy was a popular approach that emerged out of multicultural education in the 1990s. Whereas multicultural education generally focused on the broader policy goals of antiracism, inclusion, and curriculum reform in American schools, culturally responsive pedagogy specifically targeted classroom practice to gain leverage on better educating minority students. The cultural mismatch theory was at the heart of the approach. As James A. Banks explained, "[Culturally responsive pedagogy] postulates that the discontinuities between the school culture and the home and community cultures of low-income students of color are an important factor in their low academic achievement," and that "academic achievement of these students will increase if schools and teachers reflect and draw on their cultural and language strengths."[50] Gay, a professor of education at the University of Washington–Seattle, provided a qualified endorsement for the ethnic learning style idea in her book *Culturally Responsive Teaching* by insisting that learning styles were "closely related to cultural values and traits," but they were also "multidimensional and dynamic . . . rather than static descriptors of finite behaviors in all situations." To justify the learning style idea, Gay cited the Witkin-inspired typologies of Ramírez and Shade, as well as the VAK-oriented typologies of Dunn and Barbe and Swassing, even though the VAK model had proven to be race neutral. Ultimately, Gay steered an awkward course between recognizing the importance of culture and cultural clash in the classroom, while simultaneously steering teachers away from using ethnic learning styles to stereotype students of color, or to sort students of color into ethnically homogeneous groups. On this final point, Gay stated unequivocally that she did "not advocate the physical separation of students by ethnic groups for instructional purposes."[51]

Nieto, a professor of education at the University of Massachusetts–Amherst, was even more skeptical of the idea of ethnic-based learning styles. As she explained in her textbook, *Affirming Diversity*, "Exactly how culture influences learning is unclear," and the "linear process implied by this [ethnic learning style] theory is not entirely convincing." She also wrote, "A focus on rigid learning styles is problematic because of a tendency to dichotomize learning," and she cited research demonstrating that some teachers used the alleged learning style of Hispanic students to "justify a number of clearly discriminatory pedagogical decisions."[52] Just as many Black advocates for the racial integration of schools began to question the efficacy of desegregation after they witnessed the mistreatment of Black students by White teachers, many advocates for the ethnic learning style idea began to question whether the idea was doing more harm than good, especially when White teachers were using the learning style idea to justify a diminished curriculum for Black and Latine students.[53] In an article for *Newsweek*, the best-selling author and educational advocate Jonathan Kozol described how he witnessed this very thing, how "different learning styles" had become a "fashionable" method to justify "a stratified approach" to students of color. Instead of intellectual engagement, Kozol wrote, poor Black students were being taught job skills because these skills were allegedly a better fit for their learning style.[54]

Gloria Ladson-Billings, a professor at University of Wisconsin–Madison, attempted to move beyond the cultural mismatch theory altogether because the paradigm was focused mainly on explaining why many Black students failed instead of exploring why many others succeeded. "Instead of asking what was wrong with African American learners," she later reflected, "I dared to ask what was right with these students and what happened in the classrooms of teachers who seemed to experience pedagogical success with them."[55] In a pivotal 1995 article introducing the concept of culturally relevant teaching, she described the successful efforts of eight teachers who had experienced academic success with their students of color. She made little use of the research on cultural mismatch beyond a brief reference to the work of Hilliard. Instead of casting Black culture as a static list of behaviors and traits that clashed with White culture, she depicted the culture of Black students in more localized and dynamic terms: "The problem that African-America students face is the constant devaluation of their culture both in school and in the larger society. Thus the styles apparent in African-American youth culture—e.g., dress, music, walk, language—are equated with poor academic performance." The teachers Ladson-Billings documented made academic success "cool" by linking leadership and achievement to students' cultural attributes in ways that validated and encouraged them to aspire for greatness. Finally, and most significantly, Ladson-Billings documented how the successful teachers of Black students incorporated critiques of local economic and social inequality into their pedagogy. As a result, "teachers allowed students to use their community circumstances as official knowledge."[56] This critical approach to pedagogy—inspired by the Brazilian educator Paulo Freire—would continue to become more popular in subsequent decades. In fact, many psychologists and educators have continued to pursue the idea that race and ethnicity impacted classroom interactions between teachers and students. Drawing on Witkin's work, Richard Nisbett, Robert Sternberg, and Li-fang Zhang have more recently explored how culture and race effect cognitive and thinking styles, and some cognitive psychologists and researchers such as Carol Lee have continued to pursue the effects of culture on learning—but they have all done so without reference to the Black learning style idea.[57]

The Black learning style idea originally emerged from well-intended efforts at creating a liberating, engaging, and relevant experience for marginalized students. However, when misunderstood and misapplied by teachers, the race-based learning style approach came dangerously close to racial stereotyping and social sorting. With the advent of culturally responsive and sustaining pedagogy, the onus of learning has shifted from the student to the teacher. In other words, rather than identifying the learning styles and characteristics of individual students, teachers were invited to reflect on their own cultural and racial biases, assumptions, and misunderstandings, and to search for materials and methods that better aligned with the diverse experiences of their students. Research on the ways a mostly White teacher workforce interacts with a student population that is becoming more diverse with each passing year is still warranted. Even though culturally responsive educators have abandoned the Black learning style idea, it nevertheless served to inspire several relevant lines of inquiry that are still being pursued today.

*

By the end of the 2000s, most educators had abandoned the idea that Black or Latine students had a different learning style, although many scholars were still comfortable citing the work of Witkin, Cohen, Hilliard, and Hale as a general (and vague) justification for the importance of multicultural and culturally responsive education. Few recognized that the seeds of culturally responsive pedagogy could be traced to the research of Witkin, who had passed away a decade and a half earlier and who had resisted the idea that ethnic and racial groups could be aligned with cognitive styles. By the 1990s, the VAK learning style typology had overtaken Witkin's field dependent/independent typology in popularity anyway, so few noticed when the Black learning style idea gradually disappeared from the educational discourse. What the race-based and VAK-oriented learning style typologies shared was a growing tendency to link a students' learning style to their identity—something students had no control over. Because students could not change their identity, it was the job of the teacher to change their instruction to better align with their needs. Even though the learning style idea had been dismissed by many Black and Latine educators as "dangerous," it continued to be popular way for teachers to engage students of color. In fact, the learning style idea became fused with a related but far more popular idea also linked to student identity: Howard Gardner's theory of multiple intelligences. The next chapter explores the rise of Gardner's popular theory and its unwarranted conflation with the learning style idea.

4
Multiple Intelligences as Learning Styles

In 1994, the *Washington Post* published an article with the headline "How We Learn: The Multiple Intelligences Teaching Approach." The article introduced the work of Howard Gardner, professor of cognition and education at Harvard University and a MacArthur genius award recipient, who a decade earlier had introduced his theory of multiple intelligences (MI theory) in the best-selling book *Frames of Mind: A Theory of Multiple Intelligences*. The article also featured the curriculum of the Key School in Indianapolis, which was "the nation's first school designed according to the tenets of MI theory."[1] Students at the Key School (later known as the Key Learning Community) worked in pods based on one of Gardner's seven intelligences, and a few times a week they interacted with a media room in which they could choose from an assortment of activities based on their preferences and interests. Although the headline "How We Learn" belied this fact, MI theory was not actually a learning theory, nor was it a learning style theory; it was a theory about how psychologists and society defined and assessed intelligence. Nevertheless, Gardner's MI theory immediately resonated with educators from around the world and provided additional fuel to the learning style idea in the 1990s and 2000s as teachers at all levels of education confused and conflated MI theory with learning styles. This chapter explores Gardner's MI theory, its conflation with learning style idea, and Gardner's unsuccessful attempt to reign in the misapplications and overextensions of his ideas.

Frames of Mind

Gardner published *Frames of Mind* in 1983. That year was not just any year in education; it was a major turning point in the movement toward the rise of high-stakes testing in American schools. Two publications—E. D. Hirsch's article "Cultural Literacy" and *A Nation at Risk*, a report by the National Commission on Excellence in Education—appeared that year alongside Gardner's influential book. These publications paved the way for the testing revolution that would upend schools for the next three decades.

Hirsch was an English professor at the University of Virginia. In his 1983 article for the *American Scholar*, he lamented the lack of basic background among incoming college-age students, a fact he supported with evidence of falling SAT scores between 1962 and 1980: "The scores on the verbal SAT are solid evidence that literacy has been declining in this country just when our need for effective literacy has been sharply rising."[2] With encouragement from Assistant Secretary of Education Diane Ravitch, Hirsch later expanded his article into a best-selling book, *Cultural Literacy: What Every American Needs to Know*, published in 1987. The appendix to *Cultural Literacy* included a controversial list of facts, names, dates, and phrases that all Americans needed to know if they hoped to consider themselves culturally literate. Based on this list, Hirsch later developed a core knowledge curriculum that was adopted by hundreds of schools around the country, and he edited a series of best-selling textbooks (*What Your Kindergartner Needs to Know*, *What Your First Grader Needs to Know*, etc.), based on his rigorous, prescribed, and fact-based curriculum. Thus, Hirsch officially endorsed and promoted a national one-size-fits-all curriculum, which inevitably put him in direct conflict with learning style advocates.

Drawing upon the same general sense of educational discontent as Hirsch, President Ronald Reagan's secretary of education, Terrel H. Bell, commissioned the National Commission on Excellence in Education in reaction to the "widespread public perception that something is seriously remiss in our educational system." There findings appeared in 1983 as the *Nation at Risk* report. Like Hirsch, the commission noted that "the average graduate of our schools and colleges today is not as well-educated as the average graduate of 25 or 35 years ago." The report identified deficiencies in curriculum requirements, academic rigor, and teacher education. In an oft-cited passage specifically designed for maximum impact, the commission concluded: "If an unfriendly foreign power had attempted to impose on America the mediocre educational performance that exists today, we might well have viewed it as an act of war." Just as Hirsch had done in his article and his book, the *Nation at Risk* report also cited falling SAT scores to support its incendiary assertion that the "educational foundations of our society are presently being eroded by a rising tide of mediocrity that threatens our very future as a Nation and as a people."[3] Both Hirsch and the *Nation at Risk* report demanded greater rigor in American schools and recommended that national curriculum standards be created and implemented toward that goal. Both publications drew on evidence from norm-based standardized testing to demonstrate the alleged diminishment of the American intellect due to the misguided student-centered reforms of the 1960s and '70s, such as open and alternative education.

After a failed attempt at establishing national standards in the 1990s, President George W. Bush signed No Child Left Behind into law in 2001 requiring that every state develop its own local standards and that each student be tested every year in math and reading between third and eighth grade. The legislation also required that each school's test scores be disaggregated by race, disability status, and other categories, and that each school—regardless of its socioeconomic background—demonstrate annual yearly progress (AYP) in test scores or else face punitive measures. This placed unprecedented expectations on schools and ultimately created a culture of teaching to the test because, if a school failed to make annual yearly progress for three consecutive years, it would be restructured, taken over, or shut down. Against this background of rising standardization and high-stakes testing in schools, Gardner made his case for an expanded definition of intelligence that moved beyond the narrow math and literacy skills that were so valued by the SAT, intelligence tests, and other norm-referenced standardized exams. What started as a crusade to expand society's view of intelligence ended up as a plea to humanize American schooling in the face of unprecedented and rapid movement toward test-centric standardization.

Prior to the publication of *Frames of Mind* in 1983, Gardner had been codirector of Harvard's Project Zero, in which he studied the effects of art on the mind. He was also studying the effects of brain damage at the Boston Veterans Administration Hospital. Gardner did not hold a permanent professorship at this time, and so he had to fund his own position through grant work and book writing, which is why he was working on such disparate projects early in his career. Yet, as Gardner asserted in his memoir, he had a synthesizing mind that constantly looked for connections among psychology and the other social sciences, which served him well in his unique career trajectory.

Gardner was a prolific author who valued writing for a general audience. In fact, *Frames of Mind* was his seventh book. His third book, *The Scattered Mind*, published in 1975, explored the effects and cognitive implications of brain damage. His fifth and sixth books, *Artful Scribbles* (1980) and *Art, Mind, and Brain* (1982), addressed the role of the mind in the creation of art. These books paved the way for his work on multiple intelligences and led to his MacArthur fellowship award in 1981, which he used to leverage a permanent professorship at the Harvard Graduate School of Education. He considered the winning of the MacArthur award, not the publication of *Frames of Mind*, to be the biggest turning point in his life.[4] Indeed, looking across the span of Gardner's prolific career, the theory of multiple intelligences occupied only a fraction of what he studied and wrote about, both before and after the publication of the best-selling book.

In addition to Gardner's work on brain damage and art, *Frames of Mind* emerged from his work on the Harvard Project on Human Potential. In the early 1980s, Gardner began mapping "all that was known" about human cognitive potentials in pursuit of a book on the cognitive potential of humans. From this research, he drafted a list of criteria for what to include as a comprehensive list of capacities for the human mind, although he had not yet decided what to call these capacities. His criteria for naming them included the possibility that they could be isolated by brain damage, the existence of savants and prodigies in the area, an identifiable core of operations, a distinct developmental history, an evolutionary history, support from experimental tasks and psychometric findings, and susceptibility to being encoded in a symbol system. Employing this criterion, Gardner identified seven cognitive capacities: linguistic, logical-mathematical, musical, spatial, bodily-kinesthetic, interpersonal, and intrapersonal.

Had he continued to refer to these as "capacities," *Frames of Mind* would have had far less of an impact. Instead, he chose to name these capacities *intelligences*. "It was the pluralization of the single, simple, four-syllable word that turned out in the end to 'make all the difference,'" he later reflected. And: "With little doubt, it was by virtue of the decision to beg, borrow, seize, or steal the word *intelligence* that I caught the attention of so many readers, including the then all powerful members of the so-called chattering classes."[5] It was not only that Gardner employed the term *intelligence*, but also that he directly attacked the traditional concept of intelligence and the tests that narrowly assessed them. He argued that traditional IQ tests covered just a small portion of what the human mind was capable of and that most norm-referenced standardized tests, such as the SAT, focused on only two of his seven intelligences—logical-mathematical and linguistic—even though, historically, society had valued all of them. Clearly aware of the classist and racist history of IQ testing, his expansion of the term *intelligence* democratized the idea of it from a hierarchical to a horizontal and descriptive model. (He was not the only one expanding the definition of intelligence and mapping out the mind in multifaceted ways at that time. Within a few years of the publication of *Frames of Mind*, the psychologist Robert Sternberg introduced his own triarchic theory of intelligence, covered below in chapter 6; and Jerry Fodor published a related but far less accessible book called *The Modularity of Mind* (1983). Both works only made a fraction of the impact that Gardner's best-selling study did.

Frames of Mind was reviewed extensively, and educators took an intense interest in the book. They embraced Gardner's idea of multiple intelligences and applied it broadly to all areas of the curriculum and school. Gardner took a hands-off approach to the adoption of his theory by educators, and, as his idea gained greater popularity year after year, he largely observed from afar. He is fond of telling a story about how he attended a conference in Kutztown, Pennsylvania, in 1985 when he was approached by a teacher from Indianapolis who was so inspired by the argument presented in *Frames of Mind* that she planned to establish a school based on his seven intelligences. The point of this story was to underscore the fact that Gardner was surprised that educators took such an instant and enthusiastic interest in his MI theory, which he claimed he thought of as "principally as a contribution to my own discipline of developmental psychology."[6] However, this is somewhat disingenuous. Gardner had been publishing in education journals for years, and almost immediately he pitched his MI theory directly to educators. For example, the very same year he published *Frames of Mind*, he published an article in *Art Educator* outlining his MI theory and additional implications for teaching. The next year, he discussed his MI theory in the high-impact education journal *Phi Delta Kappan*. Furthermore, only a few years after that, he coauthored an article on assessing multiple intelligences for *Educational Researcher*, the flagship journal of the American Educational Research Association (AERA)—a publication that was sent to the thousands of members of the organization around the world.[7] By the late 1980s, educators had shown interest in MI theory, and the findings Gardner reported in *Educational Research* based on his work for Project Spectrum were just preliminary. Nevertheless, this publication demonstrated Gardner's eagerness not only to engage the educational research community directly and almost immediately, but to do so at highest and the most rigorous level.

However, despite these efforts to engage educators, Gardner could not have predicted the alacrity with which teachers and administrators embraced the theory and recognized its teaching implications. Within a decade, an entire professional development industry emerged around MI theory. Much as Charles Darwin rarely used the phrase *survival of the fittest* that came be associated with him, Gardner never used the actual phrase *seven kinds of smart* that came to be associated with him and his theory of multiple intelligences. What professional development personnel sold (and what many teachers and parents wanted to buy) was the idea that all students were smart in something—teachers simply had to figure out what students' intelligence strength was and how to exploit it. Gardner never quite stated it that way, but it didn't matter, because this message meshed perfectly with the then-burgeoning self-esteem movement that sought to pump up students' academic self-image.

Thomas Armstrong was one of the first to enter the MI marketplace with his books, *Multiple Intelligences in the Classroom* (1994) and *Seven Kinds of Smart: Identifying and Developing Your Multiple Intelligences* (1999). Numerous other practitioner-based books on MI followed. Many of these authors conducted professional development workshops for teachers and administrators. By 1996, there were about fifty books on MI, and twenty years later there were more than a hundred. Additional MI schools—such as the New City School in St. Louis and the Howard Gardner School in Alexandria, Virginia—opened around the country, and even an MI-based theme-park exhibit called *Explorama* that opened in Nordborg, Denmark, was meant to engage all the intelligences of its guests.

In addition to the rising impact of standardized testing, two best-selling books kept the idea of intelligence in the headlines throughout the 1990s and 2000s, which cast additional attention back onto Gardner's MI theory. The first was by the journalist Daniel Goleman, whose book *Emotional Intelligence: Why It Can Matter More Than IQ* was a bestseller in 1995. Goleman defined emotional intelligence as "self-control, zeal and persistence, and the ability to motivate one's self." Instead of the relatively fixed traits that constituted IQ, he continued, emotional intelligence could be "taught to children, giving them a better chance to use whatever intellectual potential the genetic lottery may have given them."[8] Like Gardner, Goleman targeted the limited nature of IQ and its ability to predict the destiny of the individual. Also like Gardner, Goleman lamented the narrow focus of school curricula, which he argued should be devoting more time to developing these important social skills. Gardner welcomed Goleman's focus on emotional intelligences. He also clarified that what Goleman had called emotional intelligence had originally been included in his own MI theory as interpersonal and intrapersonal intelligences. Furthermore, Gardner pondered whether emotional intelligence would even have been "discovered and so-named without my own previous work."[9] The net effect of Goleman's book was to provide addition support for Gardner's idea that psychologists and the public needed to expand their definition of intelligence—something that many teachers were more than willing to do.

The second book that kept IQ in the headlines was far more controversial: *The Bell Curve: Intelligence and Class Structure in American Life* (1994) by Richard Herrnstein and Charles Murray. Using the traditional version of intelligence as IQ, Herrnstein and Murray argued that there was a natural, genetically determined bell curve of intelligences among American citizens. They argued that those at the bottom of the socioeconomic order were there because they (and their parents) had low IQs and there was nothing schools or social policy could do to remedy this fact. Murray had first made this argument along with Arthur Jensen in the late 1960s. As covered in the last chapter, Frank Riessman devoted an entire chapter of *The Inner-City Child* to attacking the idea of IQ as genetic, unbiased, and unalterable. Nevertheless, when reintroduced in the 1990s, conservatives viewed the atavistic IQ-as-destiny argument presented in *The Bell Curve* as justification for defunding and/or abandoning social programs such as welfare, Head Start, Title 1, and affirmative action.

In 1989, Gardner responded to *Emotional Intelligence*, *The Bell Curve*, and the politicization of intelligence in an essay for the *Atlantic Monthly* titled "Who Owns Intelligence?" Gardner admitted that the psychometric research demonstrated that IQ was indeed stable and inheritable, a fact underscored by studies of twins raised in completely different environments. However, he still thought that the idea of pure intelligence as a single, quantifiable attribute was too narrow and needed to be expanded. In addition to his own MI theory, he highlighted Sternberg's and Goleman's efforts to expand the definition of intelligence. However, although he admired Sternberg's work and considered it to be more or less compatible with his own, Gardner thought Goleman had gone too far by including emotional and moral aspects in the definition of intelligence. Using the metaphor of an elastic band, he argued that definition of intelligence needed to expand to include more than just linguistic and logical computation: "So long as intelligences are restricted to the processing of contents in the world, we avoid epistemological problems," but intelligences "should not be expanded to include personality, motivation, will, attention, character, creativity" because "such stretching [was] likely to snap the band."[10] Thus, Gardner positioned his pluralistic definition of intelligence between the extremes of *The Bell Curve* and *Emotional Intelligence* by moving beyond a single, pure attribute represented by IQ while also avoiding the subjective aspects he found in emotional intelligence. Gardner's definition of intelligence as "the processing of contents in the world" was perhaps also aimed at learning style advocates, who included such subjective factors as personality, attention, and personal preferences in their assessment of students' learning profiles.

Despite its popularity, Gardner's MI theory did experience some resistance by educators. Specifically, New Left scholars pointed to the fact that, even though Gardner's attempted to broaden the definition of intelligence in a more egalitarian direction, he still did not transcend the oppressive and exploitative history of the term. As Joe Kincheloe explained in his critique of Gardner's MI theory, "What is labeled intelligence can never be separated from what dominant power groups designate it to be." Kincheloe pointed out that, as much as educators have embraced Gardner as a progressive, a radical, and a multiculturalist, Gardner nevertheless linked his MI theory "to the claim of scientific neutrality"—an orientation that still connected his theory to the racist history of intelligence testing, social sorting, and academic tracking.[11] For Kincheloe, the truly radical act would not have been to expand the definition of intelligence, but rather to abandon the idea of intelligence altogether. In fact, according to the English philosophy professor John White, replacing IQ with multiple intelligences may have created more problems than it solved. "All across the world, young people are now typing themselves as kinesthetic, spatial, interpersonal learners," White complained in 2006. "They think this is the sort of person they are; they have been made this way." Thus, the intelligence labels Gardner created constituted "as much a threat to [students'] sense of their own identity as the IQ myth was to their predecessors."[12] As explained below, Gardner opposed labeling students with a specific intelligence; still, many educators were confused by what exactly the teaching implications of MI theory were.

George A. Miller, a respected cognitive scientist, dismissed Gardner's theory outright as mere "hunch and opinion" in the *New York Times Book Review*. More significantly, Miller pointed to an issue that had plagued Gardner and learning style advocates from the very beginning: even if MI theory were true, was it the job of teachers to develop students' weaker intelligences, or was it their job to build upon their intelligence strengths? Miller noted, "Since nobody knows whether the educator should play to the student's strengths (or bolster the student's weaknesses or both), the new psychometrics does not seem to advance practical matters much beyond present psychometrics."[13] What exactly was the role of the school and the teacher, according to MI theory? Weren't schools already offering music, physical education, home economics, woodshop, and even chess? Gardner eventually developed answers for all these questions and issues, but it would take more than a decade (and the aid of collaborators and disciples) to fully work them out.

Part of the confusion was how Gardner approached intelligence, which he defined as "the capacity to solve problems or to fashion products that are valued in one or more cultural settings."[14] His interactionist definition of intelligence was not playing by the rules of the vast majority of psychometricianss who created paper-and pencil exams, such IQ tests and the SAT, specifically so they could predict future academic performance. Ontologically, psychometricians cast intelligence in essentialist terms, as something existing prior to experience, innate, and relatively stable. Gardner dismissed this traditional view of intelligence as "entirely inside baseball."[15] In contrast, Gardner defined intelligence as something one did through interaction with the world. Ontologically, he cast intelligence in pragmatist or functionalist terms—as something one performed, not as something one walked around with in one's head. As Gardner explained, "There is no 'pure' spatial intelligence; instead, there is spatial intelligence as expressed in a child's puzzle solutions, route finding, block building, or basketball passing."[16] Perry Klein found Gardner's definition of intelligence to be circular: "The definition of bodily-kinesthetic intelligence is virtually a definition of dance, so the explanation says, in effect, that Michael is a good dancer because he is a good dancer." This not only made Gardner's MI theory tautological, Klein quipped, but it also made it "trivial."[17]

Gardner's interactionist approach to intelligence recalled that of his mentor, Jerome Bruner, who declared that thinking was a process, not a product. Accordingly, Gardner refused to ever construct a transportable MI assessment tool because he thought that intelligences were activated only in specific and authentic cultural contexts, and so they could not be accurately assessed by a decontextualized pen-and-paper exam. This added additional ambiguity to the theory. When Gardner did eventually develop an MI assessment tool for his Project Spectrum in the 1990s, it involved hands-on interactions at a variety of activity centers, was appropriate only for preschool age children, and took nearly two hours and a special set of equipment to administer. Gardner never attempted to construct an assessment for older children or adults because, by those stages of development, they had likely already demonstrated their intelligence strengths. "We are well advised to assess intelligences by watching people who are already familiar with and have some skills in these pursuits," Gardner wrote, "or by introducing individuals to such domains and observing how well one can move beyond the novice stage, with or without specific supports or scaffolding."[18] Gardner's refusal to construct an official assessment instrument clashed with the learning style tradition of Barbe and Swassing, Dunn, Gregorc, Kolb, and Witkin. It also opened the door for other, less-qualified educators to step in and design their own MI assessments. For better or for worse, many did.

Gardner's Actual Learning Theory

Inspired by the reception of *Frames of Mind* (1983), Gardner spent the next decade and half writing about education and educational reform. For the tenth anniversary of the *Frames of Mind*, as well as in his books *The Unschooled*

Mind (1991), *Multiple Intelligences* (1993), *The Disciplined Mind* (1999), and *Intelligence Reframed* (1999), Gardner explained the relationship of his theory of multiple intelligences—which, again, was not a learning theory—to his actual learning theory, best described as disciplinary symbolic socialization theory. For Gardner, learning was the acculturation to the thinking of disciplinary experts. Learning involved overcoming one's intuitive—but simplistic and incorrect—interpretation of the world by developing a more nuanced, accurate version of the world through socialization to the symbols, concepts, and methods of the academic disciplines. In other words, for Gardner, learning involved decreasing the cognitive distance between a novice and a disciplinary expert. In fact, when pressed by a journalist for a label for his learning theory, Gardner referred to himself as a "disciplinarian."[19] His learning theory was an updating of the argument first presented in Jerome Bruner's 1960 classic, the *Process of Education*. Although the strength of Gardner's MI theory lay in its simplicity, an accurate understanding of his broader learning theory was far more multifaceted and complex. He also introduced it incrementally over the course of several years.

A full understanding of Gardner's learning theory involved understanding the relationship between intelligences, domains, and fields. Intelligences, Gardner explained, were individual neurological attributes; domains were "disciplines, crafts, and other pursuits in which one can become encultured and then be assessed in terms of level of competence has attained." Fields, he continued, were the "people, institutions, award mechanisms and so forth that render judgements about the qualities of individual performances."[20] Intelligences, domains, and fields interacted and overlapped, but they were not the same. Multiple intelligences contributed to but did not themselves constitute the domains and fields needed for learning and knowledge. For example, for me to write this book, according to Gardner's learning theory, I am drawing upon my interpersonal and linguistic *intelligences* to study the past; I am drawing upon my enculturation to the *domain* of history to compile my study of the past into a plausible historical narrative; I am drawing upon the previously published research of other historians (my *field*) to guide my inquiry; and I will rely on the judgment of other historians (my *field* again) to ultimately determine whether or not I did a convincing job. Thus, intelligences, domains, and fields were all involved in the learning and knowledge construction process of writing this book.

How did Gardner's learning theory relate to existing school subjects? This is where things got complicated. Some of the intelligences/domains/fields aligned directly with school subjects, but some did not. Logical-mathematical intelligence, for example, aligned directly with the domain and field of mathematics, linguistic intelligence with the domain and field of English/language arts, and musical intelligence with the domain and field of music. However, the subjects of science and social studies did not align directly with any domains and fields, because in Gardner's typology there was no scientific or social scientific intelligence—these subjects drew upon multiple intelligences, domains, and fields. Scientific domains and fields could draw heavily upon logical-mathematic intelligence (physics) or linguistic intelligence (biology), depending on which subdiscipline was being studied. Social studies is interdisciplinary by nature; it includes geography (which, in Gardner's view, aligned with spatial intelligence), history (which aligned with linguistic and interpersonal intelligence), economics (which aligned with mathematical intelligence), and the social sciences (which aligned with interpersonal, interpersonal and logical-mathematical intelligences). So not only did Gardner's seven intelligences fail to directly align with school subjects, but his domains and fields did not directly align with them either.

To address the domains that did not directly align with one of his seven intelligences, Gardner suggested that teachers approach any school topic through one of five "entry points." The entry points he suggested were a *narrational* entry point that used stories or narratives about the topic, a *logical-quantitative* entry point that used numerical considerations or deductive reasoning, a *foundational* entry point that used "the philosophical and terminological facets of the concept," an *aesthetic* entry approach that used "sensory or surface features" of the topic, and a *experiential* approach for students who learned "best with a hands-on approach, dealing directly with the materials the embody or convey the concept." Gardner wrote that if teachers could not understand a topic using its most obvious and direct entry point (say, history through a *narrational* entry point), then they should explore alternative entry points (say, a *quantitative* entry point).[21] However, he cautioned against the assumption that "a problem in one domain must be translatable" to another domain. Using the example of math, he explained how finding an "alternative route to the mathematical content" though the "medium of an intelligence that is relatively strong for that individual" would yield limited results because eventually "the learner must translate back into the domain of mathematics." If understood, this caveat greatly hindered the application of MI theory beyond elementary school, because most teachers in middle and high school only taught in a single domain such as math, English, physical education, or music. To complicate things more, Gardner warned against teaching to all the intelligences within a single subject or lesson: "To be sure, most topics can be approached in varied ways, but applying scattershot approach to each topic is a waste of effort and time."[22] Although Gardner encouraged teachers to determine students' intelligence strengths, he was against labeling as, say, a musical or interpersonal learner. In fact, Gardner never applied the term *learner* to any if his intelligences, although, as demonstrated below, this would be a very common practice among practitioners. In his refusal to label students as musical or kinesthetic learners, he again diverged from the learning style advocates.

Gardner also did not outline his learning theory all at once, but rather worked it out piecemeal over the course of a decade and a half through five books. Had Gardner authored a book called *Five Entry Points to Teaching*, this would have done much to clarify his learning theory, but no such book ever appeared. Given the complexity of his learning theory and its relationship to existing school curricula, one can understand why teachers preferred the simplicity of the seven intelligences first presented in *Frames of Mind* to the more complicated learning theory Gardner rolled out in his subsequent books. Gardner often joked about the simplicity of his MI theory as a major reason for its popularity: "You can summarize it in a sentence: This guy Gardner claims that we have seven separate intelligences, called multiple intelligences."[23] For many teachers, this was all they needed to know. As one unidentified educator suggested to a journalist, "Howard is the guru and *Frames of Mind* is the bible."[24]

Conflating Learning Styles and MI Theory

Gardner's MI theory met a receptive educational audience that not only had a preexisting antagonism to standardized testing dating back to the 1960s but had also grown comfortable with the idea of learning styles as an alternative to rote and shallow learning. In fact, one study by Mindy Kornhaber of nine schools that implemented an MI-based curriculum confirmed that the reason teachers adopted the approach so enthusiastically was because "educators' everyday observations were already aligned with the theory's idea that people learn in a variety of ways."[25] Accordingly, educators were eager to conflate MI theory with the already popular learning style theories. As the *Washington Post* article cited at the beginning of this chapter revealed, even when authors accurately described Gardner's theory as a theory of intelligence and not a learning theory, they added descriptive headings, such as "How We Learn," that implied it *was* a learning style theory. This can be seen in a 1991 article in the *Journal of Museum Education*, where the author provided an overview of the many learning style theories and presented Gardner's theory under the heading "People Learn in Different Ways." Even though the author provided a relatively accurate description of Gardner's MI theory as a theory of intelligence, not learning, her word choice showed otherwise: "Just as there are many theories of learning, there are many schools of thought regarding learning styles. Howard Gardner's model [had] important implications for museum educators."[26] The heading and the syntax of these two sentences presented MI theory as a learning style theory, and readers were led to reach this conclusion. Likewise, a 1991 article in the *Washington Post*, titled "The Ways We Learn," introduced Gardner's MI theory alongside other learning style typologies, including Dunn's LSI, McCarthy's 4MAT, Charles Litteri's Cognitive Profile, and James Keefe's Learning Style Profile. Again, the article described Gardner's theory accurately as a theory of intelligences, but by including it alongside popular learning style typologies, the implication was that MI theory was a learning style theory like the others. Could readers really recognize the difference?[27]

By the late 1990s, practitioner and research articles began appearing that introduced both learning styles and multiple intelligences. Even when introduced separately, the two became conflated; students with strengths in musical intelligence were dubbed "musical learners," students who demonstrated strength in interpersonal intelligence were dubbed "interpersonal learners," and so on. The suggested activities for these learners were not only wrong based on Gardner's own writings, but they were often misguided and absurd at face value. For example, one article on teaching science to college students suggested that "musical learners study [science by] listening to recordings related to the topic" such as "Holst's The Planets" or "Grofe's Grand Canyon Suite" Besides the fact that these classical recordings are instrumental and thus convey no scientific information about the topic whatsoever, the activity would not even develop the students' musical intelligence unless the students were composing the music themselves. "Interpersonal learners," the same article suggested, "like to work on group projects and discuss with others," and "naturalist learners see patterns and like to identify a problem and research solutions" (in the late 1990s, Gardner had added an eighth intelligence, *naturalistic*).[28] Both of these descriptions were misapplications of Gardner's theory, and they were also so vague that any number of either rigorous or vacuous activities could be assigned in the name of tapping into a student's interpersonal or naturalistic intelligence. Gardner even commented on the trivial nature of many of the activities implemented in the name of MI theory when he quipped: "'Let's sing our times tables, children!' says the teacher, and then an observer claims that musical intelligence has been used to teach mathematical thinking." In place of these vacuous activities, Gardner implored his followers to use examples "that [made] sense, not merely to invent examples that, checklist-style, will occupy every space in a preset grid."[29]

Educators consistently ignored this advice. In fact, some educators stated outright that MI was a learning style theory. As one science teacher from Florida wrote, "From my perspective as a high school Chemistry teacher, [MI] theory is another way to describe different learning styles." Thomas Hoerr, head of the New City School in St. Louis, explained how "MI has made our curriculum and instruction far more inclusive of varied learning styles."[30] And an art teacher in Maryland explained as recently as 2022: "We know that not everyone learns in the same way. Some people are kinesthetic learners, and some people are auditory learners. Arts instruction activates multiple intelligences."[31] By the turn of the twentieth-first century, educators had added MI theory to the long list of learning style theories. "You might prefer Howard Gardner's multiple intelligences, Bernice McCarthy's 4MAT system, the Myers-Brigg's personality type indicators," one administrator wrote in the *Phi Delta Kappan*. "Each of these systems provides a way to categorize individuals into types so that we can better help them learn in the classroom setting."[32] Thus, like the learning style typologies, MI theory became a way to assess and label students and offer them learning activities and content that allegedly aligned with their learning strength, profile, and/or identity.

Some of the biggest advocates of MI theory were Harvey Silver, Richard Strong, and Matthew Perini. They were part of a growing professional development industry that introduced MI theory to make classrooms more engaging and effective. The three had stepped in where Gardner was unwilling to go by designing a transportable MI assessment tool called the Multiple Intelligences Indicator. In an article for ASCD's journal *Educational Leadership*, Silver, Strong, and Perini sought to bring learning style theory and MI into conversation with one another. Their own four-category learning style typology—which drew upon the research of Jung, Myers and Briggs, and Kolb—included a mastery style learner, who "absorbs information concretely," an understanding style learner, who "focuses more on ideas and abstractions," a self-expressive style learner, who "looks for images, . . . feelings and emotions to construct new ideas," and an interpersonal style learner, who "prefers to learn socially." The authors argued that the learning style approach had limitations that MI theory could offset because the learning style idea focused on process and emotion, whereas MI theory focused on content. "Without multiple intelligence theory, style is rather abstract, and generally undervalues content," they wrote. "Without learning styles, multiple intelligence theory proves unable to describe different processes and thought and feeling."[33] They developed Integrated Intelligence Menus to combine the two approaches, and they expanded this model into a book, *So Each May Learn: Integrating Learning Styles and Multiple Intelligences* (2000). Ultimately, Silver, Strong, and

Perini had their own learning style product to sell, and they did not want it replaced with Gardner's MI theory, nor did they want to appear out of touch with the latest research—so they absorbed Gardner's theory into their own.

Rita Dunn took the opposite approach in her response to MI theory. Having spent three decades refining her LSI, Dunn felt threatened by the rapid ascendency of Gardner's MI theory. In a 2001 article, "Two Sides of the Same Coin or Different Strokes for Different Folks?," Dunn attacked Gardner's theory directly. She and her coauthors dismissed Gardner's theory for lacking the kind of experimental research that her supported her LSI, a list of studies that allegedly included more than two hundred manuscripts. Dunn's claim was erroneous because by the time she published this critique, Gardner had reported some of his initial findings from classroom-based Project Spectrum in the AERA's *Educational Researcher*. In contrast, none of Dunn's manuscripts had ever been published in an AERA journal. However, beyond questioning the rigor of the research behind Gardner's MI theory, she attacked his use of the term *intelligence* and dismissed his seven intelligences as mere talents. "It is possible to be extremely intelligent but have no developed talent," she noted. "It is also possible to be extremely talented in any of these areas and demonstrate only limited intelligence." She concluded that there was much popular support for MI theory because it was "appealing and democratic"; nevertheless, she steered her readers away from it and toward her own LSI, which, she alleged, was better supported by the research.[34]

In 2004, *Teachers College Record* dedicated a themed issue to MI theory to mark the twenty-year anniversary of the publication of *Frames of Mind*. The issue contained articles about the promise and perils of teaching through an MI approach by well-known educators such as Larry Cuban and Eliott Eisner. However, the most-cited article in the issue was Stephen Denig's "Multiple Intelligences and Learning Styles: Two Complementary Dimensions." Denig, a frequent collaborator with Rita Dunn, based his learning style theory solely on Dunn's LSI. He echoed the sentiment of Silver, Strong, and Perini that learning styles and MI theory could and should work in tandem because they complemented each other. However, unlike these researchers, who kept the two approaches distinct, Denig conflated them by asserting that "people who are smart in an intelligence learn best through methods associated with that intelligence." Accordingly, he listed each intelligence with an appropriate learning method: "Musical learn best with rhythm and melody, singing and listening to music and melody," and "Bodily-kinesthetic learn best by touching, moving, and processing knowledge through bodily sensation."[35]

Similarly, Alan Pritchard's textbook, *Ways of Learning* (2013), introduced the basics of MI theory alongside other learning style theories, with emphasis on the VAK model. He then aligned the relevant VAK categories to the seven intelligences and listed the teaching implications for each one in a way that transformed them into learning styles. For example, the linguistic/verbal learner "learns best by saying, hearing, and seeing words," the spatial/visual learner "learns best by visualizing, dreaming, and using the mind's eye and working with pictures," and the kinesthetic learner "learns best by touching, moving, interacting with space and processing knowledge through bodily sensations."[36] None of these researchers seemed interested in Gardner's actual learning theory as presented in *The Unschooled Mind* and *The Disciplined Mind*. Rather, they extrapolated a learning theory from Gardner's writing on MI theory and searched for unwarranted connections to learning style theories. The easiest way to do this was to simply convert Gardner's seven intelligences into seven learning styles, which most educators did.

Even critics of learning styles and MI theory linked the two together. In *The Schools We Need and Why We Don't Have Them* (1996)—his follow-up to *Cultural Literacy*—E. D. Hirsch linked both typologies to the progressive educational notion that every student was unique and special: "The enthusiasm for the doctrines of individual learning styles and multiple intelligences exemplifies the consistent and troublesome tendency of the educational community to elevate ideologically pleasing but non-consensus findings over ideologically troublesome ones that have achieved scientific consensus." The "scientific consensus" to which Hirsch referred was the traditional idea that *all* students learn best through direct verbal instruction, not through individual learning preferences. Hirsch dismissed the idea of learning styles in general, stating (accurately) that the "results of research on learning styles are decidedly mixed," and that "the claims for different learning styles among different ethnic groups are disputed in the literature."[37] Whereas Hirsch and Gardner found themselves on opposite ends of the ideological spectrum on the issue of curriculum and pedagogy, ironically, on the issue of the validity of the learning style idea, their views were almost completely aligned with each other.

Gardner on Learning Styles

In the early 1990s, Gardner was initially open to the idea that learning styles and his MI theory could coexist. He admitted that, "without doubt, some of the distinctions made in the theory of multiple intelligences resemble those made by educators who speak of different learning or working styles." He invited interested scholars to "chart *both* the styles and the contents, in order to determine which styles seem yoked to specific contents and which may operate across the board." He implored educators to develop "sensitivity to different intelligences and learning styles."[38] He was also open to the idea, suggested by Harvey Silver, that people with strengths in particular intelligences must still decide how to exploit those strengths and that this choice could be affected by their learning, cognitive, or personality style. "Perhaps the decision about *how* to use one's favored intelligence reflects one's preferred style," Gardner declared.[39] Despite these efforts at reconciliation, one could sense that Gardner was being diplomatic; he did not subscribe to the learning style idea, but he was initially hesitant to denounce it outright.

When Gardner was writing about learning styles in the 1990s, he seemed to be referring mostly to the personality styles of Myers–Briggs and the cognitive styles of Witkin (field dependent/independent) and Jerome Kagan (intuitive/analytic). However, by the 2000s, the VAK model had become more popular, and Gardner became more suspicious of learning styles in general, stating, "For one thing, such individuals speak about someone as having a 'visual' or 'auditory' learning style. I find this labeling scientifically ungrounded and conceptually confused." He continued: "Individuals who have trouble reading are often called 'visual learners' because they gravitate towards pictorial or graphic imagery rather than towards the text; but of course reading is visual as well, and these individuals are singled out precisely because they cannot read easily."[40] Thus, Gardner suggested that VAK learning style advocates had mistaken the cause for the effect by confusing linguistic weaknesses among students for strengths in other senses, when the real issue was that the student needed academic support in their linguistic intelligence.

Likewise, in later editions of his book *Multiple Intelligences in the Classroom*, Thomas Armstrong also hoped to differentiate learning styles from MI theory. Armstrong admitted that it was "tempting to want to relate MI theory to any number of learning-style theories that have gained prominence in the last two decades," yet he advised teachers not to do so. He echoed Gardner's assertion that learning style theories addressed only the processing of information, but MI theory addressed the learning of specific content. He directly targeted the VAK model, which he linked to Dunn's LSI: "A seemingly related theory, the Visual-Auditory-Kinesthetic model, is actually very different from MI theory in that it is a sensory-channel model," but MI theory was not "specifically tied to the senses," so attempting "to correlate MI theory with models like these is akin to comparing apples to oranges."[41] However, to most educators, correlating MI theory to learning styles was more like comparing oranges to tangerines than apples to oranges.

In the introduction to the tenth-anniversary edition of *Frames of Mind*, Gardner again clarified the differences between learning styles and his intelligences. First, he explained, he had compiled his seven intelligences not only by drawing upon empirical studies on intelligence and achievement (as many learning style typologies also did), but also by incorporating research on brain damage, savants, and evolutionary biology. This methodology, he wrote, made his approach distinct from both learning styles and other models of intelligence. Second, unlike learning styles, he linked his intelligences "to informational contents that exist in the world—numerical information, spatial information, information about other people." This underscored his interactionist approach to intelligence by emphasizing the role of real-life application to his intelligence model. Finally, he suggested that research on his MI theory undercut the idea that students had global learning styles that applied across all subjects. In *The Unschooled Mind* and other works, Gardner targeted the work of Jean Piaget, the developmental psychologist who argued that all children developed through global stages. Gardner developed his MI theory in part to dispute Piaget's idea of global developmental stages because he argued that each intelligence has its own independent stages. Had Gardner examined the research on learning styles a little closer, he would have discovered that most of the research on learning styles (or, at least, the VAK-oriented learning style typology) applied only to linguistic intelligence anyway, but that was beside the point.

In fact, Gardner's research for Project Spectrum found that the "same child that is reflective or engaged with one content can turn out to be impulsive or inattentive with another," and thus he cautioned against the "easy assumption that styles are independent of content." He and his team had also explored the idea of "working styles," which he defined in a series of dualities such as playful/serious, focused/distractible, persistent/frustrated, and reflective/impulsive. It is unclear from where his idea of "working styles" originated and exactly how they were different from learning styles. Nevertheless, he confirmed that "working styles depended . . . on the content of the area being explored." In other words, a child's working style may be "persistent" when writing, but "frustrated" when working on math; or "focused" when studying music, but "distractible when reading." He interpreted these findings as further evidence for the validity of his MI theory because it demonstrated localized separation among the cognitive domains and intelligences instead of global developmental stages and/or behaviors.[42]

In 2013, Gardner directly addressed the conflation of MI with learning styles again for an article in the *Washington Post*. Apparently unaware of research by Dunn and others, he pointed out that there was no "persuasive evidence that the learning style analysis produces more effective outcomes than a 'one size fits all approach.'" He then zeroed in on the VAK learning style typology with vitriol and frustration. Instead of suggesting that the VAK typology could somehow be reconciled with his MI theory as he had in the early 1990s, Gardner now argued that the two were not only incompatible, but MI theory disproved the existence of VAK-based learning styles altogether.

> Sometimes people speak about a "visual" learner or an "auditory" learner. The implication is that some people learn through their eyes, others through their ears. This notion is incoherent. Both spatial information and reading occur with the eyes, but they make use of entirely different cognitive faculties. Similarly, both music and speaking activate the ears, but again these are entirely different cognitive faculties. Recognizing this fact, the concept of intelligences does not focus on how linguistic or spatial information reaches the brain—via eyes, ears, hands, it doesn't matter. What matters is the power of the mental computer, the intelligence, that acts upon that sensory information, once picked up.[43]

His assault on learning styles continued. In 2019, Gardner posted a link on his blog to an article by Yasmin Anwar on how the brain reacts to reading and listening to the same story.[44] Anwar reported: "Using functional MRI, researchers scanned their brains in both the listening and reading conditions, compared their listening-versus-reading brain activity data, and found the maps they created from both databases were virtually identical."[45] In other words, human brains do not react differently to new information based on whether it has been learned visually or auditorily. As far as the brain is concerned, the information had been learned to the same degree regardless of what sense had been used to take it in. Although the article itself made no connection to learning styles, Gardner interpreted this as further refutation of the VAK learning style idea, and so he introduced the article under the heading "Why Learning Styles Based on Sensory Organs Make No Sense" and added that "the intelligence becomes operative only after information has been received by the cortex. . . . What matters is not whether the language is heard (auditory), read (visual) or perceived by touch (tactile, as with braille)."[46] By pointing solely to the VAK version of the learning style theory, he implied that other learning style models could still be valid.

By the time he published his memoir, *A Synthesizing Mind*, in 2020, Gardner declared that he "detested" the term *learning style* and unloaded his pent-up frustration. "*Multiple intelligences are not learning styles!*" he exclaimed in italics. He found the confusion of learning styles and multiple intelligences to be "appalling." He lamented how his "occasional attempts to insist on terminological distinctions [had] not been particularly successful" and so many "educators and laypersons continue[d] to collapse intelligences and styles." At the end of his career, Gardner's failure to clarify his position on learning styles was one of his biggest regrets as a researcher. "As for damage done, I regret this very much," he reflected. "I wish I could have done more to prevent it."[47] He should have had regrets, because it was own ambiguity on learning styles that contributed to the confusion in the first place.

In his 2019 blog post, Gardner insisted: "I have always taken care to distinguish 'multiple intelligences' from 'learning styles.'"[48] However, this was not entirely true. As demonstrated above, Gardner was initially quite open to the prospect that learning styles and multiple intelligences could potentially align, and at times he seemed to endorse the idea. For example, in *The Unschooled Mind*, Gardner wrote, "By the time of their entry to formal schooling, children have also developed more specific intellectual strengths and *styles*, which are part and parcel of the ways in which they will interact with the world beyond home."[49] The difference between teaching through a learning style approach and an MI approach were subtle—perhaps too subtle for most practitioners to even discern. For both approaches, teachers first identified the learning strengths of their students and then implemented alternative teaching methods that better aligned with their learning profile. Just as learning style advocates had done, Gardner openly endorsed individualized learning to "reach students who learn in different ways," and he implored teachers to "learn as much as you can about each student and teach each person in ways that they find comfortable and learn effectively."[50] Furthermore, in the preface to Armstrong's *Multiple Intelligences in the Classroom*, Gardner even wrote that "the essence of the theory is respect for . . . the multiple variations in the ways that [students] learn."[51] How, then, were "learning in different ways" and "multiple variations in the ways that they learn" different from learning styles? If they were different, these differences seemed to be largely semantic.

Even if the terminology and justification for learning styles and multiple intelligences were different, the classroom application of the competing theories were imperceptible to most teachers. For example, if an observer walked into a classroom and witnessed students creating physical models of a rockets to test scientific concepts, could the observer really determine whether the teacher justified the activity as "engaging kinesthetic learners" (i.e., VAK learning styles theory) or "developing students spatial and kinesthetic intelligence" (i.e., MI theory)? In other words, teaching to multiple intelligences and teaching through learning styles often looked the same in practice, and so the differences in terminology mattered far more to theorists than to classroom teachers.

Finally, Gardner could have done more to directly engage the literature on learning styles. In his memoir, he described himself as a great synthesizer.

Why, then, did he never do a formal literature review of research on learning styles to determine how his MI theory related to them? Throughout his career, Gardner seemed to have experienced the research on learning styles secondhand, only when it was conflated and confused with MI theory by educators. He seemed uninterested in engaging the research directly. For example, neither of his great works of synthesis, *Frames of Mind* and *The Mind's New Science*, made any reference to the research of Herman Witkin, despite Witkin being one of the most-cited psychologists of the 1970s.[52] Gardner's collaborator and competitor in intelligence theory, Robert Sternberg, did take learning style theory seriously, was very familiar with the research on the topic, and related his triarchic theory of intelligence directly to it (see chapter 6). Gardner, in contrast, showed little interest in learning style theory until it was too late.

Even though Gardner eventually came to resent the conflation of learning styles and multiple intelligences, he nevertheless benefited from teachers' confusion of the two. When he published *Frames of Mind* in 1983, the learning style theory was very much in the educational discourse. The race-specific learning style idea described in chapter 3 was peaking, and the popularity of VAK-oriented learning style model continued to rise, so the education world was primed for a new theory of intelligence based on a relativistic instead of a hierarchical model of intelligence. In other words, Gardner's theory of multiple intelligences did not flourish *despite* the learning style idea, it flourished *because* of the learning style idea. Learning style advocates had already laid the conceptual groundwork for MI theory, which educators interpreted as another example of what they knew intuitively: students learned differently from one another, and standardized testing did not account for this. Therefore, whether he wanted to acknowledge it or not, Gardner owed the popularity of his MI theory, in large part, to the very learning style idea he grew to detest.

*

As the multiple misapplications of MI theory proved, Gardner's theory was far more complicated than it appeared to be on the surface, and he struggled to describe the teaching implications of MI theory with precision. In 1998, the journalist James Traub visited the MI theory–based Key Learning Community in Indianapolis in preparation for his feature article on Gardner and MI theory for the *New Republic*. Traub admitted that he "expected Key to be one of those schools where kids learn everything in seven or eight ways, jumping up and down in math class and singing their way through English." Instead, what he witnessed were classes that looked "perfectly familiar." In fact, the only two features that distinguished the Key School from traditional schools were how "every student spent as much time on music and art as English or social studies," and how qualitative progress reports were issued to students based on their performance along a developmental continuum instead of an objective location "on invidious bell curves"—a clever choice of words in light of Gardner's role in the controversy over *The Bell Curve*.[53] Both of the Key School's innovations had little to do specifically with MI theory and could easily be aligned with the tenets of progressive education. Nevertheless, Traub was impressed by what he saw. But he doubted that most schools implemented MI theory as faithfully and with as much rigor as the Key School did, and he pondered whether misapplications of MI theory far outnumbered the faithful ones (as did Gardner).

Due to its complexity, ambiguity, and long list of caveats, MI theory was hard to implement accurately. The most relevant place to implement it was at the school and curriculum levels—not the classroom level—because the curriculum was the most appropriate place for all the intelligences to be addressed. For this reason, charter, magnet, and independent schools (such as the Key and New Schools) were the most likely to implement the theory fully and accurately. Effective implementation required a top-down reorganization of the entire school curriculum, as well as an administration fully committed to supporting it. If understood accurately, there was little that individual teachers at the high school and middle school levels could do with MI theory because math teachers worked solely in logical-mathematical intelligence and English teachers worked solely in linguistic intelligence. Thus, the irony of the popularity of multiple intelligences was that the more accurate an understanding a teacher had of MI theory, the more limited its use. Conversely, the more simplistic and inaccurate understanding a teacher had of MI theory (and the more it was conflated with learning styles), the more useful it became for teachers.

As part of his reportage for the *New Republic*, Traub handed Gardner a copy of a book full of frivolous teaching suggestions called *Celebrating Multiple Intelligences*. Gardner read it, frowned, and said, "I would not want to be in a school where a lot of time was spent doing these things."[54] Historians can never know what percentage of teachers implemented Gardner's MI theory rigorously and what percentage had students "singing their way through English." However, given the thousands of citations on MI theory in the 1990s and 2000s, one has to assume that many of the applications of Gardner's theory were misguided, trivial, or wrong. But did most teachers care that they were misapplying the theory, especially if they got results? For example, the philosopher John White, a critic of MI theory, related a story of an award-winning teacher in England who told several struggling students that they were "musically or bodily intelligent" and adopted his English teaching to "their preferred learning styles, via karate-based lessons in punctuation and silly, guitar-accompanied songs on the concept of the adverb." White wrote that "this zaniness really paid off," and, as a result of the teacher's "inspired idiocy," the students were "eating out of his hand."[55]

Meant as illustration of the absurdity of MI theory in practice, White's anecdote unintentionally revealed several things: (1) that like this award-winning teacher, most practitioners instinctually turned the multiple intelligences into a learning style theory; (2) that the metacognitive and emotional impact of telling struggling students that they had a different—not a deficient—learning style had an immediate impact on their behavior, learning, focus, and self-esteem; and (3) that educators commonly aligned struggling learners with bodily-kinesthetic intelligence. The dangerous and problematic repercussions of the kinesthetic learner classification as an identity, especially when applied to students of color, is the subject of the next chapter.

5
The Kinesthetic Learner as Identity

Even though Herman Witkin and his colleagues had found little connection between race and field dependent/independent cognitive styles, and even though Black and Latine scholars concluded that race-based learning styles were dangerous, the idea persisted. In 1993, Howard Gardner received an unexpected email from a colleague in Australia who informed him that a province there had circulated a document based on his MI theory that aligned different races and ethnicities with intelligence strengths and weaknesses.

Gardner was "stunned" that an official organization was using his MI theory to generate and justify racial stereotypes. After all, he had developed his MI theory in part to move beyond the racial biases found in traditional IQ testing. "If we had adequate measures, there may well be some differences in average profiles of intelligence across groups," he later explained, "but certainly, the variation within any demography would overwhelm any difference between demographics."[1] In other words, even if one racial group proved to have a slightly higher average in musical intelligence, say, than that of another racial group, the number of individuals with high or low musical intelligence *within* the alleged nonmusical group would likely be far greater than the average difference between the two groups. Thus, asserting that one group had musical intelligence strong enough to justify a different curriculum for those students would be unwarranted.

Gardner's point about the dangers of stereotyping across racial and ethnic groups echoed those made by critics of all biological-based racial theories throughout the twentieth century. To put an immediate end to this kind of race-based labeling, Gardner appeared on a popular Australian television news program to clarify that his "ideas were being exploited to justify unwarranted educational interventions," and the province quietly dropped the idea of aligning ethnic groups with specific intelligences.[2] Given the history of using educational assessment to label and sort ethnic minorities, and especially students of color, it was not surprising that MI theory would be used for that purpose.

Throughout his career, Gardner deliberately avoided the topic of race. In contrast, best-selling authors such as Stephen Jay Gould and Jonathan Kozol made race a central concern in their best-selling books *The Mismeasure of Man* (1981) and *Savage Inequalities* (1992), which were published within years of Gardner's *Frames of Mind* (1983). In the introduction to the revised and expanded edition of *The Mismeasure of Man*, Gould listed the ways he had supported the civil rights movement in his youth and confessed how his "convictions about social justice" inspired him to write his book, which traced and critiqued scientists' abuses of statistical methods to make unwarranted racist claims about the inferiority of certain racial groups.[3] In *Savage Inequalities*, Kozol, who won a National Book Award for reporting about the lives of inner-city children in the 1960s, exposed "the remarkable degree of racial segregation that persisted" among American schools, a trend that had only intensified during the 1980s.[4] *The Mismeasure of Man*, *Frames of Mind*, and *Savage Inequalities* would likely have been on the bookshelves of the very same liberal and progressive readers in the 1990s (all three were recommended to me by professors in graduate school in the early 2000s). In fact, many scholars cited both Gould and Gardner as evidence that IQ testing was problematic, biased, and perhaps even racist. However, unlike Gould and Kozol, Gardner chose to circumvent the issue of race and ethnicity in his work: "I suspect that if intelligent-fair tests were developed, they would reveal differences across gender and other readily identifiable groups. . . . I have elected not to pursue this question." Citing the example of the Australian province's racial profiling, Gardner related how "group differences have been exploited for politically dubious ends . . . and I prefer not to provide additional ammunition for such efforts."[5]

Gardner's race-neutral prescriptions nevertheless had racial implications, given the racialized state of education in the US. As Joe Kinechloe pointed out in his insightful critique of MI theory, "In this power vacuum Gardner is not unlike many other upper- middle-class Americans in that he cannot imagine how dominant-power-inscribed psychologies and educational practices can harm individuals—especially those marginalized in some way by the dynamics of, say, race, class, or gender."[6] As referenced above, Gardner deliberately chose to ignore race, ethnicity, and class in his work. This omission contributed to the sense that he was speaking mainly to a White, middle-class audience who welcomed the idea that their children were smart in a way that was not recognized by IQ tests and traditional schooling. Gardner never expressed much concern for marginalized populations, or the possible impact of his theory on these populations. Even though Gardner's MI theory was race blind in theory, the labeling of low-income students as kinesthetic learners forced his theory to become racialized in practice.

This chapter explores how the learning style idea interacted with the troubling history of labeling minoritized students with unique intellectual traits and deficiencies. Specifically, I demonstrate how educators have consistently aligned Black and Latine students with an alleged predilection for hands-on, vocational-based education, and as a result steered them away from the academic curriculum offered to White students. I argue that the learning style idea furthered this trend by disproportionately labeling students of color as kinesthetic learners—a classification that was included in both Gardner's MI theory and the popular VAK-based typologies.

As MI theory and VAK-based learning style theory grew in popularity, so did the tendency to label the most vulnerable and oppressed student populations with the identity of kinesthetic, tactile, or physical learners, which was then used to justify a curriculum that diverted these students away from the linguistic-based knowledge and skills they would need to be successful in college, careers, and civic life. "I feel there are great dangers in the misuse of learning style concepts," David Kolb warned in 1981. "Specifically we must avoid turning these ideas into stereotypes used to pigeon-hole individuals."[7] Unfortunately, Kolb's warning was not heeded. As demonstrated in this chapter, learning style advocates routinely and consistently aligned "culturally deprived" and at-risk students as tactile, physical, and kinesthetic learners, which well-meaning teachers then used to justify less rigorous learning activities for these marginalized students. Therefore, the tendency to use the "kinesthetic" label to divert marginalized students away from the same curriculum to which the so-called visual and auditory learners had access to was ultimately the most dangerous outcome of the learning style idea.

Industrial Learning and Minoritized Students

As discussed in chapter 3, many learning style advocates in the 1970s and '80s pursued the idea that there may be Black and/or Latine learning style. In contrast, advocates for some version of the VAK-based typology considered the learning style idea to be race neutral. However, as the VAK typology was adapted by an educational establishment with a history of structural and institutional racism, the race neutrality of this typology became harder to maintain. There was a long history in the United States of labeling students of color with alleged intellectual deficiencies and differences, and this tendency went hand in hand with offering these students a diminished, nonacademic curriculum that prepared them for manual labor and second-class social status. Therefore, the VAK learning style typology was a continuation of this longstanding trend; students of color were more likely to be labeled kinesthetic learners, and thus far more likely to be offered the kind of trivial and less rigorous activities that often went along with that classification.

The Black educator Booker T. Washington was one of the first to align his southern Black students with an industrial education during the post–Civil War years at the Hampton and Tuskegee Institutes that focused on thrift, humility, and vocational-industrial instruction, instead of the academic curriculum offered to White students. Backed by northern White philanthropists, Washington offered his recently emancipated Black population the skills for employment in low-level trades. Washington believed economic independence needed to precede political empowerment and social equality, and many White supporters agreed. As one White Alabama politician, J. L. M. Curry, argued, an academic curriculum for Black students "would spoil a good plow hand," and so he supported Washington's industrial education for Black students to keep Black workers at the socioeconomic bottom. Most of the northern White philanthropists who funded Washington's industrial education argued that Black students needed to accept their subservient role in the social order because Black people could not handle intellectually engaging work. "Time has proven that [the Negro] is best fitted to perform the heavy labor of the Southern States," the industrialist William Baldwin opined "This will permit the southern white laborer to perform the more expert labor, and to leave the fields, the mines, and the simpler trades for the Negro."[8]

White leaders extended this kind of hierarchical thinking to other minoritized groups as well. Educators of Indigenous Americans offered a vocational curriculum to its students at boardings schools, such as the United States Indian Industrial School in Carlisle, Pennsylvania. At these schools, Indigenous Americans were also offered a hands-on industrial curriculum that was meant to teach discipline, obedience, and assimilation to White society. At these boarding schools, Indigenous students were forced to cut their hair and abandon their tribal customs, language, and culture. As Estelle Reel, superintendent of Indian education from 1898 to 1919, explained, "Industrial training will make the Indian boy a useful, practical, self-supporting citizen. It will make the Indian girls more motherly."[9] Samuel T. Dutton, superintendent of schools for Brookline, Massachusetts, confirmed in 1907 the prevailing view that "the only hope of elevating the Indian and African lies in a sort of industrial reformation."[10] In the late nineteenth and early twentieth centuries, educators were convinced that Black, Mexican American, and Indigenous students did not have the intellectual capacity to handle an academic curriculum anyway, and so offering them a more useful industrial curriculum not only better prepared them for their likely subservient role in the social order, but it also better aligned with the so-called savage or primitive psychological-sociological stage they were believed to inhabit.[11]

Washington's Hampton–Tuskegee model was also extended to Indigenous populations of Cuba, Hawaii, the Philippines, and Puerto Rico when these territories came under the autonomy of the United States after the Spanish–American War in the 1900s. Charles Bartlett Dyke, who had worked with Indigenous populations in Hawaii, stated in 1909: "Psychical race differences are not eliminated in any appreciable number of generations be the education what it may. . . . [Therefore,] primitive man must be trained for vocations that fit him for life in the white man's world."[12] This racist and paternalistic thinking toward the "primitive" races justified a curriculum grounded in hands-on practical learning that engaged the body more than the mind, discouraged critical thinking, and generally taught these groups to accept their subservient place in society as manual laborers. Educational leaders did not hide their intensions. In fact, Secretary of the Interior Franklin Lane was proud of the second-class education that the US provided Blacks and Indigenous Americans. "The Indian we feel we are responsible for as a Nation, and we give him an education—a most practical one," he boasted in 1919, and "the Negro . . . is slowly, very slowly coming into that . . . knowledge of the way of making a living." Whereas hands-on learning for White students meant engaging in academic projects, for students of color, hands-on learning meant "a practical education" aimed solely at "making a living."[13]

The deficit approach to students of color continued during the Progressive Era, the Great Depression, and World War II. In the racially integrated schools outside the American South, intelligence tests were administered to all students, and guidance counselors often shunted students of color into vocational tracks. As discussed earlier, Lewis Terman recommended in *Measurement of Intelligence* that "Spanish-Indian and Mexican families of the Southwest and . . . negroes . . . be segregated in special classes and be given instruction which is concrete and practical."[14] Even leading progressive opponents to intelligence testing, such as the psychologist William Bagley and the anthropologist Ruth Benedict, had disparaging things to say about the Black intellect: Bagley asserted in 1925, "No one can seriously doubt the general superiority of the whites over the negroes in native intelligence," and Benedict stated in 1940, "Great numbers of negroes are not ready for full citizenship."[15] In the underfunded, segregated schools in the South as well as the North,

Black students graduated at much lower rates than their White counterparts. As a result, by the mid-1940s, less than half of the 4.7 million Black citizens in Alabama, Georgia, Louisiana, Mississippi, and South Carolina had completed five years of formal schooling.[16] Even when Black teachers offered their Black students an academic curriculum, they had to do so secretly because their White administrators and financiers demanded that Black students be taught an industrial curriculum.

All of this added up to diminished educational offerings for most students of color prior to the 1960s. In all cases, White educational leaders argued that these non-White populations did not have the intellectual capacity to handle the same coursework and curriculum as White students, and so they were offered a hands-on, practical, nonacademic curriculum as an alternative. For nearly a century, the exclusive offering of a hands-on, practical learning to students of color has been linked to racial segregation and oppression in American education, and this trend continued with the ascendency of the learning style idea.

As explored in the first two chapters, the learning style idea emerged from the post-*Brown* and post–civil rights context of trying to remedy the achievement gap between White students and students of color. Although this impulse was egalitarian in nature, the first learning style advocates nevertheless identified Black and Latine as more likely to be physical, tactile, or kinesthetic learners with an alleged predisposition for a hands-on, job-oriented, utilitarian curriculum. In 1954, in one of the first-ever VAK learning style assessments, Robert E. Mills confirmed that "children of low intelligence" learned best through the kinesthetic method—again aligning the kinesthetic classification with struggling learners, who were more likely to be Black or Latine.

When the learning style idea was introduced in the 1960s, scholars continued to reinforce the idea that Black and Latine students learned best through kinesthetic methods. In 1962, Frank Riessman pointed to the "anti-intellectualism and narrow practicality of the deprived" to justify his assertion that inner-city Black children had a "physical style of learning" that required "doing things, touching things." A physical learner, Riessman elaborated, "has to get one's muscles into it, and this takes time."[17] Rita Dunn likewise confirmed that low-income students were kinesthetic learners: "Our slower, or 'disadvantaged,' students frequently experience difficulty when trying to learn"; therefore, these students required "kinesthetic involvement with information, skills, attitude, or values before [they could] even begin to understand through either a visual or auditory exposure."[18] Others agreed with this assessment. Writing in the 1980s, Joy Reid found that English-language learners—especially Spanish speakers—"strongly preferred kinesthetic and tactile learning styles," and Norma Ewing and Fung Lan Yong confirmed in the 1990s that even gifted Black and Latine students "preferred kinesthetic modality of learning" and therefore required "active, real-life experiences . . . to meet their learning needs." Thus, the learning style idea was not only being used to justify the classification of students of color as less developed than their White counterparts, but it was also being used to align them with a more concrete and utilitarian curriculum grounded in "real-life experiences."[19]

Hands-on activities were undoubtedly an effective way to grab and keep the attention of struggling learners and to connect academic content to real-world applications—good pedagogy for students of any race. However, these educators were not merely suggesting relevant, hands-on activities to initially hook or interest minoritized students en route to a rigorous, academic curriculum. Rather, they were recommending that teachers assign a semipermanent label to these mostly low-income, minoritized students and introduce all new content to them solely through the kinesthetic lens. In contrast, as discussed in chapter 3, Black and Latine educators such as Asa Hilliard III and Janice Hale never included a preference or predilection for kinesthetic methods or learning in their discussions of race-based learning styles. So, the "kinesthetic learner" label was mainly something White educators applied to Black and Latine students without the input and cooperation of the minoritized communities themselves. Although these well-meaning educators did not directly align kinesthetic learning with job training as previous generations had done, they nevertheless suggested a practical, hands-on curriculum that diverged from the more academic curriculum being offered to most White students in suburban schools.

Kinesthetic Leaners as At-Risk Students

The tradition of labeling students of color and aligning them with an academically diminished curriculum continued in the 1980s when educators replaced Riessman's term *culturally deprived* with new term: *at-risk*. The term *at-risk* was originally coined to designate those students who faced socioeconomic hardships and thus could potentially be overlooked in the push toward standardized testing and academic excellence. These students were allegedly at risk of falling behind their peers and then dropping out of school. The term was intended to be race neutral; after all, plenty of White students were impoverished, struggled academically, and dropped out of school. However, given the racialized nature of American society, the term soon became racialized as well. As one definition specified, "Home conditions that contribute to being educationally at risk include poverty, low educational attainments of parents, single parent families, and non-English speaking families."[20] In other definitions, the label was extended to include any students with learning disabilities. In 1990, legislators amended and renamed the Education for All Handicapped Children Act of 1975 as the Individuals with Disabilities Education Act (IDEA). With this expansion came higher numbers of students with classifications. In fact, the number of students identified as having special needs grew from 8.3 percent to 13.3 percent of the overall student population between 1976 and 2000.[21]

Scholars debated whether this growth simply meant that previously overlooked students were getting the services they required and deserved, or whether students—specifically, Black and Latine students—were being overdiagnosed with learning and emotional disabilities. By the end of the twentieth century, Black students were three time more likely than White students to be labeled with an intellectual disability. Latine students were far less likely to have these labels than Black students, but they were nevertheless classified with learning disabilities at higher rates than White students.[22] Since a higher percentage of Black and Latine students met these criteria than White students, the "at-risk" label was disproportionately applied to minoritized students, and it soon came to serve as another term for urban Black and Latine students. As the historians Sylvia Martinez and John Rury concluded in their study: "The term [*at-risk*] has become almost exclusively used in reference to groups and individuals who are labelled 'poor' and 'minority' and who were described as 'deprived' in the past."[23] In one instance in 1994, the Austin Independent School District in Texas applied the label to 46 percent of its largely Latine student population, because these students technically met the criteria established by the state. When a letter was sent home explaining why their students (including some straight-A students) were designated at-risk, parents protested; the district issued an apology, even though it was simply following state policy of identifying students based on demographic data.[24]

The "kinesthetic learner" label could be traced back to work of Grace Fernald, but it became more common after the publication of Gardner's *Frames of Mind*. This label was the only intelligence of Gardner's original seven to overlap with the one of the channels from the VAK model, which seemed to underscore the misperception that MI was a learning style theory and that kinesthetic learning was the most significant intelligence in the classroom. As Stephen J. Denig asserted in his oft-cited article, "Multiple Intelligences and Learning Styles: Two Complementary Perspectives": "Both multiple intelligences and learning styles discuss kinesthetic learners."[25] Actually, Gardner never used the term *kinesthetic learner*. In *Frames of Mind*, he defined bodily-kinesthetic intelligence as "the ability to use one's body in highly differentiated and skilled ways, for expressive as well as goal-directed purposes." Experts who drew upon this intelligence included "dancers and swimmers—who develop keen mastery over the motions of their bodies, as well as those individuals—like artisans, ballplayers, and instrumentalists—who are able to manipulate objects with finesse."[26] Like he had done for the other six intelligences, Gardner outlined how bodily-kinesthetic intelligence met his criteria by demonstrating its role in the evolutionary history of humankind, its present use among primates, its distinct role among autistic and brain-damaged individuals, the anthropological role of dance among different cultures, and the kinesthetic aspects of comedy, acting, and athletics.

Despite his avoidance of the exact term *kinesthetic learner*, Gardner nevertheless endorsed the idea that some students learn best with their hands and bodies. In his books on pedagogy, Gardner later introduced the "experiential" approach as one of his "five entry points" for students who learned "best with a hands-on approach, dealing directly with the materials the embody or convey the concept." The experiential entry point was meant to engage students' kinesthetic intelligence, although Gardner was inconsistent about what exactly this meant.[27] In his book *Intelligence Reframed* (1999), he renamed the experiential entry point "Hands On" and declared that "many people, particularly children, most easily approach a topic through an activity in which they become fully engaged—where they can build something, manipulate materials, or carry out experiments." To address kinesthetic intelligence, Gardner gave the example of the US Holocaust Memorial Museum giving "alternative identities" to visitors as an example of a "powerful educational experience."[28] Indeed, anyone who has visited the Holocaust Memorial Museum can confirm that seeing whether your assigned victim lived or perished at the end of the exhibit is a moving aspect of the experience. But was this really a sound example of how to engage students' kinesthetic intel ligence? Would an athlete or dancer really be better at walking through a museum with an identification card (or be more affected by the experience) than anyone else? Wouldn't this be more accurately described as interpersonal intelligence? In fact, in *The Disciplined Mind*, Gardner listed historical "role play" as an example of an "interpersonal point of entry," not an experiential point of entry, thus underscoring the confusion around exactly what Gardner's kinesthetic-based learning should look like.[29]

Gardner never implied that low-income or at-risk students were more likely to have kinesthetic intelligence, but he did seem to imply that it was more common for young children to enjoy kinesthetic activities than older students. In other words, he implied there was a developmental aspect to the "kinesthetic learner" designation. No one contributed more to the trend of aligning at-risk and students with disabilities students with kinesthetic learning more than Rita Dunn. In a 2009 article, Dunn and a coauthor listed a catalog of educational deficits that characterized at-risk students: "[They are] learning disabled, grow up in isolated communities and do not begin learning English until they enter school, do not speak English because they have recently arrived from another country, live in poverty and lack educational resources in their homes, [and/or are] children of migrant workers or undocumented immigrants."[30] Based on this list of characteristics, nearly all at-risk students would likely have been Black or Latine. In fact, in a 1990 article, Dunn and her coauthors stated plainly. "Nearly one quarter of all children under age 15 are Black and Hispanic, and they are the most likely to achieve poorly in school, become at-risk, and drop out."[31] She and her husband, Kenneth Dunn, directly aligned at-risk students with a preference for tactile-kinesthetic learning: "Many at-risk adolescents in middle schools and high schools tend to be highly tactile (i.e., need hands-on learning experiences and manipulatives), kinesthetic learners (i.e., need frequent mobility) or both. The best strategies for engaging tactual and kinesthetic learners' minds are to engage their hands and bodies with manipulative instructional resources or to allow them to learn on their feet."[32] They also later confirmed that "Most Special Education (SPED) students have only tactual and/or kinesthetic strengths."[33]

Again, Dunn never suggested that the purpose of kinesthetic learning for at-risk students, students of color, and students with disabilities was for job training or preparation for second-class social status. In fact, she was careful to direct her suggested methods toward academic subject matter. Yet her insistence in aligning permanent labels to students (e.g., "only have tactile and/or kinesthetic strengths")—as well as her rejection of the idea that teachers ought to move students away from kinesthetic learning toward the more-valued visual and auditory learning—reflected a static social outlook in which students were stuck for life with their ascribed characteristics. Her labeling also reflected a general ambiguity (one that plagued the entire field of learning style) around the issue of whether learning styles were developmental or relativistic.

Kinesthetic Learners as Less Developed

In theory, according to the rhetoric of learning style advocates, kinesthetic learners were not less developed or less intelligent, they just learned differently than visual and auditory learners. However, in practice, kinesthetic learners were far more likely to be aligned with negative traits than auditory and visual learners. Thus, the "kinesthetic" label continued the long tradition of aligning behavioral and intellectual deficits with students who were more likely to be Black, Latine, or Indigenous. As one pair of teachers explained, kinesthetic learners were "poor listeners [who had] difficulty paying attention," "seem[ed] quite restless," were "not organized," and had "poor sense of time."[34] Raymond Swassing and Walter Barbe noted how kinesthetic learners were impulsive, fidgety, "not avid reader[s]," "often poor speller[s]," wore clothes that were "wrinkled through activity," and quickly lost "interest in detailed verbal discourse."[35] Dunn described kinesthetic learners as those who could not "sit at desks for more than twelve to fifteen minutes without squirming, falling out of their seats," and those who could not "listen and retain three quarters of the new and difficult academic information they hear or read."[36] As much as learning style advocates insisted that all learning styles were equal, their descriptions of the actual traits of kinesthetic learners were rarely ones that most students or parents would have wanted to be affiliated with.

Despite Dunn's aligning of the "kinesthetic" label with struggling learners, she attempted to be egalitarian by applying the term to then President George H. W. Bush. "Some children, when first introduced to difficult information, learn best by doing—running, jumping, walking, bouncing and moving," Dunn explained to the *Washington Post* in 1991. "These kinesthetic learners, like the kinesthetic President Bush, problem-solve through sport. They learn theory through simulation, concept through enactment." Whether President Bush had ever formally been assessed as a kinesthetic learner or whether Dunn diagnosed him from afar was unclear. Either way, the egalitarian message was that kinesthetic learners could accomplish anything they wanted—even become president of the United States. However, Dunn was inconsistent with this message, because elsewhere she noted the developmental aspects of the designation: "Data support the findings that many children are more tactile and kinesthetic in the primary grades. As they become 2nd and 3rd graders, their ability to remember visually becomes stronger."[37] Dunn seemed to be implying that kinesthetic learning was something that most children grew out of by third grade, but at-risk adolescents were stuck forever in the kinesthetic stage as the psychological equivalent of second- and third-graders. As Dunn stated elsewhere, "With time youngsters preferences evolve from psychomotor (learning through touching and experiencing things) to visual and then to auditory, as the learner matures."[38] Similarly, Dunn's former student and collaborator, Marie Carbo, also equated young students with at-risk learners, asserting that "most young students and at-risk readers tend to be primarily global learners," by which she meant field dependent. Carbo recommended using the “Fernald word-tracing method” with “global/tactile students.”[39] If you put these assertions together, Dunn and Carbo implied that at-risk Black and Latine students were stuck in an earlier, kinesthetic stage of development, whereas White students made it to a higher stage of development represented by the auditory and visual senses. The racist implications of this conclusion were obvious, but Dunn and Carbo were careful not to state this outright.

In fact, the controversy of whether learning styles were developmental or relativistic plagued the movement from the beginning. In a 1977 review of Witkin’s field dependent/independent cognitive styles, the educational psychologists Lee Cronbach and Richard Snow pondered whether “workers such as Witkin . . . [were] only demonstrating what Binet built into his definition of intelligence: The principle that weakness in analysis or self-discipline is a cause of poor intellectual performance.” In other words, Cronbach and Snow argued that field independence was just part of a more developed general intelligence, not a relativistic cognitive style, so individuals who were field dependent were just less intelligent than those who were field independent. Thus, the critics insisted, “the ‘field dependent’ is a deficit rather than style.” Witkin did not agree with this assessment. He responded to Cronbach and Snow via personal communication that “the field-dependent person” might have “a positive advantage in dealing with some kinds of complex situation—particularly, interpersonal situations—where the analytic person uses his intelligence badly.”[40] That is, in some contexts, a field independent person may have psychological advantages, but in other contexts a field dependent person may have an advantage.

Perhaps appreciating the racial implications of the development versus relativistic approach, both Witkin and Dunn equivocated on the issue throughout their careers. Neither wanted to state outright that the learning style more common among students of color represented an earlier stage of development than the style more common for White students. Yet both of their assessment instruments often generated results that implied this was the case. But if learning style advocates such as Carbo, Dunn, and Witkin employed their learning style inventories individually to Black and Latine students, then they could avoid racial stereotyping. However, many teachers did not have access to these inventories; nor did they have the time or inclination to administer them. Therefore, many teachers likely wondered, why even bother to assess students individually when the research has already determined that most at-risk Black and Latine students were kinesthetic learners? As Dunn generalized in 1995: “Many male adolescents . . . underachievers, at risk and drop-out students are almost exclusively tactile or kinesthetic learners.”[41]

Furthermore, at least two empirical studies of learning style interventions in predominantly Black schools—in Greensboro, North Carolina, and Freeport, Illinois—demonstrated increased achievement when teachers employed kinesthetic and tactile activities with these minoritized students.[42] A 1992 study of gifted minoritized students in Chicago public schools also found that gifted "Mexican American students" and "African-American Students" both preferred "kinesthetic modality" to the auditory and visual modalities, and a 2002 study on the learning styles of English-language learners (ELLs), including Armenian, Hmong, Korean, Mexican, and Vietnamese students, concluded: "All of the ethnic groups indicated either major or minor preferences for kinesthetic and tactile learning." The authors insisted that teachers plan "instructional activities and develop curricular materials that will require whole body involvement and provide experiential learning . . . so that they can learn by doing."[43] Even some Black educators embraced the "kinesthetic" label. "A large percentage of African American males are tactile and kinesthetic learners," the educational consultant Jawanza Kunjufu asserted in his 2011 book *Understanding Black Male Learning Styles*. Despite the overriding rejection by culturally responsive educators in the mid-1990s of the idea that there was a Black learning style (see chapter 3), the idea persisted among some Black educators, who continued to employ the cultural mismatch theory as an explanation for why many Black students struggled in school. "If at least two-thirds of your students are visual-pictures, oral, auditory, tactile, and kinesthetic learners, it should be obvious that you are now approaching the national proportion of 80 percent or more Black male students who may not be visual-print learners," Kunjufu explained. "In contrast, teachers use ditto sheets and textbooks 90 percent of the time. Is it any wonder that Black boys are struggling in school?"[44] James A. Banks continued to cite the cultural mismatch theory as justification for multicultural education in his updated versions of his popular textbook, *An Introduction to Multicultural Education*, though he made no references to kinesthetic learners. In 1986, Janice Hale updated her book *Black Children: Their Roots, Culture, and Learning Styles* to include Gardner's MI theory, which, according to Hale, knocked "language and logic off their pedestal," and thus allowed the "strengths of African-American culture" to be better recognized and celebrated. However, she too did not recognize the VAK model or make any attempts to classify Black students as kinesthetic learners.[45]

As multicultural education made inroads in American schools, educators were caught in a difficult position. On the one hand, they were asked to recognize the impact of cultural difference on classroom learning, which invited generalizations about the characteristics of racial and ethnic groups.

On other hand, to avoid racial stereotyping or racial insensitivity, educators emphasized the importance of assessing students at the individual level, because many individuals within a racial or ethnic group did not share the common characteristics aligned with the group. To this end, Dunn and her coauthor, Shirley Griggs, cataloged the cultural and learning preferences of racial groups in their book *Multiculturalism and Learning Style* (1995). According to Dunn and Griggs, Indigenous American students preferred "peer and team learning . . . low mobility and a rejection of learning in the afternoon . . . [and] simultaneous processing, field independence, and reflective learning." Latine students preferred "cooler temperatures, formal design, and peer learning . . . reveal[ed] low levels of persistence . . . [preferred] learning kinesthetically, [and needed] bright light and a quiet environment." Black students preferred "not to be auditory learners . . . high mobility," and "afternoon learning." Asian Americans preferred "significantly more quiet" and had "high motivation and persistence and need for high structure." Finally, European Americans "preferred warmer temperatures," studying independently, and auditory learning.[46] The authors were careful to report differences among ethnic groups within each race category (e.g., Chinese versus Koreans), but the whole point of the book was to determine group similarities that could be leveraged by teachers and school counselors. Interestingly, Dunn and Briggs incorporated the findings of Witkin and his associates on field dependence/independence, as well as the research on the Black and Latine learning style by Janice Hale, Manuel Ramírez, and Barbara Shade, implying that Dunn's LSI was compatible with these competing typologies. Still, Dunn also insisted that the LSI was the "instrument with the highest reliability and validity and the one based on the most research on learning styles."[47]

As related above, Dunn and her associates made numerous data-backed statements about minoritized populations, such as the fact they were more likely to be labeled at-risk and more likely to be labeled as kinesthetic learners. But, when critics pointed to the lack of research on the efficacy of teaching to learning styles in general, Dunn insisted that students needed to be assessed individually, not buried in group data. Her inconsistency on the issue of individual versus group data reflected the fact that the learning style idea was not holding up to scrutiny; having dedicated her entire career to the idea, though, she was not going to back away from it. Moreover, Dunn exacerbated a growing tendency in the 1990s and beyond to link the alleged learning preferences to student identities, so students with relative strengths in kinesthetic methods became "kinesthetic learners," as an identity that was then linked to other labels, such as "at-risk" and other racialized generalizations.

Teaching the "Really Hands-On Kinesthetic Types"

After educators assessed the at-risk students with VAK learning style assessment tools, the students were identified as kinesthetic learners and provided with hands-on and active learning activities. There is nothing inherently wrong with hands-on, active learning, especially when it used to excite and engage learners, or when it is centered around intellectually rigorous activities such as a science lab or interpreting primary source documents. In fact, well-designed hands-on activities have proven to be successful with all students, not only struggling learners. But historically in many cases, the activities suggested for kinesthetic learners were low-level, rote, and/or cognitively undemanding—that is, the kinesthetic methods were a way to keep the at-risk students occupied, whereas other students were engaged in a more academically rigorous activities involving auditory, visual, and linguistic methods.

Dunn suggested several activities to engage these tactile-kinesthetic learners, including task cards, learning stations, board games, role playing, dramatizations, and posing questions through a "pic-a-hole self-corrective tactual resource." Most of these activities were designed to get and keep the students' attention, but they still required the "visual" method of reading text or the "auditory" method of understanding directions and/or explaining things to others. Perhaps it was not that these students had a perceptual strength in kinesthetic learning, just that they needed more engaging instruction to keep them on task for activities that eventually required auditory and linguistic learning. But this is not how Dunn saw it. In fact, she insisted that they be labeled as tactile-kinesthetic learners: "Tactual and kinesthetic instruction works because the learners' strongest perceptual modalities are in these areas."[48] Ultimately, many of the activities that Dunn and her coauthors suggested were pedagogically sound, but they did not need to be justified by the VAK learning style typology to be useful and effective. And by making the connection between at-risk students and kinesthetic learning, Dunn unwittingly connected her typology to a long history of offering marginalized youth a vocationally oriented curriculum.

This was not Dunn's intention. In fact, throughout her career, she was clear that kinesthetic learning ought to be as demanding as auditory and visual learning and that all students ought to achieve the same learning goals, regardless of learning style. "Be certain . . . to emphasize to the entire class that all students will be responsible for learning and mastering the identical objectives," she and a coauthor advised, "but each will learn the information through his or her learning style strengths."[49] Clearly, though, many teachers were not getting the message. As one English teacher alleged, kinesthetic learners were those who "want to act out a situation, to make a product, and in general to be busy with their learning." Citing Barbe and Swassing, Dunn, and Gardner, this teacher suggested making library displays, comic books, mobiles, plot diagrams, and timelines; drawing portraits of characters; and role playing scenes in small groups. She also suggested having the kinesthetic learners "present their findings using a talk show format" and/or videotaped commercials. She related: "There is usually quite a clamor among the really hands-on kinesthetic types over who gets to be camerapersons."[50] Here we see the tendency to label some students the "hands-on kinesthetic type" and to assign them a nonacademic activity (e.g., camerawork, drawing, acting) instead of an academic one. In other words, the kinesthetic learners were assigned the nonacademic task of holding the camera, while the visual and auditory learners did the academic work of researching the topic, writing the script, and delivering the information. Other learning style advocates suggested representing knowledge in nonlinguistic ways, such as creating "a human illustration," performing a skit, or building a model, in addition to using "charades," "dioramas," "mind maps," "play dough representations," and "role plays."[51] There was nothing inherently wrong with any of these methods, but again, if the kinesthetic learners were playing with play dough while the visual learners were writing essays, these differentiated activities mirrored the social inequalities that existed outside the classroom, and all students were not achieving the same learning outcomes.

Furthermore, the teaching suggestions for addressing kinesthetic learners revealed the vagueness of the concept and the difficulty of isolating kinesthetic senses. Some of the suggestions that advocates made for kinesthetic learners included writing "notes to remember things," taking "notes during lectures and discussions," and drawing "pictures of what is learned."[52] Some suggested finger pointing, tracing letters and numbers, using manipulatives in math, and assembling words with wood letters to spell. Others suggested setting up learning centers, walking to the library, and presenting information through dramatic performances and/or dance routines so kinesthetic learners could move around as they learned. Besides the fact that these hands-on activities still involved visual and auditory learning, activities such as notetaking and the use of manipulatives in math have been proven to be effective for *all* students, not only those who have been labeled "kinesthetic learners." Furthermore, these suggestions demonstrate a general confusion about exactly what kinesthetic methods are and how kinesthetic learning could be isolated in pure form from visual and auditory learning.

The simplification of kinesthetic intelligence became one of the most common misapplications of Gardner's MI theory, an issue he addressed in an article on the myths of multiple intelligences. "I have seen classes in which children are encouraged to move their arms or to run around, on the assumption that exercising one's body represents itself some kind of MI statement," Gardner noted, referring in reference to teachers' misguided efforts to develop bodily-kinesthetic intelligence. He then clarified, "Random muscular movements have nothing to do with the cultivation of the mind . . . or even the body!"[53] Gardner was not solely responsible for the rise in popularity of the kinesthetic learner idea, but the publication of *Frames of Mind* and Gardner's ambiguity around the issue of kinesthetic intelligence contributed greatly to its spread.

In contrast to Gardner, Dunn was remarkably consistent throughout her career in what she considered to be tactile and kinesthetic learning strategies. For kinesthetic learners, Dunn recommended "floor games, role playing, simulations, or real life examples," and for tactile learners, she suggested the use of "Electroboards," "Flip Chutes," "Pic-a-Holes," and "Task-Cards," all of which involved interactive ways for students to use their hands to work through a series of lower order questions with behavioral reinforcements.[54] She even included directions in her textbooks for how to create these materials. These tactile activities seemed useful only in the pursuit of the rote learning of discreet facts, but not for the in-depth exploration of topics. In contrast, Gardner, Kolb, and McCarthy used their learning theories to endorse in-depth project-based explorations of fewer topics en route to a deeper conceptual understanding of the content. Gardner contrasted his multiple entry-point approach to curriculum with the shallow, fact-based learning proposed by E. D. Hirsch. Dunn's suggested activities for tactile learners aligned more with Hirsch's vision than Gardner's because they focused on the memorization of decontextualized, discreet facts. To be fair, this shallow, fact-based learning was what most standardized tests were assessing at the time, and so Dunn was merely supporting what students needed to succeed on these exams. Nevertheless, her suggested methods for both kinesthetic and tactile methods were concrete, low level, and generally less rigorous than her suggested activities for visual and auditory learners.

The trend of identifying Black and Latine students as kinesthetic learners and offering them low-level, hands-on learning activities that either steered them away from linguistic-based learning or linked all learning activities to vocational pursuits, continued into the twenty-first century. This could be seen in Jonathan Kozol's best-selling book, *Shame of a Nation: The Restoration of Apartheid Schooling in America*, published in 2005. For his research,

Kozol visited several schools in Chicago; Columbus, Ohio; Hartford, Connecticut; and the South Bronx that were made up almost entirely of Black and Latine students. Beyond the social isolation experienced by these de facto racially segregated schools, Kozol documented how these urban students were being offered a largely scripted, low-level, and job-oriented curriculum.

With academic standards and high-stakes testing in place, these schools could not explicitly teach job skills as in the days of Booker T. Washington. Nevertheless, they linked all the academic content to job activities: the schools adopted corporate-based rhetoric, rewarded students with "scholar dollars," and insisted that students choose a vocational track before they entered high school. The objective was to direct all the content to future jobs and to produce efficient and docile workers, and this was justified, in part, by the fact that Black and Latine students allegedly had a different learning style than White students. "Beginning in the early 1980s," Kozol reported, "the notion of producing 'products' who will then produce more wealth for the society has come to be embraced by many politicians and, increasingly, by principals of inner-city schools that have developed close affiliations with the representatives of private business corporations." Kozol was disgusted by the "extremes to which mercantile distortion of the purposes and character of education have been taken" and "how unabashedly proponents of these practices are willing to defend them." Kozol quoted one school leader who proudly embraced the criticism that he produced "robots," because robots, he rebutted, did not get arrested and got good jobs.[55]

It is notoriously difficult for historians and educational researchers to determine what is going on in the majority of classrooms at any given time. As a result, researchers are forced to work with anecdotal and incomplete portrayals of classroom practice collected from practitioner articles and journalistic accounts. Such incomplete evidence can only be suggestive, not definitive. Nevertheless, drawing upon these sources, a consistent pattern emerges of not only offering kinesthetic activities to Black and Latine students at a higher rate than White students, but also using the construct of the kinesthetic learner to justify this curriculum differentiation toward nonacademic work. In fact, a 2023 study that surveyed hundreds of teachers, parents, and students about their thoughts on the academic potential of visual learners and kinesthetic learners found that the vast majority of all three groups considered visual learners to be "smarter," whereas they considered kinesthetic learners to be "sportier." The authors confirmed that "perceived learning style traits may lead parents and teachers to make a host of specific (unwarranted) inferences about children's academic strengths and weaknesses . . . and are likely to trigger incorrect thinking about children's abilities by educators, parents and their peers."[56] I am not suggesting that Dunn and other learning style advocates, or teachers in general, deliberately adopted kinesthetic learning activities for Black and Latine students to preserve the existing social order or to shunt them into low-paying jobs. Nevertheless, the practice of labeling Black and Latine students as kinesthetic learners reinforced a long-standing pattern of racial profiling in schools. The rise of standardized testing exacerbated these preexisting trends.

No Child Left Behind

Between 1990 and 2010, the learning style idea became even more popular among teachers. So did the idea that kinesthetic learners, who were more likely to be Black and Latine, preferred vocational-oriented, hands-on activities that allegedly aligned with their learning style. Although the adoption of the learning style idea by teachers can be explained in part by the popularity of Gardner's MI theory and the continued efforts of Dunn and others, a broader explanation is needed. The single most impactful reform that took place during this period was the passage of No Child Left Behind, which greatly enhanced the appeal of the learning style idea for teachers.

No Child Left Behind had three major effects on schools. First, it forced educators to place a laser-like focus on low-achieving students. President George W. Bush pursued the passage of No Child Left Behind in part to overcome what he referred to as the "soft bigotry of low expectations" toward low-income students of color.[57] By this, he meant the subconscious and conscious underestimation of the academic ability of Black and Latine students by their mostly White teachers. No Child Left Behind targeted this tendency by requiring schools to disaggregate their test data by race, ethnicity, low-income status, disability status, and limited English proficiency status. To meet the requirements of annual yearly progress (AYP), schools had to demonstrate growth in test scores year after year in each of these demographics. For nearly a century prior, research had demonstrated that most students (two-thirds, in fact) learned best through auditory and visual means. Therefore, teachers who clung to the traditional teaching methods could boast that their traditional methods were, in fact, effective for most of their students—an assertion that would have essentially been valid. However, by having to disaggregate their test score data, schools could no longer bury their struggling learners in the academic achievements of the majority. In fact, under No Child Left Behind, it was precisely the bottom third of learners that determined whether a school made AYP or not. Even if a school's top students excelled, it was the academic achievement of bottom third that often determined whether the school would be rewarded, celebrated, or shut down due to the mandated punitive measures written into the legislation. This forced many educators to at least consider the idea that some of their struggling learners may have a different learning style, because the achievement of these previously overlooked students was so consequential to the future of their schools.

Second, No Child left Behind forced many schools to increase their focus on the only two subjects that were mandated to be tested: literacy and math. A 2007 study by the Center on Education Policy reported that 62 percent of school districts had increased their time and focus on reading and math, and 44 percent had decreased their time allocation of science, social studies, and the arts. Predictably, this narrowing of the curriculum disproportionately affected urban schools serving Black and Latine students. The VAK learning style typology had deep historical roots in literacy instruction stretching back to the Fernald method of the 1920s. Whereas the research on the efficacy of VAK-based literacy interventions, such as Carbo's Reading Styles Program, was mixed at best, the relative increase in school time allotted to literacy instruction likely added to the popularity of the VAK-based interventions.[58] The additional pressure of raising test scores in literacy and the search for any methods that could potentially aid in that effort likely heightened awareness and the willingness to experiment with the VAK learning style model.

Finally, when schools failed to make AYP (and some schools failed to make AYP even a single time), states were mandated to implement some form of radical restructuring to overhaul the curriculum and teaching methods. This often resulted in the implementation of scripted curricula. Some of these curricula were based on the idea that Black and Latine students had a different learning style than their White, middle-class peers. "Curriculum materials that are alleged to be aligned with governmentally established goals and standards and particularly suited to what are regarded as 'the special needs and learning styles' of low-income urban children have been introduced," Kozol reported in *Harper's Magazine* in 2005. "Relentless emphasis on raising test scores, a new empiricism and the imposition of unusually detailed lists of named and numbered 'outcomes' for each isolated parcel of instruction. . . . These are just a few of the familiar aspects of these new adaptive strategies." As Kozol explained, urban schools serving Black and Latine students took the brunt of the punitive measures aimed at improving "failing" schools, and these students disproportionately suffered the costs of the narrowing of the curriculum. In New York City, 99 percent of the students receiving the required scripted curriculum for "failing" schools were Black and Latine. "The introduction of Skinnerian approaches (which are commonly employed in penal institutions and drug rehabilitation programs as a way of altering the attitudes and learning styles of black and Hispanic children) is provocative," Kozol wrote, "and it has stirred some outcries from respected scholars."[59]

Whereas Gardner cast his MI theory and his curriculum of multiple entry points as an alternative to a teaching-to-the-test approach, Kozol documented how many schools seamlessly incorporated a learning style approach into their teaching-to-the test regimes and outlook. Ultimately, No Child Left Behind created an unprecedented focus on raising the test scores of struggling learners, as it was designed to do, which, in turn, created an intense demand for new interventions and approaches to teaching. The VAK learning style typology, due to its flexible and essentially apolitical nature, both reinforced and undermined the rigor of the curriculum during this age of high-stakes testing. Often, the "kinesthetic learning" label was used to justify low-level, rote learning for Black and Latine students, whereas the more creative and academically demanding activities were reserved for the White students in the suburban schools.

*

The "kinesthetic learner" was a problematic idea that continued the racist history of aligning students of color with alleged intellectual deficits. Kinesthetic learning was also a vague, ill-defined idea that could easily be misapplied or abused by well-meaning teachers who offered academically undemanding activities in place of linguistics-based, rigorous ones. Building the Parthenon out of sugar cubes was not the intellectual equivalent of researching and writing a paper about Roman culture, although many learning style theorists and MI theory advocates implied it was. "My son's teacher keeps talking about his learning style, which they describe as kinesthetic," one disgruntled parent wrote in 2006. "As far as I can see, he's hardly learning anything."[60] The few problematic examples of kinesthetic learning I cited above were published, and thus made it through some sort of editorial or peer review. Therefore, these examples likely reflect hundreds, if not thousands, of vacuous activities that were likely assigned to struggling learners in the name of kinesthetic learning or were generated to fill out a grid of different learning style or MI activities. There is no way of knowing how many ill-conceived kinesthetic activities were justified and assigned to students of color over the past three decades. For every pedagogically sound application, there were likely several that were problematic. The rise of the "kinesthetic learner" label and identity was tethered to the overall rise of the VAK-based learning typology, which, as will be explored in chapter 6, unexpectedly became the most popular version of the theory during the first decades of the twenty-first century.

6
The Peak Years

In October 1990, ASCD devoted a themed issue of *Educational Leadership* to the learning style idea, a topic that had grown more popular since the journal first addressed it a decade earlier. Despite this steady growth, the future of learning styles was still uncertain. Marie Carbo had witnessed a decline in interest since the late 1970s and '80s, but, she explained, a series of educational developments made a renewed interest in learning styles seem likely. The first development was the rise of standardized testing, which had educators "looking for answers" and made them "more likely to be open" to new ideas. The second development Carbo identified was "the movement for honoring diversity" that underscored the fact that students came from different cultural backgrounds and learned differently. Although Carbo was optimistic about the prospects of a learning style renaissance, others were more cautious.

Anthony Gregorc predicted that the learning style idea would muddle along in schools, "never getting enough energy to really build it in, but never dying out because it has some truth in it." James Keefe, director of the National Association of Secondary School Principals (NASSP), agreed with Gregorc, stating that learning style–based professional development had "become a ubiquitous in-service offering and many teachers speak knowingly of 'sense-feelers' and 'abstract sequentials' "—classifications that came from Gregorc's Style Delineator. Although the idea had become "almost universal in education," Keefe nevertheless estimated only 10 percent of schools did anything substantive with it beyond vaguely employing some of the learning style rhetoric. Others were concerned that the failure of the learning style researchers to coalesce around one or two major typologies was hurting its prospects for growth. "We have not moved to a unified field—everyone clings to his or her own model," one advocate stated. "Teachers ask: which one should I use? And end up saying: I won't use any."[1]

None of these learning style advocates predicted the explosion in interest that would take place over the next two decades, the ascendency of the VAK-based learning style typology, or the backlash that this popularity would later inspire. This chapter explores the growth in popularity in the learning style idea in secondary and higher education during the 2000s and 2010s, with particular focus on the ascendency of the VAK version of the idea.

VAK Triumphant

The learning style idea continued to gain ground among educational theorists and practitioners in the 1990s, 2000s, and 2010s. As the work of Rita Dunn, Gregorc, David Kolb, and Herman Witkin continued to be cited by learning style advocates during this period, the typology of Barbe and Swassing was cited with less frequency after the 1990s. Despite this decline in citations, the VAK-based typology not only continued to grow, but it quickly became the most popular version of the idea. Certainly, the work of Dunn and of Howard Gardner—who each emphasized kinesthetic learning—aided the momentum of the VAK typology. However, this alone does not explain the escalating popularity of the VAK model. The main reasons for its popularity were the simplistic and intuitive nature of the typology itself, the rise of high-stakes testing demanding that all students perform well on the exams, and the emergence of the internet as a major force in disseminating teaching ideas without the mediation of the educational research and professional development communities.

As the VAK-based learning style typology rose in popularity, Dunn became one the biggest advocates of the approach, and so she focused her research on the impact of aligning instruction to perceptual strengths. In 1988, she responded directly to critics of the VAKT approach and to the empirical studies demonstrating that these learning styles did not exist and so teaching to them was futile. Dunn admitted that many empirical studies indeed demonstrated that when groups of students who were taught by auditory methods were compared with groups of students who were taught through kinesthetic, tactile, or visual means, there was no statistically significant difference among the groups. However, she rebutted, this did not mean that certain *individuals* within these groups did not have perceptual strengths that were buried in the group data. She also continued to defend the idea that students—even young students—could accurately identify their own learning preferences, despite continued skepticism that this was the case. To further defend the efficacy of the VAK typology, Dunn pointed to "four pioneering studies"—all of which happened to be dissertations completed under her supervision—that proved the impact of VAK-based learning style interventions on student achievement.[2]

A decade and a half later, Dunn and her husband reviewed the research on the VAKT-based learning again. By then, the list of supervised dissertations supporting the efficacy of her VAK-based LSI had doubled, and the Dunns cited this research as further evidence for the validity of their approach. They made vague references to "confusing reports of only limited successes for students with perceptual strengths" and the fact that "some people don't believe" that "students with extreme learning style characteristics do achieve higher test scores when instructional conditions and resources complement how they learn," although the Dunns did not directly cite the scholarship expressing skepticism about VAKT-based learning styles.[3] Instead, they reasserted that perceptual strengths (visual, auditory, kinesthetic, and tactile) did exist and that teaching to them led to increases in student achievement, although they were unable to find a single study that validated the VAKT learning style typology that was not in some way directly related to research using their own LSI. In other words, the enormous research base supporting the existence of VAKT-based learning styles was authored exclusively by Dunn and her associates. One such study, published in 2001, compared the achievement of fifty-nine third-graders on a science unit using traditional and tactile-kinesthetic methods. Dunn and her coauthor defined traditional teaching as "lectures, discussions, textbook, and workbook activities" and defined tactile-kinesthetic teaching as using "task cards, fact fans, learning wheels, matching puzzle pieces, and electro-boards." They found that 65 percent of the students who learned through the tactile-kinesthetic method scored high (3 or 4) on the state science examination, whereas only 10 percent of students taught traditionally scored that high. This study did not assess specifically for visual and auditory learning, perhaps because these modalities were presumed to align with "traditional" learning.[4]

In addition to work by Gardner and by the Dunns, two publications appeared in 1992 that provided additional momentum to the VAK version of the learning style idea: *Learning Styles: What Research Says to the Teacher* by Judith Reiff and "Not Another Inventory, Rather a Catalyst for Reflection" by Neil Fleming and Colleen Mills. Reiff's report offered a comprehensive and readable literature review of the learning style idea, and the article by Fleming and Mills offered an updated version of the VAK typology. Reiff was a professor of education at the University of Georgia. She authored a review the literature on learning styles on behalf of the National Education Association (NEA)—the largest and most influential teacher union and professional organization in the country. Compared to other educational organizations, such as the Association for Supervision and Curriculum Development (ASCD) or Phi Delta Kappa, the NEA was relatively conservative, in close contact with classroom practice, and not prone to chasing educational fads. Although late to the game, the NEA's embrace of the learning style idea represented a critical step in legitimizing it for many teachers and administrators. Reiff's forty-page white paper was deposited in the ERIC research database, where teachers could access it for free, especially after internet connections became standard in most teachers' homes and schools.

Unlike Lynn Curry (see chapter 2), Reiff made no attempt to synthesize or critically analyze the research on learning styles. Instead, she offered an agnostic and practitioner-focused overview of the topic by addressing hemispheric learning, multiple intelligences, and the learning style typologies of Barbe and Swassing, Carbo, Dunn, Gregorc, Jung, Kolb, Myers and Briggs, and Witkin. She carefully noted controversies about the learning styles of young children and the validity of race-based learning style theories, but she steered clear of weighing in on them. For example, on the race issue, she simply reported that "Janice Hale-Benson discusses the issue of learning style from the Black perspective. How culture relates to style is a controversial but significant question." She also repeated the common belief that struggling and at-risk students were more likely to be kinesthetic learners: "One of the key reasons at-risk children have trouble with school is that they tend to be tactile/kinesthetic learners."[5] She concluded with a list of learning style–based curricula, such as the McCarthy 4MAT system, and recommended that teachers start experimenting with learning style–based instruction. Although Reiff's review offered nothing new, her levelheaded overview of the learning style idea—and her circumvention of any critiques and/or countervailing research—made her article highly citable as an overall rationale for the idea.

Fleming was a professor of education at Lincoln University in Canterbury, New Zealand. In a relatively obscure journal, *To Improve the Academy*, he and his coauthor causally introduced a slight variation of the VAK typology by adding a reading/writing modality (i.e., the *R* in VARK). Rather than engage the ballooning research on learning styles as Curry and Reiff had done, Fleming and Mills simply dismissed this scholarship as too complicated and contradictory to be of any use to teachers: "The range of style dimensions and therefore, the combinations that might occur in one particular student group are likely to be so extensive that teachers are unable to extend their repertoire of teaching methods to encompass all of them." Fleming and Mills argued that, instead of assessing students through a formal learning style inventory, educators should teach students to recognize their own learning styles as a "catalyst" toward better metacognition. To facilitate this process, the researchers used a set of thirteen questions designed to spark a conversation with students about how they *felt* they learned best. For example, the questionnaire asked: "I want to find out more about a tour that I am going on. I would a) look at details about the highlights and activities on the tour b) use a map and see where the places are, c) talk with the person who planned the tour, etc." Because these questions were merely used to "stimulate reflection and discussion," Fleming and Mills claimed that "testing for validity and reliability was unnecessary and inappropriate."[6] Through this clever evasion of construct validity, Fleming and Mills created this learning style typology through a bottom-up approach of talking directly to students about their learning style preferences instead of a top-down approach of creating a reliable instrument based on brain and empirical research.

Although Fleming's VARK model was generally continuous with the long tradition of VAK-based typologies, his definition of kinesthetic learning diverged from that of virtually all previous scholars using the term. He defined it as "one in which all or any of these perceptual modes are used to connect the student to reality." In other words, the use of any real-world examples in teaching—even if they had nothing do with the students moving around or using their hands—counted as kinesthetic learning. Under kinesthetic activities, Fleming listed using "hands-on approaches," but also listed the reading of case studies and watching videos—activities traditionally aligned with visual and auditory learning. This further muddied the already confused conceptualization of kinesthetic learning.

Due to its simplicity, the Fleming VARK model quickly became one of the most popular learning style typologies in the world. In fact, a 2011 book on teaching with learning styles included Fleming's VARK model as one of only four typologies the authors featured, along with those of Dunn, Gardner, and Gregorc (The typologies of Witkin and Barbe and Swassing had apparently already been forgotten).[7] By 2020, the Fleming and Mills article had been cited more than 1,500 times, and Fleming's books on VARK have been cited thousands of times.[8] How did such an obscure learning style model by an unknown professor in New Zealand leapfrog over half a dozen more-established learning style theories in just a matter of years? The answer was the internet, which came to prominence during the 1990s. In 1994, only 35 percent of public schools in the US had access to the internet, but by the end of the decade, 98 percent did. By the turn of the twenty-first century, schools had a 5:1 student-to-computer ratio, and 77 percent of schools had the faster "dedicated line" internet access, as opposed to the slower dial-up connection.[9] To capitalize on the rapid expansion of internet access and use in schools, Fleming and his wife created a website, www.vark-learn.com, where they made their basic questionnaire available for free. (Fleming had originally sought out the web address vark.com, but that name had already been taken by a pet shop in Pennsylvania because *vark* means pig in Dutch.)[10] Fleming reported that in 2006, more than 180,000 people completed his online VARK questionnaire in only half a year, and by 2020 their web page stated that 1.4 million from around the globe had completed it during that year.[11]

The rise of the internet as a source of information for teachers and its role in spreading the learning style idea cannot be overemphasized. No longer beholden to purchasing expensive professional development sessions or curriculum materials, teachers could access hundreds of resources online for free from around the world. In response to this sudden demand, Dunn set up learningstyles.net; Gardner set up www. multipleintelligencesoasis.com, which he dubbed "The Official Authoritative Site of Multiple Intelligences." Additional sites, such as George Lucas's edutopia.com, made a Multiple Intelligences Self-Assessment Quiz available to teachers for free, and dozens of other learning style inventories popped up, unconnected to the originators of the idea. Just google "learning style questionnaire" and more than a dozen versions emerge, many of which are housed on university web pages. The ubiquity of VAK-based learning style inventories not only helped spread the idea to teaching practitioners, but it also made it a more popular topic among educational researchers and journalists.

Dunn's Educational Empire

As the popularity of Rita Dunn's learning style typology continued to grow in the 1980s, 1990s, and 2000s, greater scrutiny followed. This could be seen in Dunn's relationship with the NASSP, the group with which she originally partnered to disseminate the learning style idea. Conflict between Dunn and the NASSP initially arose over the issue of whether to approach learning styles developmentally or relativistically. In other words, should a teacher indulge a kinesthetic learner only with kinesthetic learning methods, or did the teacher have a responsibility to gradually move the kinesthetic learner toward the more common and valued visual/auditory methods affiliated with greater analytic thinking? Most learning style advocates, including Dunn, espoused the relativistic approach, precisely to move beyond the hierarchical outlook of IQ testing. Yet at least one member of the NASSP board, Charles Letteri of the University of Vermont, thought that student learning styles needed to be developed toward improved analytic thinking. Letteri would eventually design his own learning style assessment instrument. The International Learning Styles Network (ILSN) leadership compromised by agreeing that the "cognitive" aspects of learning styles needed to be "augmented" toward, whereas the rest of the "affective and psychological" aspects found in Dunn's LSI could be indulged. By the 1990s, the relationship between Dunn and the NASSP soured even further due to Dunn's hesitancy to respond to "weak learning style model applications" and the "perceived lack of rigor" behind the LSI. In 1995, Dunn's collaboration with the NASSP ended, and the new executive director, James Keefe, pushed his own learning style assessment called the Learning Style Profile, which incorporated aspects of Witkin's embedded-figures test, and explicitly targeted the development of analytic thinking in students.[12]

In addition to forming these networks early in her career, Dunn adapted her pitch for the learning style idea in response to the emerging educational issues and concerns. As stated above, Dunn's LSI emerged from her initial work in free and alternative education in the 1960s based on her experiences teaching disadvantaged students. In the 1970s, she pivoted her justification for the learning style approach to its potential role in fending off lawsuits in the wake of the passage of the Education for All Handicapped Children Act. In the 1980s, she aligned her learning style approach with the right brain/left brain learning theory. "Hemispheric preference is a recent addition to the learning style elements," Dunn and her coauthors explained in a 1982 article. "It is likely to gain increasing attention among those who are concerned about providing maximum instructional opportunities."[13] In the 1990s and 2000s, she fused her learning style approach with multicultural education and pitched it as a method of engaging of at-risk students, students with disabilities, English-language learners, and students with attention-deficit/hyperactivity disorder (ADHD). By addressing these emerging concerns, Dunn kept her learning style approach current and underscored her belief that there was no educational problem her LSI could not solve or student population her LSI could not engage.

Dunn published research demonstrating the efficacy of her learning style approach, and many of her early collaborations with school districts required that she demonstrate academic improvement. Dunn and her students documented gains in student achievement on standardized assessments, such as the California Achievement Test, Stanford Achievement Test, Iowa Test of Basic Skills, and the Texas Assessment of Basic Skills, although most of these studies did not undergo peer review.[14] Whereas others had developed their learning style approaches as a critique of standardized testing, Dunn routinely employed standardized testing to demonstrate the efficacy of her LSI. Many of the dissertations written using the LSI won awards from the professional organizations with which she collaborated, such as ASCD, Kappa Delta Pi, NASSP, and Phi Delta Kappa. In 1998, the US Department of Education recognized Marie Carbo's Reading Styles Program, which was based on Dunn's LSI, as one of only seven research-based reform programs that its endorsed, although it later withdrew this endorsement. However, when one sorts through the hundreds of studies that provided support for the validity of Dunn's LSI, it becomes clear that most of these were unpublished dissertations conducted under her supervision, practitioner-based articles introducing her learning style theory to teachers, unpublished white papers housed at the Center for the Study of Learning and Teaching Styles at St. John's University, or solicited contributions to learning style–themed journal issues. When she and her coauthors did publish articles in research journals, they focused on the more peripheral aspects of her LSI, such as students' mobility and hemispheric preferences, and not their VAK-based learning preferences.[15] One of Dunn's articles, "Survey of Research on Learning Styles," cited only unpublished dissertations as evidence.[16]

As noted above, Dunn's research never appeared in any of the top-tiered research journals, such as the journals of the American Educational Research Association (AERA). I point to this relative lack of rigor in Dunn's empirical research not to cast aspersions on her intellect (or any other educational researchers who may not have been published in these journals), but rather because she herself made repeated references to the allegedly airtight research base that supported her theory. Just a single empirical study in one of these top journals—say, AERA's *Review of Educational Research*—could have gone a long way in dispelling the skepticism that arose around her LSI. Yet, in contrast to Witkin, Gardner, and Sternberg (see below), Dunn was either unwilling or unable to put her learning style theory up to that degree of scrutiny and rigorous review.

When defending her LSI, Dunn seemed more interested in touting the quantity of her studies over their quality. For example, in her dismissal of Howard Gardner's theory of multiple intelligences, Dunn referenced her own "20 books and 300 manuscripts" and "three decades of research" that supported her own learning style theory.[17] In other articles, she dismissed any learning style research that did not employ her LSI because such research had not "used a valid and reliable instrument to identify individuals learning styles."[18] Furthermore, many of Dunn's article titles were worded defensively, such as "Learning Style–Based Teaching . . . There's No Debate," "Thirty-Five Years of Research on Perceptual Strengths," and "A Meta-analytic Validation of the Dunn and Dunn Model of Learning Style Preferences."[19] Although she always cited research to support her ideas, she employed this research selectively and inconsistently. For example, in a dispute in the early 1980s over whether young children were more likely to be kinesthetic learners than auditory learners, Dunn cited a 1975 article in AERA's *Review of Educational Research* stating that more studies were needed on kinesthetic learning with young children. In other words, she cited the "lack of investigations into the relationship of the tactile and kinesthetic modalities" as evidence to justify her predetermined assertion that young children learned best kinesthetically.[20] Yet, she later dismissed Gardner's MI theory for this very same thing—that it didn't yet have empirical studies to back it up. In addition, Dunn often touted the comprehensive nature of her LSI because it explored eighteen elements of the learning process, yet in many of her own research articles she focused on only one of these eighteen elements, such as temperature, time of day, or perceptual strengths, which undermined her assertion that all eighteen aspects were important to the validity of her instrument.

Furthermore, Dunn adopted a messianic attitude toward the learning style idea that bordered on arrogant. A journalist witnessed Dunn at a professional development workshop in 1990 "promising" that "within six weeks . . . kids who you think can't learn will be learning well and easily." The overconfident and unqualified pronouncements such as these, he reported, "clearly rankle some researchers."[21] In a later interview, Dunn imagined a scenario in which President George W. Bush would turn to her to save American schools. " 'Tell me what to do,' " Dunn envisioned him saying. "And I would tell him exactly what to do. Learning styles. Make learning style testing part of every curriculum."[22] As her LSI accumulated more criticism, she seemed to gain confidence, even backing off her earlier caution about casting learning styles as mere preferences instead of permanent learning labels. "If learning through your preference consistently produces significantly better test scores and grades," she reasoned, "then your preference *is* your strength." As we saw in previous chapters, many other learning style advocates invited criticism of their typologies; issued caveats about exaggerating differences and permanently labeling students; and generally adopted a humbler attitude about their approach. Dunn, in contrast, expressed no such doubts or hesitations about her LSI, even on the issue of permanently labeling students. "*Everybody* has a learning style, and everybody has learning style strengths," she insisted unequivocally.[23]

Although Dunn was one of the first educators to adopt and incorporate the VAK learning style typology into her approach, ironically, her influence waned as the VAK model became more popular in schools. Few affiliated the popularity of the VAK typology with her LSI, and her name recognition among teachers never approached that of Howard Gardner. Further, Dunn guarded her LSI from misuse by issuing official trainer status to certified educators. While this effort protected her ideas from misinterpretation and misapplication, it also limited their spread during a period when teachers could access VAK-based typologies such as Fleming's for free via the internet. If Gardner's hands-off approach to his theory of multiple intelligences led to rampant misapplication, Dunn's hands-on approach, in contrast, seems to have stanched its popularity and spread. Regardless of what one thinks about the rigor of Dunn's research or the extent of its impact, she was undoubtedly one of the most pivotal figures in the history of the learning style idea.

The Thinking Styles of Robert Sternberg

Known among educators primarily for the triarchic theory of intelligences that he launched in the mid-1980s around the same time that Gardner published *Frames of Mind*, Robert Sternberg was relatively late to the learning style game. In fact, he created his learning style theory just as the idea was beginning to garner skepticism among psychologists. Ever since he was a young boy, Sternberg had a fascination with psychological assessments. Due to his anxiety, he scored poorly on an intelligence test when he was six. Several years later, he discovered a copy of the Stanford–Binet intelligence test at the public library in Maplewood, New Jersey, and he began administering it to his friends and members of his Boy Scout troop, before the school principal called him to his office and warned him not to ever bring the test to school again. Even after this discouragement, his obsession with intelligence tests continued. By posing as a graduate student, Sternberg requested additional instruments via mail and continued to examine and administer them to his friends. In college, his interest in intelligence testing led him to the field of psychology, but he initially struggled. In fact, Sternberg earned a C in his first class in the major at Yale University, but eventually graduated summa cum laude and pursued his doctorate in psychology at Stanford University. His failure to score well on traditional IQ tests as a child, as well as his initial lack of success in psychology, inspired him to examine alternative ways of conceptualizing and assessing intelligence, without dismantling the idea altogether like Gardner had attempted to do.

As a psychology professor at Yale in the 1980s, Sternberg created an expanded version of intelligence that went beyond the unity trait of traditional IQ testing, which, as Gardner had also argued a few years earlier, overlooked a lot of important mental attributes that society valued. "There are a lot of kids who have potential to be successful in their fields, but the way the system is set up, they never get a chance," Sternberg complained. He further argued that intelligences were not fixed, they were "not something you're born with, that [were] etched in invisible ink on your forehead and [could not] be changed."[24] To assess the dynamic and expanded definition of intelligence he envisioned, Sternberg created a triarchic theory of intelligence in the early 1980s that included analytical, creative, and practical intelligences. He argued that these three intelligences better aligned with the mental abilities needed for success in life than the narrow computational skills being assessed by standard IQ tests. After publishing *Beyond IQ: A Triarchic Theory of Human Intelligence* in 1985, Sternberg published extensively on intelligence over the next three decades in books such as *Intelligence Applied* (1986), *The Triarchic Mind* (1988), *Successful Intelligence* (1997), *Wisdom, Intelligence, and Creativity Synthesized* (2007), and *Adaptive Intelligence* (2021).

As he continued to develop his ideas on intelligence, Sternberg soon applied his interests to learning styles. He recognized that a theory of intelligence was incomplete without a related theory of how people learned: "Styles represent what may be an important 'missing link' between intelligence and personality."[25] As the rest of the field of cognitive psychology was mobilizing against the learning style idea (see chapter 7), Sternberg began compiling evidence that learning styles did exist and that aligning instruction to student learning styles could increase student achievement. He first unveiled his theory in a 1988 article for the journal *Human Development*. He defined intelligence as "mental self-governance," which he contrasted with the computational definition of intelligence inherent in traditional IQ tests. Sternberg's definition of intelligence also conflicted with Gardner's pragmatic definition of intelligence, which focused on the ability to create products that had social value. In other words, Sternberg's definition of intelligence extended beyond the traditional, computational approach to IQ, but it was still limited to what Gardner would later dismiss as "inside baseball."[26]

In accordance with his definition of intelligence, Sternberg extended his government metaphor to the three thinking styles that he identified as executive, legislative, and judicial. Individuals with an executive thinking style were "implementers . . . who like[d] to follow rules," those with a judicial thinking style "like[d] to evaluate rules and procedures," and those with a legislative thinking style "enjoy[ed] creating, formulating, and planning for problem solution." Furthermore, these styles were crossed with additional governmental styles of "form": monarchical, hierarchical, oligarchical, and anarchic. Individuals with a monarchical thinking style tended "to be motivated by a single goal or need at a time," those with a hierarchical thinking style tended "to be motivated by a hierarchy of goals, with the recognition that not all goals can be fulfilled equally well," those with an oligarchical style tended "to be motivated by multiple, competing goals of equal importance," and those with an anarchic style tended "to be motived by a potpourri of needs and goals that [were] often difficult for themselves, as well as others, to sort out." He related the thinking styles to additional elements of levels (global, local), scope (internal, external), and learning (liberal, conservative). Despite the familiar terminology of well-known governmental systems, Sternberg's multitiered theory was complicated, and initially he offered no assessment instrument to go with it. Nevertheless, he encouraged educators to employ his theory to "teach students to capitalize on their strengths and to remediate or compensate for their weaknesses."[27]

A couple of years later, Sternberg introduced his thinking styles theory to teachers in a publication for the National Education Association. He admitted he was still working on a thinking style assessment instrument, but he speculated on how thinking styles might impact learning, especially if there was a mismatch between teacher and student styles. As Sternberg suggested, "On the whole schools most reward executive types—children who work within existing rule systems and seek the rewards that the schools value." Like Gardner, Sternberg initially made no attempt to align racial and ethnic groups with specific thinking styles, and he seemed to be completely unaware of the ongoing Black/Latine learning style controversy. Nevertheless, he unwittingly contributed evidence to the cultural mismatch theory by concluding that "unrecognized differences in teachers' and students' intellectual styles, and the match between them, may result in substantial differences in the way students are perceived by teachers, and the way that teachers are perceived by students."[28] A similar observation had been made by Witkin a decade earlier, but Sternberg did not initially cite or otherwise recognize Witkin's work on cognitive styles.[29]

By the mid-1990s, Sternberg began a fruitful collaboration with his graduate student Elena Grigorenko that brought him into closer communication with the existing literature on learning/cognitive styles and allowed him to pilot and develop his thinking style assessment with students and teachers. Realizing that his growing interest in learning styles was moving against the grain of the profession, he and Grigorenko copublished an article for the *American Psychologist* in 1997, defensively titled "Are Cognitive Styles Still in Style?," in which they attempted to revive the idea among their peers. The article offered a rich but concise literature review that recognized the previous attempts at learning/thinking/cognitive styles by Jung, Myers and Briggs, Witkin, Dunn, Gregorc, Kolb, and others. They pitched Sternberg's thinking styles typology as "a bridge between what might seem to be two fairly distinct areas of psychological investigation: cognition and personality."[30] They reported the results of several studies that employed their Thinking Style Inventory and Thinking Styles Questionnaire for Teachers that assessed the impact of alignments and misalignment between the two populations, and they confirmed that mismatched thinking styles did affect how many students learned, but many others were able to socialize themselves to the style of the teacher. During this time, Sternberg also pitched his typology directly to teachers via a book, *Thinking Styles* (1997), and practitioner-focused articles in the *Phi Delta Kappan* and *Educational Leadership*.[31] By the 2010s, Sternberg had coedited two massive volumes on thinking and learning styles that positioned him as the leading academic proponent of the learning style idea.[32] Despite these efforts to bring his theory to practitioners, his thinking styles typology failed to make much of an impact with teachers. In fact, Sternberg's research program on thinking styles could serve as a cautionary tale about doing everything right, but still only making a minimal impact on educational theory and practice.

Unlike Gardner, Sternberg constructed and validated a reliable assessment instrument, the Thinking Styles Inventory (TSI), that could be administered easily to students and drew on existing psychometric research. Sternberg revised and tweaked his instrument and subjected it to the rigorous peer review, and his work on thinking styles appeared in top peer-reviewed journals such as the American Psychological Association's *American Psychologist* and AERA's *Educational Researcher*. He developed a substantial empirical base for the efficacy of his ideas in practice before he launched his thinking style typology widely, and he never made his TSI widely available on a website. In other words, he rolled out his thinking style theory cautiously and was careful not to overstate what his research had and had not established at any given time. Sternberg's thinking style typology employed a user-friendly terminology based on preexisting and familiar vocabulary (e.g., executive, legislative, judicial). Most significantly, he extensively reviewed the preexisting research in cognitive, thinking, learning, and personality styles and pitched his typology as a culmination of the work of previous scholars. His two edited books attempted to provide the kind of theoretical and empirical synthesis that Lynn Curry had asked for as early as 1983. Ultimately, Sternberg and his collaborators did everything scientists were supposed to do when meticulously developing and introducing a theory to the public, and avoided all the mistakes, missteps, and unwarranted overextensions made by previous learning style advocates. And yet, his thinking styles typology remains obscure.

So why did Sternberg's thinking styles typology fail to make an impact? There were several reasons. First, Sternberg had bad timing. Writing in the late 2010s, Sternberg was aware of how the learning style theory had "gone out of fashion for a number of years" with psychologists when he first launched his typology, but he seemed to underestimate how popular Gardner's theory of multiple intelligences and the VAK typology had become with teachers who were not really looking for another theory to add to these more popular and simpler ones.[33] Second, Sternberg's barrage of books and theories published between 1985 and 2021 on the psychology of intelligence, wisdom, creativity, problem solving, love, and thinking styles got in one another's way and essentially canceled one another out. In contrast, Gardner was a prolific writer during this period, and he was far better than Sternberg was at articulating exactly how his MI theory interacted with his later books on "disciplined" learning theory. Gardner was building momentum from his previous research; Sternberg's work piled layer upon layer of psychological models and metaphors that never seemed to add up to a coherent scheme. Third, Sternberg's impulse to synthesize and build on the work of prior learning style advocates left him without a straw man against which to pitch his ideas. Again, Gardner consistently pitched his MI theory against the idea of a unity IQ, and he later pitched his disciplined inquiry approach against the low-level rote learning espoused by traditionalists such as E. D. Hirsch. As a result, Gardner tapped into ongoing pedagogical debates about educational equity and student-centered pedagogy, whereas Sternberg's work seemed disconnected from these broader educational contexts and debates. Gardner later offered as one explanation for why his theory resonated with teachers whereas Sternberg's did not: "I'm more of an engaging writer than [Sternberg] is, and I am better able to draw people in."[34]

In the battle for the hearts and minds of teachers, not only did Gardner's MI theory win over Sternberg's triarchic theory of intelligence, but sadly, its popularity overshadowed Sternberg's thinking styles as well, despite the fact that Sternberg had stronger scientific support for his theory, not to mention that Gardner never intended his MI theory to be treated as a learning style theory in the first place. Ultimately, one review of learning style typologies dismissed Sternberg's model with a single sentence: "An unnecessary addition to the proliferation of learning styles models."[35] As explored in the next chapter, Sternberg would later collaborate with his former student, Li-fang Zhang, to simplify his theory and launch a counteroffensive against learning style skeptics.

Learning Styles in Ed Schools

In a 2019 op-ed for the *Chronicle of Higher Education*, the history professor Erik Gilbert linked the learning style idea to the growing menace of "bad ideas" that emerged from colleges of education and were slowly disseminating throughout the rest of higher education. Gilbert related a story about how he once polled the education majors in his history class about the topic of learning styles. Gilbert was appalled to discover that "not only did they know about learning styles, they all knew the acronym VARK." Despite this small sample size, Gilbert considered this to be compelling evidence that the "theory . . . was alive and well" in educational circles and that "learning styles still apparently pervade colleges of education." The persistent belief in learning styles, according to Gilbert, was just further evidence of the broader problem that "colleges of education serve as the refuge for bad ideas and sloppy thinking," such as whole-language instruction and the excessive use of assessment rubrics.[36]

As demonstrated in previous chapters, the learning style idea did not emerge solely or primarily from colleges of education. Witkin's field dependent/independent typology emerged from his laboratory studies in psychology at Brooklyn College, and his first attempts at exploring the implications of his typology for education were on college students, not K–12 students. Frank Riessman, who promoted an early version of the VAK typology during the 1960s, was a social psychologist who had little interaction with colleges of education. Barbe and Swassing, Dunn, and Fleming, who helped spread the VAK typology, were professors of education, but Sternberg and Gardner were psychologists, not professors of education. More significantly, the figure who was most successful at spreading the learning style idea in higher education was the business professor David Kolb. A 2015 study revealed that Kolb's learning style typology was the most popular model with college professors: 34 percent of those who addressed learning styles in their classroom employed Kolb's model, whereas another 33 percent employed some version of the VAK model.[37] The learning style idea clearly did not emerge solely from colleges of education, but to what extent did schools of education spread it?

There are more than two thousand state-approved teacher education programs in the US, the vast majority of which are traditional programs that reside at US colleges and universities.[38] It is difficult to quantify what percentage of schools of education have embraced or continue to embrace the learning style idea. As mentioned previously, many educational psychology textbooks still introduce the idea as plausible, and many online learning style inventories are housed on university web pages. However, it just takes one or two faculty members to create or disseminate these resources, so these facts tell us little about the extent to which teacher education faculty have formally or fully embraced the learning style idea. Journal articles on learning styles in K–12 education number in the thousands, but the topic has not appeared in the most prestigious educational journals since the turn of the twenty-first century. As of this writing in 2024, the premier educational research organization, AERA, has not published articles endorsing the use of learning styles since the 1980s, and the idea has not had a strong presence in the most selective journal that publishes research on the education of teachers, the *Journal of Teacher Education*, since the 2000s. Some of the more specialized education journals have published articles on the learning styles in teacher education between the 1990s and the 2010s; but many of these addressed the role of using learning style inventories to sort and instruct the teacher candidates themselves in ways that aligned with their learning style, rather than focusing on the role of teaching candidates to address learning styles in their future classrooms. More significantly, this literature revealed the inability of teacher educators to coalesce around a preferred learning style typology because researchers have employed more than a dozen different inventories, including those of Dunn, Gardner, Keefe, Kolb, and Myers and Briggs.[39] One teacher educator even reviewed the dozens of available typologies and recommended what she, in her opinion, considered to be the top five, but her list excluded the most popular typologies of Barbe and Swassing, Dunn, Fleming, Gardner, Keefe, Kolb, Sternberg, and Witkin.[40] If teacher educators were friendly to the learning style idea in general, there has been no consensus on which typology they prefer.

Perhaps a better way to gauge the role of the learning style idea in teacher education than its representation in research journals is to determine its prevalence among teacher education standards and accreditation. In fact, as the learning style idea was gaining a foothold in American schools in the 1980, 1990s, and 2000s, teacher education was undergoing far-reaching reforms that greatly expanded and clarified what teachers were expected to know and do. What was thc rolc of the learning style idea in these reforms?

Ever since the beginning of the twentieth century, critics charged that teacher certification was too easy, it attracted academically weak students, and the courses in teacher education were too frivolous, theoretic, and divorced from both the rigor of academic content and the realities of classroom practice. However, after the publication of *A Nation at Risk* in 1983, these criticisms began to be taken more seriously, and decades of reform recommendations began to be heeded. In response to recommendations issued by the Carnegie Corporation and the Homes Group of Education Deans in 1986, state departments of education began to increase the selectivity of teacher certification programs by raising grade-point average requirements, insisting that teacher candidates complete an academic degree in additional to an education major, and adding testing requirements in basic skills and subject matter content knowledge. Furthermore, many universities added five-year programs that made teacher certification a graduate degree. More significantly, both the Carnegie and the Homes Group reports recommended the creation and implementation of professional teaching standards to make teacher certification more selective and rigorous.[41]

To this end, the first teaching standards emerged in 1987 from the Stanford Teacher Assessment Project and the National Board for Professional Teaching Standards. Both employed a portfolio assessment system that had practicing teachers demonstrate their impact on student learning via video and written reflections. By 1997, nine hundred experienced teachers had achieved the prestigious National Board certification through the submitted teacher portfolio process. The National Board standards quickly became the gold standard of teaching excellence, and they became the basis for new national standards designed by the Interstate New Teacher Assessment and Support Consortium (InTASC), a voluntary group of educational leaders dedicated to improving teacher education to which thirty-three states belonged. The participating states used the InTASC standards to revise their teaching requirements, and some states even used the standards to design teacher assessments to judge the efficacy of their in-service teachers.

Furthermore, the National Academy of Education's Committee on Teacher Education published its own report in 2005. Led by Stanford University Professor Linda Darling-Hammond, *A Good Teacher in Every Classroom* looked a lot like the InTASC standards. This was no accident—Darling-Hammond had also played an instrumental role in the development of both the National Board and the InTASC standards. *A Good Teacher in Every Classroom* only briefly referenced the learning style idea: "To instruct students who learn in different ways, teachers need a repertoire of teaching strategies that respond to different learning styles and approaches." However, the authors were careful to link the accommodation of learning styles specifically to "students of different cultural and language backgrounds" and students with "auditory or visual processing problems."[42] The authors did not suggest an across-the-board approach in which *all* students were assessed for their learning style using a formal assessment instrument, such as Dunn's LSI, nor did they suggest that there was a Black or Latine learning style.

In addition to playing a role in the reform of teacher education programs, the InTASC standards also served as the basis for the standards for the National Council for the Accreditation of Teacher Education (NCATE) and the Council for the Accreditation of Educator Preparation (CAEP), the two most popular accreditors of teacher education programs in the twenty-first century. During the 2010s and 2020s, hundreds of national and regional teacher education programs updated their coursework and requirements to receive national NCATE/CAEP accreditation. In many states, teacher education programs were required to attain national recognition by these groups. Given the central role of the InTASC standards in teacher education in most US states, they provided a fairly accurate overview of what was valued and taught by teacher education programs during the first decades of the twenty-first century, just as the popularity of the learning style idea was peaking. Thus, if the learning style idea was being embraced and disseminated through colleges and schools of education, then the idea should have a central and conspicuous role in these standards. However, this was not the case.

Despite the alleged centrality of learning style theory in schools of education, the InTASC standards made no overt mention of learning styles, or even Gardner's theory of multiple intelligences. However, in the glossary of terms at the end of the standards, one can find a few passing references to learning styles. For example, under the entry "Diverse Learners and Learning Differences," the standards state: "Learner differences are manifested in such areas as . . . preferred learning modalities"; under the term "Diversity," the standards asked teachers to account for "individual differences," including "personality" and "learning modalities;" and under the heading "Cultural Relevance," the standards asked teachers to accommodate the "performance styles of diverse learners to make learning more appropriate and effective for them." The influential InTASC standards were clearly open to the idea that students had characteristics such as "learning modalities" and "performance styles," which could have been interpreted as a vague endorsement of the learning style idea. But ultimately, the learning style idea had only marginal role in what the authors of the InTASC standards thought effective teachers needed to know and do.[43]

In summary, the National Board, National Academy of Education, InTASC, and NCATE/CAEP did not exert any top-down pressure on teacher education programs to include learning styles as part of the teacher education curriculum; they implied the significance of the learning style idea, but they never overtly mentioned or required it. Furthermore, none of these standards cited the work of Dunn, Fleming, Gardner, Gregorc, Sternberg, or Witkin. Therefore, if teacher educators pushed the learning style idea onto their teacher candidates, they did so largely through the grassroots efforts of individual professors. The lack of explicit endorsement of the learning style idea by these influential organizations underscored the fact that the idea existed largely in the gray area between the prestigious journals that mostly ignored the idea, and the wisdom of practitioners in the trenches who enthusiastically embraced it—a gap that consultants, publishers, and professional development organizations gladly filled with their own learning style materials.

The continued rise of the learning style idea during the 2000s, which took place outside the purview of the most prestigious and rigorous educational research organizations, put teacher educators in a familiar yet awkward position: if teacher educators ignored the learning style idea, then they would be considered out of touch with practitioners in the classrooms, but if they embraced the learning style idea, then they would be vulnerable to ridicule by social scientists and academic professors like Gilbert because the idea did not have the backing of the scientific community. As two historians of teacher education noted:

> Schools of education . . . have seldom succeeded in satisfying the scholarly norms of their campus letters and science colleagues, and they are simultaneously estranged from their professional peers. The more forcefully they have rowed toward the shores of scholarly research, the more distant they have become from public schools they are bound to serve. Conversely, systemic efforts at addressing the applied problems of public schools have placed schools of education at risk on their own campuses.[44]

This tension between theory and practice was more pronounced at prestigious and research-oriented universities than it was at regional state universities, where two-thirds of teachers were and still are certified. Nevertheless, the learning style idea underscored an ongoing tension that existed between professors in arts and sciences, education professors, and educational practitioners. However, to the extent that the learning style idea even had a presence in schools of education, this was not its exclusive or even primary home. To the contrary, the learning style idea flourished on the main campuses of colleges and universities, as well as professional schools, such as medical and business schools.

Learning Styles in Higher Education

Higher education eventually embraced the learning style idea as enthusiastically as their elementary and secondary counterparts had a couple of decades earlier. A 1987 report authored by Charles Claxton and Patricia Murrell on behalf of the Association for the Study of Higher Education generally endorsed the use of the learning style idea with some hesitation and caveats. For example, the report equivocated on the issue of whether teachers ought to be teaching to or challenging students' learning strengths, and it reported the mixed results of teaching to Witkin's field dependent/independent cognitive types. More significantly, just as many K–12 educators had argued, the authors saw potential in the learning style idea to teach Black and Latine students more effectively: "The most pressing need is to learn more about the learning styles of minority students—a particularly important subject in the face of participation and graduation rates that indicate higher education is not serving black students well."[45] The diversification of the student population became a recurring theme in the literature on the need for attending to students' learning styles in college. "Most of the research on learning style in the US has been done from a Western, white, middle-class perspective and value system," a professor from Claremont Graduate School wrote in 1995. "However, the rich racial and cultural diversity of American society underscores the critical need for more research into the learning styles of diverse student groups."[46] Similarly, a 2001 article demanded that professors incorporate Gardner's theory of multiple intelligences into their teaching to accommodate students with different strengths. The author suggested revising the admissions process, in addition to updating college teaching, to accommodate the multiple intelligences and diverse cultures of students coming to college.[47]

The audience for learning styles in higher education continued to grow. In 2000, Dunn coedited a book on learning styles in higher education that included entries on uses of the idea in health, engineering, law, and business schools.[48] Furthermore, the reviewers of a 2006 study of learning styles in higher education found evidence of the implementation of Kolb's learning style theory in the fields of accounting, arts education, business management, economics, education, engineering, English, geography, history, marketing, mathematics, medicine, nursing, political science, psychiatry, and theater.[49] The medical and nursing fields were perhaps the most popular fields for the learning style idea in higher education. In fact, a 2015 article, "The Learning Style Myth Is Thriving in Higher Education," described a study that found that nearly a quarter of all peer-reviewed articles on learning styles in higher education published between 1975 and 2015 appeared in publications dedicated to life sciences and biomedicine.[50] Intuitively, one may think that medical students and instructors would be the least likely to implement a learning model supported by studies that did not employ the kind of experimental design required by the Food and Drug Administration (FDA). However, medical educators were some of the most enthusiastic adopters of the theory.

Recall that Lynn Curry—whose influential 1983 article on learning styles would go on to become one of the most cited in the entire field—was in the profession of medical education, and her article was originally directed toward other medical educators. Other critics pointed to the irony of the field of medicine "owing so much of its success to its reliance upon evidence-based treatments," while medical educators implemented a learning style approach that could not hold up to "thorough empirical scrutiny."[51] Although it would be convenient to blame colleges of education for the rise of the learning style idea, it was embraced and spread by the entire educational community from kindergarten through graduate and professional schools. A 2017 study on professors in the UK found that 33 percent of those surveyed admitted to using learning styles as a teaching method in the previous twelve months, and out of these, a third had administered a learning style questionnaire to their students.[52] Medical and business professors were some of the biggest advocates for the learning style idea, a fact confirmed by a massive 2004 study of learning styles in "post-16" education.

Peddling Poppycock

In 2004, the Learning and Skills Development Agency (LSDA) commissioned Frank Coffield, David Moseley, Elaine Hall, and Kathryn Ecclestone to review, evaluate, and synthesize the literature on learning styles with a focus on its use by university students in the United Kingdom. This was (and still is) the most comprehensive and massive review of the learning style idea ever conducted; the two reports—*Learning Styles and Pedagogy in Post-16 Learning* and *Should We Be Using Learning Styles?*—totaled more than two hundred pages of analysis. The authors admitted up front that they "found the field to be much more extensive, opaque, contradictory and controversial than we thought at the start of the research process."[53] The report initially identified seventy-one learning style typologies and covered more than eight hundred experimental research articles on the topic. Based on the popularity and prevalence of certain typologies, Coffield and his coauthors narrowed their focus to thirteen models, including Dunn, Gregorc, Kolb, Myers–Briggs, and Sternberg. The authors provided a brief history, description, review of the empirical literature, and strengths and weaknesses of each typology. Oddly, they did not analyze Gardner's theory of multiple intelligences, nor did they specifically discuss the VAK learning style model beyond its role in Dunn's LSI.

Addressing Dunn's LSI, Coffield and his coauthors praised some aspects of her typology, but they criticized "the idea that preferences are relatively fixed" and worried that "a view that preferences are fixed or typical of certain groups may lead to labelling and generalizing." They also questioned the so-called objective nature of Dunn's LSI "when many learners have limited self-awareness of their behaviors." Finally, they were disturbed by Dunn's intellectual arrogance and sense of moral self-righteousness when promoting and defending her model. "It is exactly this inability of Rita Dunn to conceive that other professionals have the right to think and act different from the injunction of the model that constitutes its most serious weakness," the authors vented. "This anti-intellectual flaw makes the Dunn and Dunn Model unlike any other evaluated in this review."[54]

The Myers–Briggs Type Indicator (MBTI) was not specifically designed to be used in classrooms, but its enormous popularity in the business, religious, and medical worlds made its application in educational settings likely, so it was included in the review. According to Coffield and his coauthors, two million copies of the MBTI were sold each year and hundreds of research articles applied the model. Despite its popularity, the authors found that the evidence for its effectiveness in increasing learning was "inconclusive at best." Regarding Kolb's learning style inventory, Coffield and his coauthors noted the previously discussed problems (see chapter 1) with validity and reliability of his LSI, and they also noted the fact that Kolb's approach was often misinterpreted and misapplied by other educators who adopted it: "It may be asked if too much is being expected of a relatively simple test which consists of nine to 12 word sets of four words. What is indisputable is that such simplicity has generated complexity, controversy, and an enduring and frustrating lack of clarity." The authors' dismissal of Sternberg's theory was even more direct and ironic. Because Sternberg had reviewed the literature on learning styles so extensively, he had much to say about the shortcomings of previous approaches, including the "balkanization" of the learning/thinking style concept. Coffield and his coauthors concluded by using Sternberg's own words against him: "It is also arguable that Sternberg has himself contributed to such balkanization and that the answer to his own question—do we need another theory of learning styles?—is probably best answered in the negative."[55]

The *Learning Styles and Pedagogy* report was way too long, technical, and nuanced to be considered a wholesale takedown of the learning style idea. Nevertheless, the authors identified several enduring problems with the field, such as theoretic incoherence, conceptual confusion, vested interests, overblown claims, psychometric weaknesses, unwarranted faith in simple inventories, no clear indications for pedagogy, decontextualized views of learners, and lack of communication between different research perspectives. They concluded the report by pointing to areas of further research and endorsed the few learning style typologies and assessments they felt were the least problematic: those by Michael J. Apter, Noel J. Entwistle, Ned Herrmann, and Jan D. Vermunt. Not only were these typologies some of the least popular ones, but they were virtually unknown in the United States.

Although Coffield and his coauthors voiced harsh criticism of many of the most popular learning style typologies being used in higher education, their overall tone of the LSDA report was constructive and conciliatory. However, writing alone in a 2006 editorial for the *Guardian*, Coffield had a far more embittered and direct message about the use of learning style assessments: "Next time you see a learning styles questionnaire, burn it." In fact, Coffield dismissed the entire learning style industry. He advised that the next time teachers were introduced to a learning style inventory through professional development, they should respond that they were "professionals trying to build a solid base of knowledge about teaching and learning . . . informed by evidence, not by the unexamined hunches of some guru who's making a fortune from peddling poppycock." The "guru" comment seemed to be aimed at Anthony Gregorc, whose later learning style typology included religious and metaphysical elements. Coffield also related several anecdotes of oversimplified and pedagogically unsound applications of the learning style idea, including one instance in which "pupils had labels on their desks indicating their learning style." He concluded that "we do students a serious disservice by implying they have only one learning style, rather than a flexible repertoire from which to choose, depending on the context."[56]

Coffield's editorial reflected a growing dissatisfaction with the learning style field, which seemed to be splintering and multiplying rather than converging and building momentum as the theory became more popular. Whereas many critics were willing to forgive well-meaning but overworked K–12 teachers for adopting the idea, they were less forgiving of college and university professors, who should have known better. The fact that medical professionals were some of the greatest advocates of learning styles pointed to the perception that there was a much larger problem in educational research that needed to be remedied.

*

According to research conducted through Google Scholar, articles on learning styles and multiple intelligences (often treated as a learning style) peaked in the first decade of the twenty-first century.[57] This peak aligned with the ascendency of the VAK learning style typology and was supported by the availability of free learning style assessment instruments on the internet. Counterintuitively, the evidence suggests that learning styles were just as popular in higher education and professional schools as they were in colleges and schools of education. Furthermore, by the 2000s, the research on learning and cognitive styles had essentially split into VAK-based models that had relatively weak support in the literature and cognitive/thinking style models that traced their origins to Herman Witkin and had a far more convincing and robust research base. As we shall see in the next chapter, the onslaught of attacks on the learning style idea that emerged in the wake of Frank Coffield's critiques conflated these two learning style orientations.

7
Debunking the Myth of Learning Styles

In 1972, Anthony Gregorc was first inspired to explore the learning style idea after reading about a study on personality types in the magazine *Psychology Today*. Fifty years later, *Psychology Today* published a feature article on "Ten Myths about the Mind," which included the myth that people have learning styles. "Tailoring education to 'visual learners' and 'auditory learners' doesn't make sense," the writer posited, because "scientific reviews have found scant justification for the practice."[1] This article represented a general shift against the learning style idea by psychologists and the mainstream media that took place during the 2010s. Frank Coffield's 2006 attack on the learning style idea was just the tip of the iceberg, as numerous critiques of the idea were published over the next decade.[2] By the 2020s, many of the same publications that had once introduced the learning style idea as promising and intuitive later dismissed it as a "neuromyth" that needed to be "debunked" and sought to explain why teachers stubbornly clung to the disproven idea. Gone were the admiring profiles of innovative teachers engaging their students with learning style–based methods. In their place, journalists explored the widening gap between the so-called science of learning and the obstinate and irrational beliefs of teachers.

The Problematic Research Base of Learning Styles

As demonstrated in previous chapters, the research supporting the learning style idea had been problematic and inconclusive since its origins. Although learning style advocates including David Kolb as well as Walter Barbe and Raymond Swassing cited the work of Maria Montessori and John Dewey, they did not endorse the labeling of students and/or the isolation of certain senses at the expense of others. The VAK model originated with the German psychologist Ernst Meumann's "ideation types" (auditory, visual, motor), which related to how students recalled words after they had been learned, but not how students had learned the words in the first place. Meumann pitched his own learning style theory based on rapid and slow learners; for whatever reason, though, his learning style model did not catch on, whereas his three ideation types did. The kinesthetic aspects of learning gained additional attention through Grace Fernald's work with struggling readers in the 1920s. However, she insisted that her kinesthetic method was appropriate only for students who had "failed to learn to read by visual and auditory methods."[3] She also pointed out that most students employed a mix of visual, auditory, and kinesthetic methods in learning new words, and that many students often shifted among the preferred learning channels when doing so. Neither Meumann or Fernald recommended that students be identified permanently with a learning style label, and neither suggested that the learning (or sensory recall) channels had any relevance beyond learning to read. When Frank Riessman introduced the VAK model in the 1960s in his explanations of the alleged learning style of so-called culturally deprived children, he provided no research to support the idea, so it is difficult to determine where or how he came up with his theory.

Herman Witkin's research on cognitive styles had a firmer empirical basis than the VAK-based typology, but when his field dependent/independent model was initially applied in educational settings, the findings were not encouraging. In one of the first-ever studies that matched teaching methods to students' cognitive styles, the researcher Max Rennels found that "contrary to expectations," most students learned best through an analytic approach that aligned with field independence, regardless of whether any given student had been identified as field dependent or field independent.[4] A 1975 review of the literature on the role of perceptual channels in literacy published that same year found conflicting results for the effects of visual and auditory teaching methods, and the review also found virtually no research on the effectiveness of kinesthetic methods at all.[5] Similarly, an oft-cited book by Lee Cronbach and Richard Snow published in 1977 found that the research on diagnosing a learning style and prescribing specific learning methods aligned to that style was inconclusive because "some instructional treatments seemed to be beneficial to one subgroup while at the same time having negative effects on another subgroup."[6] When Sara Tarver and Margaret Dawson reviewed ninety studies on the role of VAK modality strength in learning how to read in 1978, they concluded that the "validity of the modality strength concept finds strikingly little support; thus practical wisdom is not supported by research data."[7]

As more studies were conducted on modality-based learning, the research supporting the idea became even thinner. Lynn Curry's 1983 review and synthesis of the different learning style typologies asserted that "learning style researchers have not yet unequivocally established the reality or utility of this concept," and a meta-analysis on learning styles conducted by Kenneth Kavale and Steven Forness in 1987 concluded that "although the notion of modality-based instruction remains intuitively appealing, the evidence is not supportive [because] . . . neither modality testing nor modality teaching were shown to be efficacious."[8] When the Yale professor Edmund Gordon reviewed the literate on race-based learning styles for the New York State Board of Regents the next year, he also found "little support in the accumulated studies of efforts at matching learner traits and instructional practices."[9] A similar review by Jacqueline Jordan Irvine and Darlene Eleanor York in 1995 for the *Handbook of Research on Multicultural Education* concluded: "Despite the continuing popularity of the instruments, the surrounding research has not fully supported the underlying idea of learning styles."[10] Counterintuitively, it seemed like the more that the empirical researchers questioned the validity of the learning style idea, the more popular the idea became among advocates and practitioners. These reviews may have been buried in somewhat obscure research publications and thus were outside the purview of most educators. However, a steady stream of more conspicuous attacks on the learning style idea started to appear in the 1990s.

The 1990 *Educational Leadership* article cited at the beginning of chapter 6 included a sidebar section entitled "Findings of Styles Research Murky at Best," reporting how "allegations and countercharges of shoddy scholarship and vested interests have clouded the issue and made it all the more difficult for practitioners to decide what's worth pursuing." The journalist interviewed several experts who expressed doubt about the learning style idea, especially Dunn's VAKT-based version of it. Although not naming Dunn, James Keefe, director of the National Association of Secondary School Principals (NASSP), admitted that most of the research demonstrating the efficacy of modality-based learning had been conducted by the authors of the learning style inventories themselves. Furthermore, Anthony Gregorc found a lot of the research on learning style to be suspect, stating, "One of the reasons that some of these scores are going up is . . . the kids sense that someone cares." He added a subtle attack on Dunn: "It may have very little to do with a beanbag chair or something else." Richard Snow, professor at Stanford University, reiterated his earlier assessment that the research supporting learning styles was "rather slim," and that most advocates did not "really validate their ideas with strong, scientifically based methods." Robert Slavin, who was a professor at Johns Hopkins University and a respected researcher whose advocacy for cooperative learning met the highest research standards, also expressed doubts about learning style–based interventions because the research did not include control groups, so it could not be proven that the achievement gains were solely because of the learning style intervention and not something else.[11]

The same issue of *Educational Leadership* included a pivotal article by Lynn Curry. Back in 1983, Curry had provided a thoughtful synthesis of the different learning style typologies and proposed a three-tiered conceptualization that attempted to reconcile these divergent models (see chapter 2). Her three-tiered proposal was cited dozens of times over the next decade in support of the learning style idea. Generally, educators would make a broad statement about the significance and popularity of learning styles and then cite Curry's review paper as evidence of its plausibility, implying that she supported the learning style idea. However, this was not really the case. Frustrated by the tendency to be viewed as a learning style advocate, Curry published a 1990 article on learning style that left no ambiguity about her position: "A Critique of the Research on Learning Styles."

Curry attacked this research from three angles. First, she reiterated the fact that the scholars pitched a "bewildering array" of learning style theories without making any attempt to relate their typologies to one another.[12] Learning style advocates apparently had no problem with the coexistence of nearly two dozen conflicting theories. In fact, every few years, a new typology would be added to the mix; by 2004, there were over thirty learning style typologies.[13] The same year, Frank Coffield and his coauthors identified seventy-one typologies.[14] Rather than viewing these conflicting and irreconcilable theories as evidence of the problematic nature of the learning style idea, advocates viewed the cumulative nature of the typologies as evidence that learning styles *must* exist because there were so many models out there. Furthermore, Curry pointed out, most learning style advocates had pitched their typologies directly to practitioners while mostly circumventing any experimental laboratory research and/or rigorous peer review. Instead, advocates simply stated that their typology was the best (or at least the most user friendly), and then introduced it directly to teachers and administrators via textbooks, learning style instrument manuals, or professional development workshops.[15]

Second, Curry targeted the weaknesses in the "reliability and validity of measurements" in the studies on learning styles. She complained that, rather than tweaking the learning style assessment instruments over years through trial and error and rigorous evaluation, advocates tended to "rush prematurely into print and marketing with very early and preliminary" findings.

In addition, Curry continued, most studies on the efficacy of learning style–based interventions had "not been designed to disconfirm hypotheses," nor did they "involve wide enough samples to constitute valid tests in educational settings."[16] All of this was to suggest that learning style advocates often cited empirical studies and statistics to convince practitioners that they knew what they were talking about, but most of these studies did not meet the minimal standards of rigorous statistical research. That is, learning style advocates employed statistics and statistical rhetoric to make their instruments look scientific to practitioners without really being scientific.

Third, Curry echoed the fact that several overlooked empirical studies had found that matching students with their alleged learning style was not beneficial. "Effects on improved test scores with testing conditions matched to every student style have been published," she wrote, "but there are also studies showing no discernable effect attributable to learning style variation." The studies showing no effect of teaching to learning styles essentially canceled out the ones that did, yet many advocates—and especially the media—ignored these conflicting studies because the learning style idea seemed so intuitive and promising. Equally problematic was the fact that certain learning styles (such as field independence and auditory learning preferences) aligned with students' IQ, which undermined the argument that these were really styles at all, instead of differences in general intelligence. In one final comment clearly aimed at Rita Dunn, Curry repeated Keefe's observation that "many studies conducted in the learning styles literature have been conducted by graduate students preparing their PhD theses under the direction of faculty members with a vested interest in substantiating a particular learning style conceptualization."[17]

As theorists argued among themselves about the validity of the learning style idea, in the 1990s psychometricians evaluated the instruments being employed to assess student learning styles. Predictably, they had nothing encouraging to say. One psychometrician concluded bluntly in the *Eleventh Mental Measurement Yearbook* that Dunn's LSI had "no redeeming values." Another who reviewed Dunn's LSI wrote, "There is no evidence that the instrument provides any valid or reliable information about learning styles," and asserted that "there currently is little reason to believe the instrument should be used as a diagnostic tool for teaching, learning, and curriculum planning." Another reviewer who pointed to the lack of scientific support for learning style assessment instruments, stated, "Not a single shred of evidence concerning the reliability and validity of either Learning Style or Teaching Style Inventories appears in the manual"; yet another concluded that there were "no reasons to consider these tests adequate for their intended purposes."[18]

Even Howard Gardner pointed out, "There is not persuasive evidence that the learning style analysis produces more effective outcomes than a 'one size fits all' approach."[19]

However, learning style advocates largely ignored these concerns, and practitioners and the media appeared to be unaware of the critiques. This would all change when a recently formed journal called *Psychological Science in the Public Interest* published a widely read article titled "Learning Styles: Concepts and Evidence" in December 2009.

Cognitive Scientists Weigh In

At a 1997 meeting, the board of directors of the then American Psychological Society (APS) discussed the possibility of launching a new journal that would be available for free to the public and focus on impartial literature reviews of "topics of pressing national importance," such as the effectiveness of Drug Abuse Resistance Education (DARE), phonics instruction in reading, or/and sex education. The organization went ahead with the plan, and the first issue of *Psychological Science in the Public Interest* appeared in May 2000. The lofty hope for the new journal was that its "juried analyses" would "inform decision making by consumers, courts, opinion makers, legislators, and leaders in business, the military and education." The editors warned that "some cherished assumptions may be shattered, and some popular interventions may be judged useless or even harmful," yet they pledged to appoint balanced reviewers and publish honest assessments of what the research concluded, regardless of the political implications.[20] Although research questioning the existence of learning styles and the efficacy of teaching had been in existence for decades, most practitioners and journalists continued to believe that the science supported the learning style idea. Debunking such popular beliefs was exactly why the *Psychological Science in the Public Interest* had been launched. The editors appointed Harold E. (Hal) Pashler of the University of California San Diego to lead a study of this particular topic, and, predictably, Pashler and his coauthors, Mark McDaniel, Doug Rohrer, and Robert A. Bjork, concluded that the science did not support the idea that teaching to learning styles would improve achievement. After the publication of this article, it would become more common for critics to dismiss the learning style idea as a "myth" or "neuromyth."

Pashler and his coauthors insisted that for the learning style idea to have any "credible validation," studies supporting it needed to have a "robust documentation of a very particular type of experimental finding" based on a specific research design. First, students needed to be divided into two groups based on learning style, and then each student had to be randomly assigned to receive instruction in one of the two methods (e.g., auditory or visual). Second, all the students needed to be given the same test. Finally, the students needed to be divided and taught through their alleged learning style strength and then tested again. For learning style research to be convincing, researchers needed results that not only proved students' scores improved when taught via their identified modality strength, but also demonstrated that this improvement exceeded the improvement that all students experienced when taught through any single modality. In other words, for learning styles to be valid in accordance with the highest standards of scientific research, advocates had to prove not only that certain students learned best through either visual or auditory methods, but also that *all* students did not learn best through either visual or auditory methods. This required a complex experimental design that most studies did not meet. "Although the literature on learning styles is enormous, very few studies have even used an experimental methodology capable of testing the validity of learning styles applied to education," Pashler and his coauthors reported. "Moreover, of those that did use an appropriate method, several found results that flatly contradict the popular meshing hypothesis [of matching learning style to method]."[21] Beyond offering specificity about what counted as acceptable experimental research, there was nothing new about this overall conclusion that the research did not support matching teaching methods to learning styles. However, unlike previous literature reviews, the Pashler study gained the immediate attention of the educational and mainstream press.

Psychological Science in the Public Interest was launched to achieve maximum impact, and its article on learning styles succeeded in drawing immediate attention. Both the *Chronicle of Higher Education* and *Education Week* issued stories on the Pashler article within a week of its publication. The *Chronicle*'s article, "Matching Teaching Style to Learning Style May Not Help Students," provocatively reported how there was "no scientific evidence to support the 'matching idea,'" so there was "absolutely no reason for professors to adopt it in the classroom." Pashler, who was interviewed for the article, admitted to the journalist that he employed a high bar for what research to include in his review: "Lots of people are selling tests and programs for customizing education that completely lack the kind of experimental evidence that you would expect for a drug. Now maybe the FDA model isn't always appropriate for education—but that's a conversation we need to have." Pashler pointed out that not only had his review found that very few studies could prove the efficacy of teaching to learning styles, but it also found that "almost every well-designed study . . . discovered that one instructional style actually works best."[22]

Rita Dunn had recently passed away, so the *Chronicle* reached out to the so-called "grandfather of this territory," David Kolb, who was then a professor of organizational behavior at Case Western Reserve University, for a rebuttal and comment. Kolb agreed that Pashler's high bar for which research to include in his review omitted a lot of important studies that may have problematized his conclusions. Nevertheless, Kolb generally accepted Pashler's findings. Kolb reiterated that he opposed assigning a permanent label to students, such as kinesthetic or visual learner, and instead advocated that teachers approach all topics through the "full learning cycle," touching on all four of his learning style profiles across a single lesson. "Matching is not a particularly good idea," Kolb added. "The paper correctly mentions the practical and ethical problems of sorting people into groups and labelling them. Tracking in education has a bad history."[23] Indeed, as explored in chapter 5, sorting and labeling students did have a bad history, especially for students of color.

Education Week employed even more direct language in its headline, "Cognitive Scientists Debunk Learning-Style Theories." This was the first time that the term *debunk* had been applied to research questioning the validity of the learning style idea, but it would appear commonly in the years that followed. Although the brief article did little beyond report the major findings of the study, the journalist asked Pashler why he and his coauthors failed to include Gardner's MI theory in his review; Pashler responded that they "strictly focused on the question of whether there is evidence to support the utility of testing students' learning styles and selecting instructional methods accordingly."[24] The conflation of MI theory and learning styles fed into the discussion of Pashler's controversial findings. For example, Peter DeWitt, a former principal and regular contributor to *Education Week*, wrote, "I spent years thinking there were learning styles. . . . I was highly influenced by Howard Gardner and spent a great deal of time matching up students to how I thought they learned best." However, after becoming aware of the findings in Pashler's article, as well as Gardner's own dismissal of learning styles on his blog, DeWitt admitted, "I was wrong." When he was a principal, DeWitt had used Fridays to offer activities aligned with the multiple intelligences and encouraged his teachers "try to hit all of the intelligences that [they] could." Although he did not label students exclusively with a particular intelligence or learning style, he confessed that his Friday curriculum had been justified by a "strong" belief "that each student had a learning style." DeWitt reflected that, in retrospect, it may have been "harmful" to "box students into one way of learning." Nevertheless, he still supported a "multi-modal approach" to teaching that used a variety of methods and entry points to a topic—an approach that, ironically, Gardner had recommended all along in his books such as *The Disciplined Mind* and *The Unschooled Mind*.[25]

Over the next decade, the tide turned against the learning style idea, and psychologists attacked it relentlessly. A 2014 study on the impact of learning styles on reading comprehension likewise found "no statistically significant relationship between learning style preference (auditory, visual word) and instructional method (audio-book, e-text)."[26] Another literature review conducted by Joshua Cuevas in 2015 focused exclusively on the research published since the pivotal 2009 Pashler article. Cuevas wrote, "The empirical evidence for the validity of the learning styles hypothesis seems to have gotten weaker in recent years," and he noted how previous studies supporting the efficacy of learning styles failed to appear in any "reputable psychology journals or high-level educational journals."[27] In an even bigger blow to the learning style idea, a group of thirty psychologists and neuroscientists from Canada, Germany, the US, and the UK sent a letter to the *Guardian* in 2017 declaring that learning styles were a "neuromyth" and that teachers should stop referencing the idea. "Such neuromyths create a false impression of individuals abilities," the letter warned, "leading to expectations and excuses that are detrimental to learning in general, which is a cost in the long term."[28] Even the *Phi Delta Kappan*, which, along with ASCD's *Educational Leadership*, had done more than any other publication to legitimize the learning style idea in the 1980s and '90s, turned against the approach. In 2015, the journal ran an article by Benjamin Riley, executive director of Deans for Impact, espousing the science of learning as an antidote to learning styles. Under the subheading "Students Do Not Have Different Learning Styles," Riley reported: "While the theory sounds plausible enough, scientists have studied it time and time again, and the data overwhelmingly suggest that students do not learn when presented with information in their preferred style."[29]

As more articles appeared debunking the learning style myth, the titles and headlines became more sensationalistic. The authors of a 2018 study that focused specifically on the validity of Neil Fleming's VARK learning style model titled their article "Another Nail in the Coffin for Learning Styles?" and concluded that "the conventional wisdom about learning styles should be rejected by educators and students alike."[30] This study inspired an article in the *Atlantic* on the "Myth of Learning Styles" with the tagline "A popular theory that some people learn better visually or aurally keeps getting debunked."[31] A story for the Toronto newspaper *Globe and Mail* appeared under the headline "Is the Theory of Unique Learning Styles Dragging Down Our Education System?," reaffirming that "the concept of learning styles—applied universally, to the general student population, beyond learners with special needs—appears to be a myth."[32] A decade after the Pashler review article, the educational and mainstream media had reached a consensus that the learning style idea was "neuromyth" or "myth" that teachers ought to abandon. No one pursued this message more consistently or to a larger audience than the psychologist Daniel Willingham.

The Learning Style Grinch

During the 2000s, Daniel Willingham became the public face of learning style skepticism and a self-professed "Grinch" on the topic. Years before the Pashler review was published in *Psychological Science in the Public Interest*, Willingham had carefully and respectfully dismantled the core concepts of learning styles for an educational audience that likely believed in—and perhaps even cherished—the learning style idea. Willingham graduated in 1990 from Harvard with his doctorate in cognitive psychology. As a professor at the University of Virginia, in 2002 he began writing a column called "Ask the Cognitive Scientist" for *American Educator*, the journal of the American Federation of Teachers, which was the second-largest teacher union in the United States. In 2005, Willingham was asked, "Do visual, auditory, and kinesthetic learners need visual, auditory, and kinesthetic Instruction?" Drawing upon some empirical studies on cognition, he offered three major critiques of the VAK learning style typology in his column.

First, Willingham pointed out, cognitive science had demonstrated that the storage of memories was independent of the sense modality through which it was learned: "You typically store memories in terms of meaning—not in terms of whether you saw, heard, or physically interacted with the information." In other words, the focus on the sense modality was misplaced because the nature of what was learned was more important for memory than how it was learned. Second, he explained, the mind cannot substitute images for words and vice versa because "different representations are more or less effective for storing different types of information." Images of maps or paintings, for example, are not translated into sounds or movements by the minds of so-called auditory or kinesthetic learners. Instead, maps and paintings are remembered as images, even if the student is allegedly an auditory or kinesthetic learner. Finally, citing the meta-analysis of Kenneth Kavale and Steven Forness, Willingham related how "substantial evidence" demonstrated that "tailoring instruction to students' modality [was] not effective; across these very well-designed studies, such tailoring had no educational effect."[33] This assertion would be reinforced a few years later with the publication and reception of the Pashler review.

In 2004, Willingham shifted his offensive from learning styles to Howard Gardner's theory of multiple intelligences. He published his critique of MI theory in a new, reform-oriented journal called *Education Next* that advocated for curriculum standards, charter schools, vouchers, and merit pay for teachers. As discussed in chapter 4, the standards advocate E. D. Hirsch had linked MI theory and learning styles to the wishful thinking of progressive-minded educators who allegedly refused to accept what hard science stated was true about how students learned. Willingham's attack on MI theory likely met a receptive audience of reformers who were also critical of progressive pedagogical ideas. In the article, Willingham charged Gardner with misrepresenting the state of psychometrics by positing that most psychologists believed in a "unitary trait" of intelligence, when in fact most psychometricians believed in a hierarchical model of intelligence, with mathematical thinking and linguistic thinking operating atop an underlying general intelligence. Second, Willingham found Gardner's criteria for intelligence to be too pliable and so vague that—using Gardner's criteria—memory, humor, olfactory, and/or spelling intelligences could also be justified. Many of the seven intelligences, Willingham argued, were better characterized as talents. Willingham also disputed whether the intelligences Gardner identified were as distinct as he claimed. "Intellectual abilities are correlated, not independent," Willingham insisted. "Distinguishable abilities do exist, but Gardner's description of them is not well supported."[34]

Regarding pedagogical misapplications of MI theory, Willingham related Gardner's own clarifications about how his theory had been misused to justify trivial classroom activities, but he also pointed out that Gardner had carelessly endorsed Thomas Armstrong's *Multiple Intelligences in the Classroom*, the 1994 book that included such trivial ideas as "singing spellings and spelling with leaves and twigs." Gardner's inconsistency, Willingham pointed out, sent a mixed message to practitioners about appropriate uses of his theory. Moreover, Willingham speculated that teachers' misapplication of MI theory was likely tied to Gardner's decision to call his mental capacities *intelligences* in the first place: "The term intelligence has always connoted the kind of thinking skills that make one successful in school, perhaps because the first intelligence test was devised to predict likely success in school." Finally, Willingham pointed out that the hard data supporting the efficacy of teaching to multiple intelligences was lacking, making "Gardner's theory . . . not all that helpful" to teachers; he recommended that they "turn their time and attention elsewhere."[35] That same year, Willingham was interviewed for a *Washington Post* article on the endurance of Gardner's MI theory, where he again expressed his criticisms of Gardner's work.[36]

When Pashler and his coauthors published their review essay in 2009, Willingham must have felt somewhat vindicated by the attention the paper and topic garnered in the press, which drew further attention to own previous critiques of learning styles. Accordingly, Willingham cited the Pashler review in his own subsequent attacks on the learning style idea. When National Public Radio's *Morning Edition* broadcast a story on learning style skepticism in 2011, the journalist interviewed Willingham for the story, demonstrating that he had become the public face of learning style skepticism. At the prompting of his editors, he continued to publish on the topic in the years that followed, despite having moved beyond learning styles in his research interests.[37]

In his 2009 book, *Why Don't Students Like School?*, he devoted an entire chapter to debunking both learning style theory and MI theory. Based in part on his columns for *American Educator*, the subtitle to his book was *A Cognitive Scientist Answers Questions about How the Mind Works and What It Means for the Classroom*. To this end, Willingham addressed the question "How should I adjust my teaching for different types of learners," to which he responded: "Children are more alike than different in terms of how they think and learn." After recounting his previous critiques of learning style theory and multiple intelligences, Willingham shared that he "felt a bit like a Grinch as I wrote this chapter . . . about the optimistic ideas others have offered regarding student differences." Although he supported the general idea of having teachers differentiate their instruction for different students, when teachers did so, he insisted, "they should know that scientists cannot offer any help."[38]

During the next few years, Willingham continued—sometimes reluctantly—to address the ineffectiveness of teaching to learning styles by publishing in a variety of journals and other outlets. He and his coauthors also added a few caveats that closed the gap slightly between what the science said about the existence of learning styles and what most teachers and the public believed to be true. Nevertheless, the overriding message was that learning styles were a "myth" that teachers should stop propagating. In fact, "myth" is exactly what he and his coauthor called the learning styles idea in a 2010 article in *Change*. The authors began their article with commonly held assumptions that the science *did* support, such as the fact that students had preferences about how they think they learned best; that these preferences affected the *way* they studied (but not how much they learned); and that important differences among students, such as background knowledge and personal interests, impacted how and what they learned. This was all to acknowledge that "in claiming that learning styles do not exist, we are not saying that all learners are the same"—a message that somewhat contradicted the more simplistic message he had published in his book a year earlier, about how students' minds were more similar than different.[39]

Furthermore, in a 2015 article for *Teaching of Psychology*, Willingham and his coauthors asserted that "learning styles theories ought to be debunked and a great place for this to take place is on our psychology classrooms." Willingham recognized that the learning style myth was as pervasive in college teaching as it was in elementary and secondary schools, including his own field of psychology (see chapter 6).[40] Furthermore, Willingham's work was featured in a 2016 white paper, *Science of Learning*, by the Deans for Impact. The paper identified "Students do not have different learning styles" as the number-one misconception about learning that the so-called science of learning hoped to correct.[41] These publications were aimed at changing the minds of college professors, proving that the perception that the learning style idea had become popular in undergraduate, graduate, and professional education.

To reach an audience even broader than teachers and professors, Willingham published an editorial for the *New York Times* in 2018 titled "You Are Not a Visual Learner." This time he avoided the more inflammatory language of "debunking" and "myths," and instead briefly explained the methodologies and findings of recent studies demonstrating that aligning learning styles with teaching methods was not effective, even though people believed it was. "The theory is wrong, but curiously, people act though it's right—they try to learn try to learn in accordance with what they think is their style," he reported. Although such a discrepancy between how people learn best and how they think they learn best may not seem to make much of a difference, Willingham suggested that thinking that you learn best in one way "can cost you," because "one mental strategy may be much better suited than another to a particular task."[42] In other words, certain problems and tasks required certain kinds of thinking to master them, regardless of what students might think their best learning style is, and so learning style theory could potentially steer students away from the most effective methods.

That same year, Willingham revisited the learning style topic for *American Educator* in his "Ask the Cognitive Scientist" column. Although he reasserted that "using learning-styles theories does not bring an advantage to students," he also updated this answer with a new twist: research showed that "people believe that they have learning styles, and they try to think in their preferred style, but doing so doesn't help them think." In other words, people may differ in the way they process information, but these divergences ultimately made no difference in how much people learn because some styles were better for certain tasks, no matter what their alleged style was. "Reflective thinking is much better than intuitive thinking for probability problems," Willingham wrote. "Imagery is much better than verbalizing for sentence memory."[43] This may have been a confusing message for teachers to digest because it seemed like Willingham was stating that learning styles *did* exist, they just did not necessarily improve learning. If this was the case, was it still accurate to call learning styles a "myth"?

Willingham's message on learning styles evolved subtly over a decade and half. Whereas he initially set out "debunk" the "myth" of the learning style idea outright, he later added a more nuanced assessment. Drawing on the research of David Kraemer at Dartmouth College, Willingham and his coauthors explained how learning styles did affect how people preferred to learn new information and this, in turn, impacted how they chose to study; however, matching learning styles to preferred methods did not improve the learning process in any demonstrable way.[44] Willingham pledged to report what the science said about learning styles as it emerged, but when the science got a little more complex, he may have lost some clarity and force in his message. He tried to redirect teachers toward research-based methods that were proven to enhance student learning, as outlined in his book *Why Don't Students Like School?* and his *American Educator* columns, but it was unclear how successful he was in this effort.

Perhaps Willingham and his colleagues overestimated the desire of practitioners to justify and update their methods based on what the research said; or perhaps they did not present a very compelling case for any harm that was being done to students by teaching to learning styles. "It's not like anything terrible is going to happen to you [do buy into learning styles]," Willingham later admitted.[45] Although the research disproved the efficacy of teaching to learning styles, it also confirmed that doing so was generally just as effective as not teaching to them. In other words, no real harm was being done by teachers' belief in and implementation of the myth. Despite the efforts of Willingham and his peers to disabuse educators of the theory, educators continued to believe in it, and some even chose to defend it.

The Persistence of Learning Styles

Perhaps psychologists and journalists naively thought that the learning style idea, which in one form or another had been around for nearly a century by the 2010s, would suddenly vanish upon the publication of these highly visible attacks. The fact that teachers did not immediately abandon the idea became a story in its own right, as well as a topic of research. That is, in the wake of the Pashler review and Willingham's attacks on the theory, researchers and journalists began to pivot away from the fact that learning styles were a myth and began to investigate the extent to which teachers still believed the myth, and why it just wouldn't go away after the scientific community decided it should.

First, journalists pointed to the persistence and extent of the belief. One shocking study from 2014 found that well over 90 percent of teachers from around the UK, the Netherlands, Turkey, Greece, and China still believed in the learning style myth, and a 2019 study confirmed that over 90 percent of teachers in the US believed it.[46] Despite all the studies attacking the learning style idea, teachers seemed to be unmoved. One metanalysis of teacher beliefs conducted in 2020 concluded, "There is no evidence that this belief [in learning styles] is decreasing, despite research going back to 2004 which demonstrates that such an approach is ineffective and potentially harmful."[47] More than three-quarters of US teachers also believed that right brain/left brain thinking impacted learning—a theory that had likewise been dismissed by cognitive scientists. Most teachers surveyed reported that they had learned about these myths through conference presentations and professional development workshops, and from their peers. "It's really not the fault of teachers—we have a system that does not give them enough support in terms of what the research says," one critic said to a journalist from *Education Week* in an article entitled "Teachers Still Believe in Learning Styles and Other Myths about Cognition."[48] A 2015 study of two hundred English teachers in the US and Canada found that 88 percent of them agreed with the statement that teaching to preferred learning styles improved student achievement.[49] Moreover, a 2019 review of introductory educational textbooks found that over 80 percent of them still included a discussion of learning styles, and a quarter of these texts still explicitly recommended matching instructional methods to them.[50] This demonstrated that textbooks were incorporating the new learning style skepticism, but slowly and awkwardly.

In one instance of this, Alan Pritchard added a section to the end of his chapter on multiple intelligences and learning styles in the fourth edition of his textbook, *Ways of Learning*, that related the concerns raised by Pashler, stating, "The findings of [Pashler's] study call into question the strong claims made for matching teaching to pupil learning." But that was an odd way to end his twenty-page discussion of MI theory and learning styles that included numerous teaching suggestions for how teachers could incorporate both these theories in their classrooms.[51] Nevertheless, adding skepticism to the end of book chapters or articles that more or less endorsed the learning style idea was a common response to the debunking literature. One study conducted in 2015 reported that, if a teacher were to type "learning styles" into an open-access teaching research database such as ERIC, "most (94%) of the current research papers [would] start out with a positive view of learning styles, despite the aforementioned research which discredits their use."[52] Whereas many learning style advocates ignored the research on learning style skepticism altogether, others simply referenced it briefly and then moved ahead with their study anyway, as if the skepticism wasn't convincing and/or it contradicted the commonsense knowledge of teachers. One journalist implored teachers to "step up and put this myth to bed"; the problem was that teachers and many researchers were not eager or willing to do so.[53]

As early as 2010, Catherine Scott, a senior research fellow at the Australian Council for Educational Research, speculated on why educators continued to act on the debunked theory. First, she cynically pointed out, "If there is money to be made, someone will take advantage of the opportunity." She cited the enormous number of companies, textbooks, and websites devoted to profiting from the learning style idea. The constant marketing of learning style–based materials kept the idea in the forefront of teachers' minds. Second, she argued that despite evidence to the contrary, teachers continued to think of human attributes in terms of fixed traits instead of "processes that can be influenced and shaped by effort and experience"—as explained in earlier chapters, the learning style idea had essentially replaced IQ as a quick and easy label that could be easily applied to all students. Finally, Scott argued, the learning style idea jibed "well with the individualist value system of our culture" that valued egalitarianism, encouraged social mobility, and celebrated difference.[54]

Willingham and the psychologist Cedar Riener added their own reasons why they thought teachers clung to the debunked theory. They pointed to the fact that the underlying premise—that students were different—was essentially true, so the learning style idea seemed accordingly plausible. Second, echoing Scott, they agreed that the idea "[fit] into an egalitarian view of education. . . . Everyone has value . . . everyone has strengths." Third, because the learning style idea had become commonsense knowledge, teachers were affected by confirmation bias: "When evaluating our own beliefs, we tend to seek out information that confirms our beliefs and ignore contrary information, even when we encounter it repeatedly."[55] Similarly, the Deans for Impact devoted an entire white paper to the question of "why mythbusting fails." The authors, Michael Pershan and Benjamin Riley, suggested that the learning style controversy had become politicized in the same way climate research had. Teachers, instead of tweaking their practice or being more nuanced with their rhetoric, viewed the attack on learning styles as a winner-takes-all battle between the knowledge of distant, lab-bound scientists and the hard-earned but disrespected wisdom of teachers. Forced to choose sides, most teachers aligned with their teaching peers. As Pershan and Riley put it: "Beliefs about science can become entangled with our self-identities, even if they didn't start out that way."[56]

A 2001 study suggested otherwise. Lenna Ojure and Thomas M. Sherman investigated how and why teachers still believed in the learning style idea when the research questioned its existence. They offered a more nuanced explanation. Rather than being "duped" or "succumbing to the bandwagon effect," teachers made their decisions about what to believe based on a "complex set of factors rooted, for the most part, in sound professional concerns." Whereas researchers "investigate[d] the absolute or comparative effects of matching learning styles," practitioners were looking for strategies they could adapt to help specific students in specific contexts. That is, the teachers were less concerned with the theoretical and empirical underpinnings of learning styles than they were with the practical methods and activities that went along with them. As demonstrated by Mindy Kornhaber's research on Gardner's MI theory, teachers were also interested in finding a language to describe and justify pedagogical methods they knew already worked for their students. Kornhaber explained: "That a Harvard psychologist's theory validated their experiences encouraged educators to learn more."[57] These findings suggested that teachers had always been critical consumers of educational research, that they approached new ideas with powerful preconceptions, and that they valued their own local experience and wisdom over the findings of distant scientists who did not know their students. "In fact," Ojure and Sherman noted, "teachers often express doubts about swallowing whole hog the prescribed teaching strategies that accompany learning-styles models. Expressly rejecting a package deal, it is far more likely that teachers will adapt and adopt methods that fit the conditions of their own particular classrooms and the children they teach."[58]

Others suggested that journalists and researchers had exaggerated the extent of teachers' belief in learning styles in the first place because critics had conflated teachers' belief in learning styles with a belief in the power of diversifying instruction over the course of a single lesson. "If, when teachers talk about learning styles, they really mean that they try to use a variety of representations and activities in class, that is a separate pedagogical strategy, and one that many more educators agree with," wrote one math teacher and blogger, Dylan Kane, in 2017. "My experience is that it's actually fairly rare for a teacher to attempt to determine student learning styles and tailor instruction to those styles." In other words, most teachers employed learning style theory to justify diversifying instruction across a single lesson, whereas very few formally assessed their students, labeled them with a learning strength, and then taught their students solely through that single modality. Nevertheless, when teachers read headlines declaring that learning styles were a "myth," some interpreted this as an unwarranted attack on diversifying instruction in general—a method that their experience had proven worked with students. "I think this is worth noting because discussions between educators on learning styles can quickly become angry and bitter," Kane added.[59]

One California teacher, Heather Wolpert-Gawron, stated bluntly that her personal experience trumped what scientists such as Pashler and Willingham had found in their studies. "I have conducted my own field studies of students in their natural habitat—my own classroom," she wrote in an opinion piece for *Education Week*. "And despite what this study claims, I have found that individuals do learn differently from one another." Wolpert-Gawron pitted the wisdom of her practical knowledge directly against the decontextualized laboratory studies of cognitive scientists such as Pashler and Willingham: "I am, after all, a classroom teacher, and pretty savvy about how kids learn . . . and I'm not so sure these scientists can boast the same depth of knowledge about their test subjects." She questioned the wisdom of dismissing a theory that justified teachers diversifying their instruction and thinking about the needs of individual students because these ideas inspired many teachers to try new methods that students would not think were "boring." She concluded, "Common sense and long experience proves to me, that there are different learning styles."[60]

Cedar Riener responded directly to Wolpert-Gawron's piece with his own op-ed, "Learning Styles: What's Being Debunked." He clarified that the researchers in the Pashler review were not debunking the idea that students differed in important ways from one another; they were merely debunking the idea that students could and should be labeled with specific learning styles, especially when the evidence pointed to the fact that most students learned best through visual methods. Although frustrated with Wolpert-Gawron's general defense of learning styles, Riener was even more ruffled by her flippant dismissal of the science of learning. Accordingly, Riener devoted most of his response to defending the integrity of the scientific endeavor. "How do we decide between the scientist in his sterile lab vs. the expert teacher with 11 years [of] experience and 2500 students?" Riener pondered. He responded: "Because despite the fact that personal experience is very compelling and convincing, human beings are notoriously bad at direct observation of complex relationships." Because "the history of common sense has been remarkably wrong," Riener explained, it was the job of scientists to test commonly held myths and report their unbiased finding to practitioners. However, there was still a place for teachers to implement their wisdom and experience in determining how to best implement the scientific findings of cognitive psychologists.[61]

The vision Riener presented was very much a top-down approach in which the mostly male cognitive scientists delivered their scientific findings to the mostly female teaching population. This contradicted recent trends toward including the voices of practitioners in educational research that emerged during the 1980s and '90s. After the many failed top-down and so-called teacher-proof educational reforms of the '60s and '70s, scholars expanded their research toolkits to include anthropological approaches to educational study, such as ethnography, participant-observer, case study, and action research. These new methodologies were designed to capture the meaning perspectives of teachers in context and to make research something that was done *with* teachers instead of something that was done *on* teachers and *to* teachers. As a result, qualitative studies of teaching became more common because scholars sought to understand how and why—not only to what degree—educational reforms did or did not work. They sought out the perspectives and collaboration of teachers and presented themselves as correctives to the kind of control experiments valued by learning style skeptics.[62]

In fact, much of the popularity of Rita Dunn's LSI could be explained by her ability to speak the language of practitioners in ways that spoke *to* them instead of *at* them. As one set of authors added after a lengthy quotation by Dunn in their book on learning styles: "These are not the words of a researcher, but a practitioner." Their assessment of Dunn as a "teacher in the trenches" was meant to be a compliment, not a criticism.[63] However, unbeknownst to these authors, Dunn had spent most of her career trying (unsuccessfully) to convince skeptics that she was not merely a practitioner, but also a serious scholar with scientific credentials. Nevertheless, if pressed to choose between scholarly respect and impact on practice, Dunn likely would have preferred the influence on practitioners over the respect of researchers, because classroom influence was the only result that really mattered in the end. Dunn defended her LSI against critics in scholarly journals, not necessarily to defend her scholarly reputation, but mainly because these attacks were a potential threat to the hard-earned influence she had in American classrooms. Ultimately, if an administrator needed to raise test scores immediately, they were far more likely to hire Dunn, who had a proven track record of raising student achievement in actual schools (albeit much of it not peer reviewed) than did Pashler, Riener, or Willingham, who could offer nothing more than a set of scientifically backed pedagogical prescriptions that still needed to be translated into practical methods. For this reason, the learning style idea persisted among many teachers who felt they had gotten results because of the theory.

Rescuing the Learning Style Idea

Although there appeared to be a consensus among cognitive scientists that learning styles were problematic, there was at least one prominent psychologist who refused to abandon the idea: Robert Sternberg. When interviewed for the *Chronicle* about Pashler's findings, Sternberg, who was then president of Tufts University, defended learning styles by insisting that Pashler and his coauthors drew "negative conclusions about a field they fail adequately to review."[64] At a time when many of the most respected advocates for the learning style idea, such as Witkin and Dunn, were no longer around to defend it, Sternberg stepped in to give it a continued sense of legitimacy and momentum. Working with his former graduate student, Li-fang Zhang, Sternberg continued to develop the learning style idea throughout the 2010s by synthesizing, critiquing, and adding to the research on what he now called intellectual styles.

In a 2015 book review for the *American Journal of Psychology*, Sternberg directly challenged the claims of Pashler, Riener, and Willingham. First, Sternberg critiqued Riener and Willingham for suggesting that learning styles were a myth because the authors relied entirely on the Pashler review of the literature, which did not use the term *myth*. Second, Sternberg questioned the extremely high bar that Pashler and his coauthors employed to review the literature on learning styles that left out hundreds of relevant studies, including many of Sternberg's own. As Sternberg quipped: "So because no study met the authors' criteria, the authors concluded that learning styles are not useful in education. That is a quite a leap of logic!" In other words, just because educational studies did not meet the highest standards of scientific research did not automatically mean that these studies were worthless and wrong, or that the learning style idea had been disproven. Sternberg then elaborated how, based on his own experiences, it was extremely difficult to conduct FDA-style research in real-world educational settings because random assignment of students in schools was nearly impossible. Finally, after praising Pashler and his coauthors as "superb scientists," Sternberg nevertheless dismissed the entire premise of the Pashler article as problematic because it sought to disprove an idea outright rather than review the idea's plausibility. "One learns in elementary statistics that one cannot prove the null hypothesis," he reminded readers, "but the article by Pashler and colleagues comes pretty close to trumpeting its proof of the null hypothesis."[65] By this Sternberg meant that statisticians set up their studies to disprove that the relationship between two variables is due merely to random variation or chance. To do this, they set up their investigations to disprove the null hypothesis (that the relationship between two variables, such as learning in general and learning style–based instruction, are due to chance) rather than prove the hypothesis (that addressing learning styles leads to better learning). A published response by Pashler and his coauthors defended their methodology and pointed out that learning styles were not only "an interesting academic topic," but also "an industry" with a large impact on teachers. Pashler and his colleagues were charged with determining whether the research supported the claims made by "the industry," and they stood by their conclusion that it did not.[66]

This debate represented a missed opportunity because Sternberg and Pashler were essentially talking past each other. The main target of Pashler, Riener, and Willingham was VAK-based learning style typology that historically had the weakest support in the literature and yet had become the most popular typology among educators and the broader public by the 2000s. Despite the thousands of pages Sternberg had written about learning styles over two decades, he had very little to say about the VAK-based version. He made little use of Dunn's extensive research; neither did he recognize the popular VAK-based work of Fleming or Barbe and Swassing. As a cognitive psychologist, Sternberg built on the major theorists in that field, such as Witkin and Kagan, but remained silent on the most popular version of the theory that had emerged largely outside mainstream cognitive psychology.

Sternberg's defense in the *American Journal of Psychology* essentially represented his final stand on the learning/thinking/intellectual style idea because he soon diverted his attention toward administrative leadership and its accompanying scandals. However, with Sternberg's blessing, Zhang carried his learning style idea forward by authoring three books on the topic in little over a decade: *The Nature of Intellectual Styles* (with Sternberg, 2006), *The Malleability of Intellectual Styles* (2013), and *The Value of Intellectual Styles* (2017).[67] Through these three books as well as dozens of peer-reviewed articles, Zhang rescued the learning style idea from professional obsolescence. But to do so, she upended some of its most cherished assumptions.

Zhang was a professor of psychology and education at the University of Hong Kong who conducted numerous studies in her home city, as well as the United States and mainland China, on the role of intellectual styles in learning, life, and psychological health. Through her work, she made four major contributions to the learning style idea. First, to move Sternberg's intellectual styles theory into the twenty-first century, Zhang simplified it. As early as 2005, Zhang reduced Sternberg's thirteen-term typology (e.g., executive, internal, global, conservative) to just three. Type I individuals "denote preferences for tasks that have low degrees of structure, that require the individuals to process information in a more complex way and allow for originality and high levels of freedom." Type II individuals "suggest preferences for tasks that are structured, that allow for individuals to process information in a more simplistic way, and that require conformity to traditional ways of doing things." Type III individuals "manifest the characteristics of both Type I and Type II intellectual styles, depending on stylistic demands of a specific task and on an individual level of interest in the task." Zhang's simplified categorization not only was based on Sternberg's previous thinking styles typology, but also incorporated other popular models, including Curry, Gregorc, Guilford, Jung, Kagan, Myers–Briggs, and Witkin.[68] Although it was far too late to enter the popular collective consciousness of teachers, Zhang's threefold intellectual style typology was far more transportable than Sternberg's earlier version.

Second, in a repudiation of over a half century of learning style conceptualization, Zhang boldly declared that the Type I intellectual style was superior to the Type II intellectual style in almost all situations. As explained in chapters 1 and 2, the entire field of learning styles had ascended largely on a relativistic paradigm suggesting that all styles were equal. Zhang disagreed. As she stated: "With very few exceptions, higher intelligence scores are related to Type I intellectual styles, suggesting that Type I styles carry more adaptive value than do Type II styles." Furthermore, she asserted, the "60 studies reviewed 'essentially' demonstrated the superiority of Type I intellectual styles over Type II styles."[69]

Third, after jettisoning the relativistic baggage of learning styles, Zhang reconciled the work on intellectual styles with research from developmental psychology—something most learning style advocates had been hesitant to do out of fear of prioritizing one style over another, especially when races were aligned with higher or lower learning styles or developmental stages. Building on the work of Jean Piaget and William G. Perry, Zhang predictably concluded that "the higher level of cognitive development (relativistic reasoning) was predominantly associated with Type I thinking styles, and the lower level of cognitive development (dualistic reasoning) was only associated with Type II thinking styles."[70] Thus, not only was the Type I intellectual style more adaptive and more valued by society and academia, but it also represented a higher developmental stage. Fourth, lest she cast intellectual styles as just another form of IQ, Zhang provided evidence on the malleability of intellectual types over time. Students were not stuck with their intellectual style for life, as Dunn, Myers and Briggs, and others had argued. Instead, Zhang insisted, "intellectual styles could be modified through both socialization and purposeful training."[71]

Like her mentor Sternberg, Zhang made little mention of VAK-based versions of the learning style idea in her work. In fact, in the forty pages of references at the end of *The Value of Intellectual Styles* there is not a single reference to the work of Barbe and Swassing, Dunn, or Fleming. She had essentially written these figures and their research out of the history of the field. The failure to engage the most popular version of the learning style idea blunted the broader impact of Zhang's work on practitioners and the media. She seemed much more interested in salvaging the respectability of the idea for her colleagues in cognitive psychology than she was in making the idea more palatable to teachers and the broader public.

Although impressive in scope and intellectual detail, the updated work of Sternberg and Zhang on intellectual styles failed to make any impact on schools or the popular imagination. Furthermore, by aligning learning styles with IQ and developmental psychology, they betrayed the entire history of a field that had developed largely in opposition to these hierarchical ideas. The learning style idea emerged from well-meaning attempts to describe learner attributes in nonhierarchical ways in the service of inclusion and educational equity. Ultimately, it was unclear what advantage there was in describing a student as a Type I intellectual as opposed to simply describing the student as having a higher IQ or being at a higher developmental stage; in all cases, students were being assessed against a universal norm. In this sense, the work of Sternberg and Zhang moved the learning style idea back to where it had begun in the 1950s—an academically respectable but largely irrelevant idea buried among dozens of other developmental and cognitive theories espoused by academic psychologists.

*

By the 2010s, many in the scientific community had decided that the learning style idea was a dangerous one and that the research had thoroughly debunked it. They cited the reams of empirical studies and literature reviews conducted over thirty years that proved scientifically that, despite the idea's intuitive nature, aligning teaching methods to student learning styles was not more effective than teaching through other methods. Many of these scientists extended their arguments beyond merely debunking the myth by suggesting that possible harm was being done to students by teachers' persistent belief in the theory. Ironically, despite their allegiance to the scientific method, critics did not have a shred of empirical evidence that the learning style theory *had* done any actual harm to students, because they ignored the issue of race and tracking. Nevertheless, the tide had clearly turned against the idea, and the efforts of Sternberg and Zhang are unlikely to revive the learning style idea among educational and cognitive psychologists.

CONCLUSION

The learning style idea has permeated the culture in ways I could never cite or formally document in this book. In the two years during which I wrote the majority of this manuscript, my older son, now a high school sophomore, was administered two learning style assessments at his school—one by a teacher, one by a guidance counselor—although it's unclear if anything was ever done with this information; a sports broadcaster on television chided a coach for not using a whiteboard during a time-out, claiming he was a "visual learner and needed to see the play drawn out"; an administrator at my university presented a chart on student enrollment, which she prefaced by saying that the chart was "for my visual learners out there"; a character on the Emmy Award–winning show *Abbott Elementary* opined about the role of "Howard Gardner's theory of multiple intelligences" and how some students might have "naturalistic" or "musical intelligence";[1] a dance instructor in the comedy, *Girls5eva*, asked a preschooler whether he was a "kinesthetic learner or a socio-interpersonal learner";[2] I read over two dozen teaching philosophies by teacher candidates pledging to "teach to all the learning styles," even though we had never introduced learning styles in our teacher education program; and I read about the "myth of learning styles" in a copy of *Psychology Today* in the waiting room of my younger son's doctor's office.[3] If you keep your eyes and ears open, you are likely to see numerous references to the learning style idea in your day-to-day life as well, demonstrating that the idea is far from defeated.

The danger of the learning style idea was never that teaching through visual, auditory, and kinesthetic methods was harmful to students; the learning style idea could be used to justify any number of either rigorous or frivolous learning activities. The danger of the learning style idea lay in the act of sorting and labeling students with permanent style identities, because there was a potential to divert certain students away from the knowledge and skills they needed for academic success. Gordon Allport, one the progenitors of personality studies, insisted in the 1930s that the assignment of learner identities "place[d] boundaries where boundaries do not belong" by "taking bits of people and forcing them into a category of special delight to some investigator."[4] Likewise, David Kolb—the most popular learning style advocate among college professors—warned against "turning these ideas into stereotypes used to pigeon-hole individuals" and "sorting people into groups and labelling them" because, as he accurately pointed out, "tracking in education has a bad history."[5] Daniel Willingham and other critics also recognized the dangers of assigning learner identities and suggested that, instead of labeling students with learning styles, teachers should focus on what pedagogical methods and learning modalities best fit the nature of the content being taught. In other words, rather than labeling students as visual, auditory, or kinesthetic learners, teachers ought to be labeling the activities as visual, auditory, or kinesthetic and then using the most appropriate method for the content or topic at hand.

This solution of focusing on the nature of the methods instead of the essential nature of the student had first been worked out at the tail end of the Black learning style controversy in the early 2000s. In an article for *Educational Researcher*, Kris Gutierrez and Barbara Rogoff issued a warning about the dangers of aligning students of color with permanent learner identities or traits based on their culture. Such a practice, they argued, "has led to tracking in which instruction is adjusted merely on the basis of a group categorization." Instead of focusing on the labeling of individual students as Black, Latine, or at-risk, teachers should focus on children's "learning repertoires" in context and how those may or may not be shaped by a student's cultural history. The prescription of "learning repertoires" was a bit vague, but their overall point was clear: aligning students of color with any essential traits or attributes betrayed the dynamic and contextual nature of both learning and culture, and thus was just another form of racial stereotyping. As Gutierrez and Rogoff concluded, "Ethnic and other cultural descriptions may fruitfully help researchers examine cultural practices if they are not assumed to imply an essence of the individual or group involved."[6]

Today, most teacher educator programs teach some form of culturally responsive or culturally sustaining pedagogy. The approach asks teachers to employ a curriculum that appeals to students and allow them to see themselves in course materials, to engage them with activities that have some relevance and connection to their lived experiences, and, most of all, to listen to students, parents, and local community members about what they value instead of imposing middle-class White norms upon them. This is not an easy process; it involves a lot of listening and trial and error. But above all, it asks teachers to question and reflect on their own assumptions and biases rather than sort and categorize students against a predetermined set of criteria. As I have argued throughout this book, the learning style idea has largely served as an impediment to this more thoughtful process by imposing artificial and unnecessary identities upon students.

Peter DeWitt, the former principal who had admitted in *Education Week* that had been "wrong" in his misplaced belief in learning styles, suggested a similar solution to the learning style dilemma. "We have to make sure we are not so concerned about helping our students that we hurt them by putting them in boxes labeled with learning styles," DeWitt admonished, ". . . and understand if we are using different strategies, teaching them to our students so they know what to do when we aren't there."[7] DeWitt urged a shift from learning styles to learning strategies, an approach he wholeheartedly endorsed. It remains to be seen whether teachers accept this rhetorical shift, or if they even know or care about the research questioning the efficacy of learning styles. However, to move beyond the learning style idea, teachers will need to abandon the comfortable rhetoric of visual, auditory, and kinesthetic learners.

If there is a lesson to be learned from the history of learning styles, it is to approach new educational ideas with healthy skepticism. I am not arguing that teachers and policymakers ought to dismiss any new educational idea, nor I am endorsing a back-to-basics approach to curriculum and pedagogy that restores some imaginary rigorous and traditional past.[8] However, the learning style idea contained many red flags that should have invited more caution from both scholars and educators. How, for example, could seventy—or even twenty or ten—learning style typologies all be true? Would scientists ever tolerate seventy models for the solar system, or how to classify the animal kingdom? Did Sternberg really expect us to believe that fifty years of international research on learning styles justified his ethnocentric conclusion that the human mind just happened to align with the three branches of the US government? How can a purely kinesthetic learner exist? Don't all able-bodied students also use their eyes and ears when working with their hands? Specifically, such a wide range of activities were justified by kinesthetic pedagogy that its existence should have invited more skepticism. Everything from watching a how-to video on YouTube (with your eyes and ears, I presume) to notetaking to holding a camera to going on a field trip were justified with the "kinesthetic" label, regardless of whether these activities were the pedagogical equivalent of visual and auditory learning. Furthermore, the idea of blindfolding students in accordance with kinesthetic learning, as both Montessori and Barbe and Swassing prescribed, was absurd. When could blindfolding a student during learning or assessment ever be justified?

When approaching a new or established educational idea, I suggest that educators ask three questions. First, ask, *Where did this idea come from?* This book originated with this very question, and it took me nearly two decades to come to a satisfactory answer. Many of the books and articles I have cited provided superficial histories of the learning style idea by assuming that any historical reference to student difference by Aristotle, Montessori, Dewey, Jung, or Allport was a justification for learning styles. That was not the case. As I have explained, none of these figures supported the learning style idea, and many, like Allport, spoke directly against the labeling of students. The fact that no one knew where the idea had come from should have set off some intellectual alarms. Second, ask, *May I see the research that supports this idea?* Such a simple question should have pointed educators to the half dozen published literature reviews conducted before the turn of the twenty-first century revealing that the research did not support the use of learning styles, especially the VAK-based version, in the classroom. Finally, ask, *Would I want my child to be taught this way?* I wonder whether the well-educated and professional classes would have tolerated their children being labeled as kinesthetic learners and provided with play dough, while immigrant, minoritized, and Indigenous populations were labeled as visual learners and provided with books. I highly doubt it. Many students of color did and do face real challenges and barriers that should not be ignored. However, the struggles of these students would have been better explained by disparities in access to healthcare, housing, healthy food, and qualified teachers, than explaining their struggles with the poorly supported idea of learning styles.

If we apply these lessons of the learning style idea to the current trend of the "science of learning" or the "science of reading," they invite some caution. Whenever the term *science* is invoked, it implies that what came before was somehow unscientific. Many of the learning style advocates stated that "the science" allegedly supported the idea when it supported only a limited use of only few typologies. Therefore, educators need to approach this term carefully. The subtitle to Montessori's *The Montessori Method*, published in 1912, was *Scientific Pedagogy as Applied to Child Education*, demonstrating that the phrase has been around for over a century. Whereas many of Montessori's insights on child development have been confirmed by contemporary research, her scientific racism as demonstrated in her lesser-known book, *Pedagogical Anthropology*, has not.[9] The point is that science is tool that can and has been used to liberate and to marginalize students throughout the twentieth and twenty-first centuries. Asking the three questions above can help educators think through the use of term *science*. Thus, the science of learning should neither be dismissed outright nor championed as a full-scale corrective to what came before. Rather, educators should look carefully at the research, be open to future developments and updates, and be ready to question even their most intuitive assumptions.

Acknowledgments

Two decades ago, I was teaching my very first class as a professor in a teacher education program. As part of the class, teacher candidates were required to submit a lesson plan. One ambitious student submitted a lesson plan on teaching Hamlet that was more than forty pages long. Actually, it wasn't one lesson plan; it was seven lesson plans designed to align with Howard Gardner's seven intelligences. The teacher candidate who submitted the lessons was an excellent student, and she had clearly put a lot of thought and effort into this assignment. In fact, she would go on to win an award at graduation for being the top English major in the class. The problem was that most of the MI-based activities she came up were frivolous and/or too difficult for students to succeed with. For example, the lesson had her so-called musical learners rapping about Hamlet and her so-called kinesthetic learners writing an additional scene to Hamlet and acting it out, as if both activities didn't primarily require linguistic intelligence.

I remembered struggling over how to grade her ambitious but misguided lesson. On the one hand, she had written seven lessons when her peers had written only one. Furthermore, she had taken an educational theory that she had learned in another class and applied it to her lesson planning. On the other hand, she conflated learning styles with multiple intelligences, misinterpreted the intelligences, and created unrealistic activities that were far too difficult for students. Nevertheless, she was probably just implementing exactly what she had been taught earlier in the program.

It was then that I realized I was dealing with a much larger problem. I went to the university library to research where the problematic learning style idea had come from. I came across a few references to Jung, but for most part I came up empty.

I want to thank this student for launching my inquiry into the origins and development of the learning style idea. I also thank the members of the New York University History of Education Writing Group, led by Zoë Burkholder and Natalia Petrzela, who provided feedback on an early draft of chapter 1. I thank Daniel Willingham for proving feedback and encouragement on chapter 7. I thank Shayan Doroudi for first bringing the work of Ernst Meumann to my attention. I thank M. Judy Matthew and the support staff at William Paterson University's David and Lorraine Cheng Library for help with the many interlibrary loans. Portions of chapters 1 and 2 appeared as "The Long Origins of the Visual, Auditory, and Kinesthetic Learning Style Typology, 1921–2001," in *History of Psychology* 26, no. 4 (November 2023): 334–54. I thank the American Psychological Association for permission to reprint this. Much of chapter 3 appeared as "Herman Witkin and the Rise and Fall of the Black Learning Style Idea, 1960–2003," *Teachers College Record* 125, no. 4 (April 2023): 67–94. I thank Sage Publishing and Teachers College, Columbia University, for permission to reprint this.

I thank my wife of twenty years, Dr. Victoria Fantozzi, for reading the book prospectus and various drafts throughout the process. I thank the anonymous reviewers for helpful feedback and suggestions, and Elizabeth Branch Dyson for showing such early and sustained enthusiasm for the project.

Finally, I want to note that this book was written during a time of austerity, layoffs, and budget cuts at my university. As a result, this research was completed with absolutely no grant support, travel funds, course releases, sabbaticals, or graduate or teaching assistantships. I mention this not out of bitterness, but perhaps so it can serve as inspiration for other scholars who may find themselves in similar circumstances.

Notes

Introduction

1. Paul A. Howard-Jones, "Neuroscience and Education: Myths and Messages," *Nature Reviews Neuroscience* 15 (2014): 817–24; Carol Lethaby and Patricia Harries, "Learning Styles and Teacher Training: Are We Perpetuating Neuromyths?," *ELT Journal* 70, no. 1 (October 2015): 21.

2. See Kristina L. Dandy and Karen Bendersky, "Student and Faculty Beliefs about Learning in Higher Education: Implications for Teaching," *International Journal of Teaching and Learning in Higher Education* 26, no. 3 (2014): 362.

3. Katrina A. Meyer and Vicki S. Murrell, "A National Study of Theories and Their Importance for Faculty Development for Online Teaching," *Online Journal of Distance Learning Administration* 17, no. 2 (2014): 1; Steven R. Wininger, Jenni L. Redifer, Antony D. Norman, and Mary K. Ryle, "Prevalence of Learning Styles in Educational Psychology and Introduction to Education Textbooks: A Content Analysis," *Psychology Learning & Teaching* 18, no. 3 (2019): 221.

4. Harold Pashler, Mark McDaniel, Doug Rohrer, and Robert Bjork, "Learning Styles: Concepts and Evidence," *Psychological Science in the Public Interest* 9, no. 3 (2008): 106.

5. Daniel T. Willingham, *Why Don't Students Like School? A Cognitive Scientist Answers Questions about How the Mind Works and What It Means for the Classroom* (Jossey-Bass, 2009), 153

6. See, for example, Randall A. Silverston and John W. Deichman, "Sense Modality Research and the Acquisition of Reading Skills," *Review of Educational Research* 45 (Winter 1975): 149–72; Herman A. Witkin, Carol Anne Moore, Donald R. Goodenough, and Patricia W. Cox, "Field-Dependent and Field-Independent Cognitive Styles and Their Educational Implications," *Review of Educational Research* 47, no. 1 (Winter 1977): 1–64; Laura Shea Doolan, *The History of the International Learning Styles Network and Its Impact on Instructional Innovation* (Lewiston: Edwin Mellon Press, 2004); Rita Dunn and Kenneth Dunn, "Thirty-Five Years of Research on Perceptual Strengths: Essential Strategies to Promote Learning," *Clearing House* 78, no. 6 (July/August 2005): 273–76; and Li-fang Zhang, *The Value of Intellectual Styles* (Cambridge University Press, 2017).

7. See, for example, Walter Burke Barbe and Raymond H. Swassing. *Teaching through Modality Strengths: Concepts and Practices*, with Michael N. Milone Jr. (Zaner-Bloser, 1979); David A. Kolb, *LSI: Learning Style Inventory Technical Manual* (McBer, 1976); and Rita Dunn, Kenneth Dunn, and G. E. Price, *Learning Style Inventory* (Price Systems, 1975).

8. Frank Coffield, David Moseley, Elaine Hall, and Kathryn Ecclestone, *Learning Styles and Pedagogy in Post-16 Learning: A Systematic and Critical Review* (Learning and Skills Research Centre, 2004).

9. Philip M. Newton, "The Learning Styles Myth Is Thriving in Higher Education," *Frontiers in Psychology* 6 (2015): 1908, https://doi.org/10.3389/fpsyg.2015.01908. Newton found that 34 percent of articles on learning styles in higher education employed Kolb's typology; VAK was employed in 33 percent of the articles.

10. "Multiple intelligences are not learning styles," Gardner insisted in his 2020 autobiography. Howard Gardner, *A Synthesizing Mind: A Memoir from the Creator of Multiple Intelligences Theory* (MIT Press, 2020), 164.

11. Manuel Ramírez III and Douglas R. Price-Williams, "Cognitive Styles of Children in Three Ethnic Groups in the United States," *Journal of Cross-Cultural Psychology* 5, no. 2 (1974): 218.

12. John O'Neil, "Making Sense of Style: While Critics Grumble, Advocates Make a Case for Transforming Classrooms Based on Students' Individual Learning Styles," *Educational Leadership* 48, no. 2 (October 1990): 8.

13. Lynn Curry, "A Critique of the Research on Learning Styles," *Educational Leadership* 48, no. 2 (October 1990): 51.

14. Erik Gilbert, "How Ed Schools Became a Bastion of Bad Ideas: A Tale of Assessment, Learning Styles and Other Notorious Concepts," *Chronicle of Higher Education* 66, no. 13 (2019), https://www.chronicle.com/article/how-ed-schools-became-a-bastion-of-bad-ideas/.

15. Janet Nelson, "What's Your Learning Style?," *New York Times*, April 25, 1993, A78.

16. Gordon Allport, *Personality: A Psychological Interpretation* (Henry Holt, 1937), 296.

17. Xin Sun, Owen Norton, and Shaylene Nancekivell, "Beware the Myth: Learning Styles Affect Parents, Children's, and Teachers' Thinking about Children's Academic Potential," *npj Science of Learning* 8, no. 1 (2023): 7.

18. Max Planck, *Scientific Autobiography and Other Papers* (Philosophical Library, 1950), 33.

19. See, for example, Heather Hollingsworth, "Why More US Schools Are Embracing a New Science of Reading," *PBS NewsHour*, April 20, 2023, https://www.pbs.org/newshour/education/why-more-u-s-schools-are-embracing-a-new-science-of-reading; and Mary Ellen Flannery, "The Science of Learning," *NEA News*, September 29, 2021, https://www.nea.org/advocating-for-change/new-from-nea/science-learning.

Chapter One

1. Howard Gardner, *Frames of Mind: The Theory of Multiple Intelligences*, 10th anniv. ed. (Basic Books, 1993).

2. Frank Riessman, "Styles of Learning," *NEA Journal* 55, no. 3 (March 1966): 15, 17.

3. Maria Montessori, *The Montessori Method: Scientific Pedagogy as Applied to Child Education* (Frederick Stokes, 1912), 198–99. Italics in original.

4. Henry W. Holmes, introduction to Montessori, *Montessori Method*, xxxv.

5. John Dewey, *My Pedagogic Creed & the Demands of Sociology upon Pedagogy* (E. L. Kellogg, 1897), 7.

6. John Dewey, *How We Think* (Heath, 1910), 191.

7. Ernst Meumann, *The Psychology of Learning: An Experimental Investigation of the Economy and Technique of Memory* (D. Appleton, 1913), 180, 181.

8. Meumann, *Psychology of Learning*, 169.

9. Stephen Sheldon Colvin, *The Learning Process* (Macmillan, 1911), 21. I thank Shayan Doroudi for first bringing Meumann's text to my attention. Meumann is also discussed in Lester Mann, *On the Trail of Process: A Historical Perspective on Cognitive Processes and Their Training* (Grune and Stratton, 1979).

10. Lewis Terman, *Measurement of Intelligence: An Explanation of and Complete Guide for the Use of the Stanford Revision and Extension of the Binet-Simon Intelligence Scale* (Houghton Mifflin, 1916), vii, xi, 92.

11. Lewis Terman, *The Intelligence of School Children: How Children Differ in Ability, the Use of Mental Tests in School Grading and the Proper Education of Exceptional Children* (Houghton Mifflin, 1919); Lewis Terman, *Intelligence Tests and School Reorganization* (World Book, 1922).

12. W. S. Deffenbaugh, *Uses of Intelligence and Achievement Tests in 215 Cities* (City School Leaflet 20, US Bureau of Education, 1925).

13. Grace M. Fernald and Helen Keller, "The Effects of Kinesthetic Factors in the Development of Word Recognition in the Case of Non-readers," *Journal of Educational Research* 4, no. 5 (December 1921): 355, 375, 376.

14. Blanche Loudon and Grace Arthur, who employed the "Fernald method" with a struggling male reader, did align the success of the method with the "intellectual idiosyncrasy of the boy," implying that the boy may have been a kinesthetic learner. Loudon and Arthur, "An Application of the Fernald Method to an Extreme Case of Reading Disability," *Elementary School Journal* 40, no. 8 (April 1940): 606.

15. Grace M. Fernald, *Remedial Techniques in Basic School Subjects* (McGraw-Hill, 1943), 182, 167, 168.

16. Fernald, *Remedial Techniques in Basic Subjects*, 109.

17. Samuel Orton, "Word Blindness in School Children," *Archives of Neurology and Psychiatry* 14, no. 5 (November 1925): 581–615; James Hinshelwood, "Congenital Word-Blindness," *Lancet*, May 26, 1900, 1506–8.

18. Samuel Orton, *Reading, Writing, and Speech Problems in Children* (Norton, 1937), 159. See also Marion Monroe, *Children Who Cannot Read* (University of Chicago Press, 1932).

19. See Anna Gillingham and Bessie Stillman, *Remedial Work for Reading, Spelling and Penmanship* (Sackett and Wilhelms, 1936); and Anna Gillingham and Bessie Stillman, *Remedial Training for Children with Specific Disability in Reading, Spelling and Penmanship* (Cambridge, MA: Educators Publishing Service, 1960). See also Kristin L. Sayeski, Gentry A. Earle, Rosalie Davis, and Josie Calamari, "Orton Gillingham: Who, What, and How," *Teaching Exceptional Children*, January/February 2019, 240–49.

20. For a thorough discussion of the relationship between the faculty psychology and the origins of learning modalities, see Mann, *On the Trail of Process*.

21. John M. O'Donnell, *The Origins of Behaviorism: American Psychology, 1870–1820* (New York University Press, 1985).

22. Helmer Myklebust, *Auditory Disorders in Children* (Grune and Stratton, 1954), 158. See also Karl Taylor, "'People Hearing without Listening': Problems of Auditory Processing in the Classroom," *Research in the Teaching of English* 12, no. 1 (February 1978): 61–75.

23. Robert E. Mills, "An Evaluation of Techniques for Teaching Word Recognition," *Elementary School Journal* 56, no. 5 (January 1956): 225.

24. Samuel A. Kirk and James J. McCarthy, "The Illinois Test of Psycholinguistic Abilities—an Approach to Differential Diagnosis," *American Journal of Mental Deficiency* 66 (1961): 403.

25. John D. King and Larry J. Masat, "Implications of the Illinois Test of Psycholinguistic Abilities for Teachers of Mentally Retarded Children," *Education and Training of the Mentally Retarded* 2, no. 3 (October 1967): 108.

26. William James, *Principles of Psychology in Two Volumes* (Henry Holt, 1910), 227; William James, *Pragmatism: A New Name for Some Old Ways of Thinking* (Longman, Green, 1907), 11–12.

27. Merve Emre, *The Personality Brokers: The Strange History of Myers-Briggs and the Birth of Personality Testing* (Doubleday, 2018).

28. William H. Whyte, *The Organization Man* (Simon and Schuster, 1956), 174.

29. Gordon Allport, *Pattern and Growth in Personality* (Holt, Rinehart, and Winston, 1961), 19, 350, 352.

30. Gordon Allport, "The Psychologists Frame of Reference," *Psychological Bulletin* 37, no. 1 (January 1940): 1. See also Ian M. Nicholson, "Gordon Allport, Character, and the Culture of Personality," *History of Psychology* 1, no. 1 (1998): 52–68.

31. Thomas Fallace, *In the Shadow of Authoritarianism: Education in the Twentieth Century* (Teachers College Press, 2018); Jamie Cohen-Cole, *The Open Mind: Cold War Politics and the Sciences of Human Nature* (University of Chicago Press, 2014).

32. Arthur M. Schlesinger Jr., *The Vital Center: The Politics of Freedom* (Riverside Press, 1949), 250.

33. Theodore Adorno, Else Frenkel-Brunswik, Daniel Levinson, and R. Nevitt Sanford, *The Authoritarian Personality*, abridged version (New York: Norton, 1982), 10. Originally published in 1950.

34. See Richard Christie and Peggy Cook, "A Guide to Published Literature Relating to the Authoritarian Personality through 1956," *Journal of Psychology* 45, no. 2 (1958): 171–99; and Howard Gabennesch, "Authoritarianism as World View," *American Journal of Sociology* 77 (March 1972): 857–75. Witkin and his coauthors did find "some evidence of a relationship between measures of authoritarianism and field dependence . . . however[,] these relationships need to be explored further before their basis can be adequately determined." Herman A. Witkin, R. B. Dyk, H. F. Faterson, D. R. Goodenough, and S. A. Karp, *Psychological Differentiation: Studies in Development* (John Wiley and Sons, 1962), 146.

35. Riesman quoted in Richard H. Pells, *The Liberal Mind in a Conservative Age: American Intellectuals in the 1940s and 1950s* (Harper and Row, 1985), 243, 244.

36. Glenn M. Blair, "Personality and Social Development," *Review of Educational Research* 30, no. 5 (December 1950): 375.

37. Sol Cohen, "The Mental Hygiene Movement, the Development of Personality and the School: The Medicalization of American Education," *History of Education Quarterly* 23, no. 2 (Summer 1983): 123–49; Stephen Petrina, "The Medicalization of Education: A Historiographical Synthesis," *History of Education Quarterly* 46, no. 4 (Winter 2006): 503–31; Catherine Gavin Loss, "Public Schools, Private Lives: American Education and Psychological Authority, 1945–1975" (PhD diss., University of Virginia, 2005).

38. Diane Ravitch, *Left Back: A Century of Failed School Reform* (Simon and Schuster, 2000), 363.

39. Sarah E. Igo, *The Known Citizen: A History of Modern America* (Harvard University Press, 2018), 130.

40. Christopher Lasch, *The Culture of Narcissism: America Life in Age of Diminishing Expectations* (Norton, 1979), 22.

41. George S. Stevenson, "Trends in Mental Hygiene: An Interpretation," *Review of Educational Research* 10 (December 1940): 407.

42. Gordon Allport, *Personality: A Psychological Interpretation* (Henry Holt, 1937), 23.

43. Gordon Allport, *Becoming: Basic Considerations for a Psychology of Personality* (Yale University Press, 1955), 100.

44. Herman A. Witkin, "The Perception of the Upright," *Scientific America* 200, no. 2 (February 1959): 53, 56.

45. Karen Elizabeth Robinson, "Intellectual Biography of Herman Witkin and His Theory of Psychological Differentiation" (PhD diss., Carlos Albizu University, 2001).

46. Howard Gardner, *The Quest for Mind: Piaget, Lévi-Strauss, and the Structuralist Movement* (University of California Press, 1973).

47. Hunter Heyck, *Age of System: Understanding the Development of Modern Social Science* (Johns Hopkins Press, 2015), 18. According to Heyck's analysis of the journals *American Anthropologist, American Economic Review, American Journal of Sociology, American Political Science Review*, and *Psychological Review*, zero articles published before 1940 sought to "model" something, but "by the 1970s half of all articles in those journals did so" (XXX). See also the prologue to Daniel T. Rogers, *Age of Fracture* (Belknap, 2011).

48. See Herman A. Witkin, *Personality through Perception: An Experimental and Clinical Study* (Harper and Brothers, 1954).

49. Samuel Messick, "Obituary: Herman A. Witkin (1916–1979)," *American Psychologist* 35, no. 1 (December 1980): 99–100.

50. Witkin et al., *Psychological Differentiation*, 70.

51. S. M. Miller and Frank Riessman, "'Working-Class Authoritarianism': A Critique of Lipset," *British Journal of Sociology* 12, no. 3 (September 1961): 263–76.

52. S. M. Miller and Frank Riessman, "The Working Class Subculture: A New View," *Social Problems* 9, no. 1 (Summer 1961): 90–91.

53. Michael Harrington, *The Other America: Poverty in the United States* (Penguin, 1962), 22–23.

54. Frank Riessman, *Strategies for Education of the Disadvantaged* (paper presented at the Conference on Curriculum Innovation for the Culturally Disadvantaged, April 1965), 2.

55. The book Riessman endorsed was *Education and Income: Inequalities of Opportunity in Our Public Schools* by Patricia Cayo Sexton, "Backmatter," *American Sociological Review* 26, no. 6 (December 1961). Riessman wrote, "Dr. Sexton does as excellent job of precisely illuminating the various ways in which educational discrimination functions against the culturally deprived child." Riessman, *Strategies for Education*, 7, 13. Riessman also claimed that the term "is in current usage," although I could not find extensive use of the term prior to his book. Frank Riessman, *The Culturally Deprived Child* (Harper & Row, 1962), 3.

56. Riessman, *Culturally Deprived Child*, 115.

57. Riessman, 115.

58. Riessman, xiii, 129.

59. Cynthia P. Deutsch, "Education for Disadvantaged Groups," *Review of Educational Research* 35, no. 2 (April 1965): 143.

60. Kenneth Johnson, *Teaching the Culturally Disadvantaged: A Rational Approach* (Palo Alto: Science Research Associates, 1970), 33, 36–39.

61. Thomas Fallace, "The Savage Origins of Child-Centered Education, 1971–1913," *American Educational Research Journal* 52, no. 2 (February 2015): 73–103.

62. Johnson, *Teaching the Culturally Disadvantaged*, 3.

63. Ralph Ellison, *Going to the Territory* (Random, 1963), 65, 67.

64. J. Castro, "Untapped Verbal Fluency of Black Schoolchildren," in *The Culture of Poverty: A Critique*, ed. Eleanor. B. Leacock (Simon and Schuster, 1971), 81–108.

65. Bernard Mackler and Morsley Giddings, "Cultural Deprivation: A Study in Mythology," *Teachers College Record* 66, no. 7 (April 1965): 611.

66. Frank Riessman, "The Overlooked Positives of Disadvantaged Groups," *Journal of Negro Education* 33, no. 3 (July 1964): 230.

67. Frank Riessman, "The Strategy of Style," *Teachers College Record* 65, no. 6 (March 1964): 484.

68. Allport, *Pattern and Growth in Personality*, 349.

69. Riessman, "Strategy of Style," 485.

70. Frank Riessman, *The Inner-City Child* (Harper and Row, 1976), ix.

71. Frank Riessman, "Students' Learning Styles: How to Determine, Strengthen, and Capitalize on Them," *Today's Education* 65 (1975): 94–98. See also Beth S. Atwood, "Helping Students Recognize Their Own Learning Styles," *Learning* 3, no. 8 (1975): 72–8; and Daniel R. Miller and Guy E. Swanson, *Inner Conflict and Defense* (Henry Holt, 1966).

72. See Milton J. Horowitz, "Learning Styles and Learning Outcomes in Medical Students," *School Review* 74, no. 1 (Spring 1966): 48–65.

73. Robert Strom, *Teaching in the Slum School* (Charles E. Merrill Books, 1965), 78.

74. See Herman A. Witkin, "Perception of the Upright When the Direction of the Force Acting in the Body Is Changed," *Journal of Experimental Psychology* 40 (1950): 93–106; and Herman A. Witkin, Carol Anne Moore, Donald R. Goodenough, and Patricia W. Cox, "Field-Dependent and Field-Independent Cognitive Styles and Their Educational Implications," *Review of Educational Research* 47, no. 1 (Winter 1977): 1–64.

75. See Herman A. Witkin, *The Role of Cognitive Style in Academic Performance and in Teacher-Student Relations* (paper presented at Graduate Record Examination Board, Montreal, Canada, November 8–10, 1972).

76. See M. R. Rennels, "The Effects of Instructional Methodology in Art Education upon Achievement on Spatial Taks by Disadvantaged Negro Youth," *Journal of Negro Education* 39 (1970): 116.

77. See Herman A. Witkin, "Some Implications of Research on Cognitive Style for Problems of Education," in *Personality and Learning: A Reader Prepared by Personality and Learning Course Team at the Open University*, ed. Joan Whitehead (Open University Press, 1975), 29.

78. See James S. Coleman, *Equality of Educational Opportunity* (US Department of Health, Education, and Welfare, Office of Education, 1966), 14, 21, available at https://files.eric.ed.gov/fulltext/ED012275.pdf.

79. James S. Coleman, *The Concept of Equality of Educational Opportunity*. ERIC ED 015 157 (1967): 14, 21, https://files.eric.ed.gov/fulltext/ED012275.pdf.

80. Johnson quoted in Daryl Michael Scott, *Contempt and Pity: Social Policy and the Image of the Damaged Black Psyche* (University of North Carolina Press, 1997), 151.

81. Horace M. Kallen, "Alain Locke and Cultural Pluralism," *Journal of Philosophy* 54, no. 5 (February 1957): 120.

82. Anthony Gregorc, "Style as a Symptom: A Phenomenological Perspective," *Theory into Practice* 23, no. 1 (Winter 1984): 54.

Chapter Two

1. See, for example, Edward A. Purcell Jr., *The Crisis of Democratic Theory: Scientific Naturalism and the Problem of Value* (University Press of Kentucky, 2013); Andrew Jewett, *Science, Democracy, and the American University: From the Civil War to the Cold War* (Cambridge University Press, 2014); and Jamie Cohen-Cole, *The Open Mind: Cold War Politics and the Sciences of Human Nature* (University of Chicago Press, 2014).

2. Diane Ravitch, *Left Back: A Century of Failed School Reform* (Simon and Schuster, 2000), 366–408; Thomas Fallace, "John Dewey and the New Left, 1960–1988," *Journal of Curriculum Studies* 52, no. 5 (2020): 593–607; Louis Menand, *The Free World: Art and Thought in the Cold War* (Farrar, Straus, and Giroux, 2021).

3. "Students Learn How to Study—and Like It: Matching Education and Individuals Can Raise Grades One School Is Finding," *U.S. News and World Report*, December 31, 1979, 75.

4. "Students Learn How to Study," 76.

5. David A. Kolb, "Management and the Learning Process," *California Management Review* 18, no. 3 (Spring 1976): 23.

6. Kolb, "Management and the Learning Process," 24.

7. Kolb, "Management and the Learning Process," 22, 26, 28–29.

8. Elizabeth Rees Gilbert, "Using the Learning Style Inventory," *Journal of Museum Education* 16, no. 1 (Winter 1991): 7–9; Bernice McCarthy, *The 4MAT System: Teaching to Learning Styles with the Right/Left Mode Techniques* (Excel, 1980). See also Betty Edwards, *Drawing on the Right Side of the Brain* (Penguin Putnam, 1979); and "Betty's Books," Drawing on the Right Side of the Brain (website), n.d., drawright.com/bettys-books.

9. Harriet Mann, Miriam Siegler, and Humphrey Osmond, "Four Types of Personalities and Four Ways of Perceiving Time," *Psychology Today* (December 1972): 78–84.

10. Anthony Gregorc, "Matching Inservice Activities with Teacher Personalities," *NASSP Bulletin*, December 1975, 24.

11. Anthony Gregorc, "Style as a Symptom: A Phenomenological Perspective," *Theory into Practice* 23, no. 1 (Winter 1984): 53.

12. Gregorc, "Style as a Symptom,"54.

13. Anthony F. Gregorc and Helen B. Ward, "A New Definition for Individual," *NASSP Bulletin*, February 1977, 21, 22, 23.

14. Quotation from Anthony F. Gregorc, Ph.D. (website), n.d., last accessed August 2024, https://www.anthonyfgregorc.com/.

15. A. S. Neill, *Summerhill* (Hart, 1960), 4.

16. See James Herndon, *The Way It Spozed to Be* (Simon and Schuster, 1968); Herbert Kohl, *36 Children* (New American Library, 1967); and Jonathan Kozol, *Death at an Early Age: The Destruction of the Hearts and Minds of Negro Children in the Public Schools* (Bantam Books, 1968).

17. Sherry Lancaster, "The Open Classroom's Debt to John Dewey," *New Voices in Education* 3 (Winter 1974): 14. See also Theodore J. Czajkowski and Melon King, "The Hidden Curriculum and Open Education," *Elementary School Journal* 75 (February 1975): 279–83.

18. Mary Anne Raywid, "The First Decade of Public School Alternatives," *Phi Delta Kappan* 62, no. 8 (April 1981): 552.

19. Rita Dunn, Kenneth Dunn, and G. E. Price, *Learning Style Inventory* (Price Systems, 1975), 5.

20. Dunn, Dunn, and Price, *Learning Style Inventory*, 6.

21. Rita Dunn and Kenneth Dunn, *Educator's Self-Teaching Guide to Individualizing Instructional Programs* (Parker Publishing, 1975), 89.

22. Dunn and Dunn, *Educator's Self-Teaching Guide*, 105. The schools included Floral Park, Chappaqua, Briarcliff Manor, and Wantagh, New York.

23. Aimee Lee Ball, "The Secrets of Learning Styles—Your Child's and Your Own," *Redbook*, November 1982, 74, 76.

24. Gregorc quoted in Edward B. Fiske, "Teachers Adjust Schooling to Fit Students' Individuality," *New York Times*, December 29, 1981, C1.

25. Dunn quoted in Ball, "Secrets of Learning Styles," 76.

26. Rita Dunn, Kenneth Dunn, and Gary E. Price, "Diagnosing Learning Styles: A Prescription for Avoiding Malpractice Suits," *Phi Delta Kappan* 58, no. 5 (January 1977): 418–20.

27. Laura Shea Doolan, *The History of the International Learning Styles Network and Its Impact on Instructional Innovation* (Edwin Mellon Press, 2004), passim.

28. Walter B. Barbe and Raymond H. Swassing, *Teaching through Modality Strengths: Concepts and Practices*, with Michael N. Milone Jr. (Zaner-Bloser, 1979), 5, 6.

29. Walter B. Barbe and Michael N. Milone Jr., "What We Know about Modality Strengths," *Educational Leadership* 38, no. 5 (February 1981): 378.

30. Barbe and Swassing, *Teaching through Modality Strengths*, 4, 34.

31. Barbe and Swassing, 13, 56, 57.

32. David P. Cavanaugh, "Student Learning Styles: A Diagnostic/Prescriptive Approach to Instruction," *The Phi Delta Kappan* 63, no. 3 (November 1981): 203. See also David Cavanaugh, "An Approach to Diagnostic and Prescriptive Education at Worthington High School," *American Secondary Education* 9, no. 4 (December 1979): 31–40.

33. Ball, "Secrets of Learning Styles," 73.

34. Sara G. Tarver and Margaret M. Dawson, "Modality Preference and the Teaching of Reading," *Journal of Learning Disabilities* 11, no. 1 (January 1978): 5, 25.

35. Lynn Curry, *An Organization of Learning Styles Theory and Constructs*. Paper presented at the Annual Meeting of the American Educational Research Association (Montreal, Quebec, April 11–15, 1983), 2.

36. Curry, *Organization of Learning Styles Theory*, 9, 1, 14.

37. Leonard Davidman, "Learning Style: The Myth, the Panacea, the Wisdom," *Phi Delta Kappan* 62, no. 9 (May 1981): 642, 643, 644.

38. Barbe and Milone, "What We Know about Modality Strengths," 378–80.

39. Richard Freedman and Stephen Stumpf, "Learning Style Theory: Less Than Meets the Eye," *Academy of Management Review* 5, no. 3 (1980): 446, 447.

40. David A. Kolb, "Experiential Learning Theory and the Learning Style Inventory: A Reply to Freedman and Stumpf," *Academy of Management Review* 6, no. 2 (April 1981): 295.

41. See, for example, Glen Gish, "Adult Development and Adaptation: An Empirical Test of the Experimental Learning Theory and Adaptive Flexibility" (PhD diss., Case Western Reserve University, 1980); and Dena Lister, "Comparisons between the Learning Styles of Underachieving and Regular Education Sixth-Grade Bermudian Students and the Effects of Responsive Instruction on the Former's Social Studies Achievement and Attitude Test Scores" (PhD diss., St. John's University, 2004).

42. See Jack Schneider, *From the Ivory Tower to the Schoolhouse: How Scholarship Becomes Common Knowledge in Education* (Harvard Education Press, 2014).

43. Cavanaugh quoted in "Students Learn How to Study," 75.

44. Ellen Blum Barish, "Learning May Turn Out to be a Matter of Styles," *Chicago Tribune*, November 26, 1989, 2.

45. David Tyack and Larry Cuban, *Tinkering towards Utopia: A Century of Public School Reform* (Harvard University Press, 1995), 9. On the resiliency of school structures, see Larry Cuban, *How Teachers Taught: Constancy & Change in American Classrooms, 1880–1990* (Teachers College Press, 1993); Linda McNeil, *Contradictions of Control: School Structure and School Knowledge* (Routledge, 2013); and Jack Schneider and Ethan L. Hutt, *Off the Mark: How Grades and Rankings Undermine Learning (but Don't Have To)* (Harvard University Press, 2023).

46. Schneider, *From the Ivory Tower*, 9.

Chapter Three

1. This work had precedent in the cultural gifts/intercultural education movements of the 1920s, '30s, and '40s. See Zoe Burkholder, *Color in the Classroom: How American Schools Taught Race, 1900–1954* (Oxford University Press, 2011); Diana Selig, *Americans All: The Cultural Gifts Movement* (Harvard University Press, 2008); Michael C. Johanek, *Leonard Covello and the Making of Benjamin Franklin High School: Education as if Citizenship Mattered* (Temple University Press, 2007); and Lauri D. Johnson and Yoon K. Pak, "Teaching for Diversity: Intercultural and Intergroup Education in the Public Schools, 1920s to 1970s," *Review of Research in Education* 43, no. 1 (2019): 1–31.

2. *Increasing High School Completion Rates: A Framework for State and Local Action* (Albany: New York State Board of Regents, 1987); Anthony DePalma, "The Culture Question," *New York Times*, November 4, 1990, A22.

3. See Gunnar Myrdal, *An American Dilemma: The Negro Problem and American Democracy* (Harper, 1944); and Gordon Allport, *The Nature of Prejudice* (Addison-Wesley, 1954).

4. Leah N. Gordon, *From Power to Prejudice: The Rise of Racial Individualism in Midcentury America* (University of Chicago Press, 2015); Walter Jackson, *Gunnar Myrdal and America's Conscience* (University of North Carolina Press, 1990); James B. McKee, *Sociology and the Race Problem: The Failure of a Perspective* (University Illinois Press, 1993)

5. Daryl Michael Scott, *Contempt and Pity: Social Policy and the Image of the Damaged Black Psyche* (University of North Carolina Press, 1997).

6. Kenneth Clark quoted in James T. Patterson, *Brown v. Board of Education: A Civil Rights Milestone and Its Troubled Legacy* (Oxford University Press, 2001), 44. Clark rejected Myrdal's and Allport's idea that prejudice was a personality disorder. "Having in mind the stereotype that the negro is childlike and irresponsible by nature," Clark argued, provided "an elaborate façade of justification and rationalization" for White supremacy. See Gordon, *From Power to Prejudice*, 116.

7. Daniel Patrick Moynihan, *The Negro Family: The Case for National Action* (MIT Press, 1965), 29; James S. Coleman, Ernest Q. Campbell, Carol J. Hobson, James McPartland, Alexander M. Mood, Frederic D. Weinfeld, and Robert L. York, *Equality of Educational Opportunity* (US Government Printing Office, 1966).

8. Frank Riessman, *Inner City Child* (Harper and Row, 1976), 69.

9. Herman A. Witkin, Hanna F. Faterson, Donald K. Goodenough, and Judith Birnbaum, "Cognitive Patterning in Mildly Retarded Boys," *Child Development* 37, no. 2 (June 1966): 302.

10. Herman A. Witkin, "A Cognitive-Style Approach to Cross-Cultural Research," *International Journal of Psychology* 4, no. 2 (1967): 249.

11. Rosalie Cohen, "Conceptual Styles, Culture Conflict, and Nonverbal Tests of Intelligence," *American Anthropologist* 71, no. 5 (October 1969): 838, 843.

12. Stephen S. Baratz and Joan C. Baratz, "Early Childhood Intervention: The Social Science Base of Institutional Racism," *Harvard Educational Review* 40, no. 1 (Winter 1970): 30–31, 32, 17, 42, 40–41.

13. Edward T. Hall, *The Silent Language* (Anchor Books, 1959); Edward T. Hall, *The Hidden Dimension* (Doubleday, 1966), 2.

14. Edward T. Hall, "Listening Behavior: Some Cultural Differences," *Phi Delta Kappan* 50, no. 7 (March 1969): 380.

15. Edward T. Hall and Mildred Reed Hall, "Nonverbal Communication for Educators," *Theory into Practice* 16, no. 3 (June 1977): 143.

16. Walter N. Gantt, "Language and Learning Styles of the Educationally Disadvantaged," *Elementary School Journal* 73, no. 3 (December 1972): 138–42; George O. Cureton, "Using a Black Learning Style," *Reading Teacher* 31, no. 7 (1978): 751–56.

17. Cureton, "Using a Black Learning Style," 755.

18. Manuel Ramírez III, "Cognitive Styles and Cultural Democracy in Education," *Social Science Quarterly* 53, no. 4 (March 1973): 903; Manuel Ramírez III and Douglas R. Price-Williams, "Cognitive Styles of Children in Three Ethnic Groups in the United States," *Journal of Cross-Cultural Psychology* 5, no. 2 (1974): 218.

19. Asa Hilliard III, *Alternatives to IQ Testing: An Approach to the Identification Gifted "Minority" Children* (California State Department of Education, Sacramento Division of Special Education, 1976), 14.

20. Hilliard, *Alternatives to IQ Testing*, 15.

21. Hilliard, 46, 53.

22. Hilliard, 53–54.

23. Janice E. Hale, *Black Children: Their Roots, Culture, and Learning Styles* (Johns Hopkins University Press, 1982), xxii, 10, 103, 153.

24. Hale quoted in DePalma, "Culture Question," A22.

25. Asa Hilliard III, "Behavioral Style, Culture, and Teaching and Learning," *Journal of Negro Education* 61, no. 3 (Summer 1992): 371.

26. Max Raymond Rennels, "The Effects of Instructional Methodology in Art Education upon Achievement in Spatial Tasks by Disadvantaged Negro Youths," *Journal of Negro Education* 39, no. 2 (Spring 1970): 123.

27. Barbara J. Shade, "Racial Variation in Perceptual Differentiation," *Perceptual and Motor Skills* 52 (1981): 243–48; Theodore Conway Schmults, "The Relationship of Black Ethnicity to Field Dependence and Adjustment" (PhD diss., University of Rhode Island, 1975), 65.

28. Walter Burke Barbe and Raymond H. Swassing. *Teaching through Modality Strengths: Concepts and Practices*, with Michael N. Milone Jr. (Zaner-Bloser, 1979), 47.

29. Rita Dunn, Josephine Gemake, Fatimeh Jalali, and Robert Zenhausern, "Cross-Cultural Differences in Learning Styles of Elementary-Age Students from Four Ethnic Backgrounds," *Journal of Multicultural Counseling and Development* 18, no. 2 (April 1990): 73; Rita Dunn and Shirley Griggs, "Research on the Learning Style Characteristics of Selected Ethnic and Racial Groups," *Journal of Reading, Writing, and Learning Disabilities International* 6, no. 3 (1990): 261.

30. Barbara J. Shade, "Afro-American Cognitive Style: A Variable in School Success?," *Review of Educational Research* 52, no. 2 (Summer 1982): 238.

31. Mark Ulig, "Learning Style of Minorities to Be Studied," *New York Times*, November 21, 1987, 29.

32. Ulig, "Learning Style to Be Studied," 29; Koff quoted in Sara Rimer, "Do Black and White Children Learn the Same Way?," *New York Times*, June 24, 1988, B1.

33. Scott, *Contempt and Pity*, 96.

34. Kenneth B. Clark, "The Effects of Prejudice and Discrimination," in *Personality in the Making; The Fact-Finding Report of the Mid-century White House Conference on Children and Youth*, ed. Helen Leland Whitmer and Ruth Kotinsky (Harper and Brothers, 1951), 48.

35. Zoe Burkholder, *An African American Dilemma: A History of School Integration and Civil Rights in the North* (Oxford University Press, 2021), 87–129.

36. Kenneth B. Clark, *Dark Ghetto: Dilemmas of Social Power* (Wesleyan University Press, 1965), 117, 126, 147

37. Blake and Moore quoted in DePalma, "Culture Question," A22.

38. Janice E. Hale, "Rejoinder to . . . 'Myths of Black Cultural Learning Styles': In Defense of Afrocentric Scholarship," *School Psychology Review* 22, no. 3 (1993): 558.

39. Edmund W. Gordon, *Report of the New York State Board of Regents' Panel on Learning Styles* (State Board of Regents, 1988), 8.

40. Hale quoted in DePalma, "Culture Question," A22; Hilliard quoted in Rimer, "Do Black and White Children," B1.

41. Hilliard, "Behavioral Style, Culture," 373, 374.

42. James A. Banks, "Ethnicity, Class, Cognitive, and Motivational Styles: Research and Teaching Implications," *Journal of Negro Education* 57, no. 4 (Autumn 1988): 462, 463, 465. See also William J. Wilson, *The Declining Significance of Race*.

43. James A. Anderson, "Cognitive Styles and Multicultural Populations," *Journal of Teacher Education* 39, no. 1 (January/February 1988): 6, 7, 8.

44. Linda Darling-Hammond, *The Flat World and Education: How America's Commitment to Equity Will Determine Our Future* (Teachers College Press, 2010), 19. For data on desegregation, see Jason M. Breslow, Evan Wexler, and Robert Collins, "The Return of School Segregation in Eight Charts," *Frontline*, n.d., last accessed August 2024, https://www.pbs.org/wgbh/frontline/article/the-return-of-school-segregation-in-eight-charts/. For data on the achievement gap, see "Student Group Scores," NAEP Long-Term Trend Assessment Results: Reading and Mathematics, Nation's Report Card, last accessed August 2024, https://www.nationsreportcard.gov/ltt/reading/student-group-scores/?age=13.

45. Banks, "Ethnicity, Class, Motivational Styles," 466.

46. Barbara G. Cox and Manuel Ramírez III, "Cognitive Styles: Implications for Multiethnic Education," in *Education in the 80s: Multiethnic Education*, ed. James Banks (National Education Association, 1981), 61, 62, 65.

47. Craig L. Frisby, "One Giant Step Backward: Myths of Black Cultural Learning Styles," *School Psychology Review* 22, no. 3 (1993): 540, 555.

48. Hale, "Rejoinder," 558.

49. Jacqueline Jordan Irvine and Darlene Eleanor York, "Learning Styles and Culturally Diverse Students: A Literature Review," in *Handbook of Research on Multicultural Education*, ed. James A. Banks and Cherry McGee Banks (MacMillan, 1995), 485, 494.

50. James A. Banks, series foreword to Geneva Gay, *Culturally Responsive Teaching: Theory, Research, and Practice*, 2nd ed. (Teachers College Press, 2010), x.

51. Gay, *Culturally Responsive Teaching*, 178, 177.

52. Sonia Nieto, *Affirming Diversity: The Sociopolitical Context of Multicultural Education*, 4th ed. (Pearson, 2004), 150.

53. Burkholder, *African American Dilemma.*

54. Jonathan Kozol, "The New Untouchables," *Newsweek*, vol. 114, no. 27 (January 1990): 53.

55. Gloria Ladson-Billings, "Culturally Relevant Pedagogy 2.0: a.k.a. the Remix," *Harvard Educational Review* 84, no. 1 (Spring 2014): 74.

56. Gloria Ladson-Billings, "Toward a Theory of Culturally Relevant Pedagogy," *American Educational Research Journal* 32, no. 3 (Autumn 1995): 485, 476.

57. See Richard E. Nisbett, *The Geography of Thought: How Asians and Westerners Think Differently* (Nicholas Brealey Publishing, 2011); Li-fang Zhang and Robert Sternberg, "Thinking Styles across Cultures: Their Relationship with Student Learning," in *Perspectives on Thinking, Learning, and Cognitive Styles*, ed. Sternberg and Zhang (Routledge, 2001), 197– 226; and Carol D. Lee, *Culture, Literacy, and Learning: Taking Bloom in the Midst of the Whirlwind* (Teacher College Press, 2007).

Chapter Four

1. Linda Chion-Kenney, "How We Learn: The Multiple Intelligences Teaching Approach," *Washington Post*, May 3, 1994, B5.

2. E. D. Hirsch Jr., "Cultural Literacy," *American Scholar* 52, no. 2 (Spring 1983): 160.

3. National Commission on Excellence in Education, *A Nation at Risk: The Imperative for Educational Reform* (April 1983), 6, 13, 9.

4. Howard Gardner, *A Synthesizing Mind: A Memoir from the Creator of Multiple Intelligences Theory* (MIT Press, 2020), 125.

5. Gardner, *Synthesizing Mind*, 110, 122.

6. Howard Gardner, *Frames of Mind: The Theory of Multiple Intelligences*, 10th anniv. ed. (Basic Books, 1993), ix.

7. See Howard Gardner, "Artistic Intelligences," *Art Educator* 36, no. 2 (March 1983): 47–47; Gardner, "Assessing Intelligences: A Comment on Testing Intelligence without IQ Tests," *Phi Delta Kappan* 65, no. 10 (June 1984): 699–700; and Howard Gardner and Thomas Hatch, "Multiple Intelligences Goes to School: Educational Implications of the Theory of Multiple Intelligences," *Educational Researcher* 18, no. 8 (November 1989): 4–10.

8. Daniel Goleman, *Emotional Intelligence: Why It Matters More Than IQ* (Bantam Books, 1995), xix.

9. Gardner, *Synthesizing Mind*, 170.

10. Howard Gardner, "Who Owns Intelligence?," *Atlantic Monthly*, February 1989, 74.

11. Joe Kincheloe, "Twenty-First-Century Questions about Multiple Intelligences," *Counterpoints* 278 (2004): 6.

12. John White, "The Trouble with Multiple Intelligences," *Teaching Geography* 31, no. 2 (Summer 2006): 83.

13. Miller quoted in E. D. Hirsch, *The Schools We Need and Why We Don't Have Them* (Anchor, 1999), 105.

14. Gardner and Hatch, "Multiple Intelligences Goes to School," 5.

15. Gardner, *Synthesizing Mind*, 137.

16. Gardner, *Frames of Mind*, xvi.

17. Perry D. Klein, "Multiplying the Problems of Intelligence by Eight: A Critique of Gardner's Theory," *Canadian Journal of Education* 22, no. 4 (Autumn 1997): 378–79.

18. Gardner, *Frames of Mind*, xvi.

19. Gardner quoted in James Traub, "Multiple Intelligences Disorder," *New Republic*, October 26, 1998, 22.

20. Gardner, *Frames of Mind*, xvi, xvii.

21. Howard Gardner, *Multiple Intelligences: The Theory in Practice: A Reader* (Basic Books, 1993), 203–4.

22. Howard Gardner, *Intelligence Reframed: Multiple Intelligences for the 21st Century* (Basic Books, 1993), 90.

23. Gardner, *Synthesizing Mind*, 130.

24. James Traub, "Multiple Intelligence Disorder: Howard Gardner's Campaign Against Logic," *New Republic*, October 26, 1998, 22.

25. Mindy Kornhaber, "Multiple Intelligences: From the Ivory Tower to the Dusty Classroom—but Why?," *Teachers College Record* 106, no. 1 (January 2004): 68.

26. Lynn Dierking, "Learning Theory and Learning Styles: An Overview," *Journal of Museum Education* 16, no. 1 (Winter 1991): 6.

27. Linda Chion-Kenney, "The Ways We Learn: There Isn't Just One Right Path That Leads to Knowledge," Education, *Washington Post*, October 7, 1991, D05.

28. Barbara M. Manner, "Learning Styles and Multiple Intelligences in Students: Getting the Most Out of Your Students' Learning," *Journal of College Science Teaching* 30, no. 6 (March/April 2001): 393.

29. Gardner, *Disciplined Mind*, 188.

30. Teacher quoted in Trent Daniel, "Atomic Activities: Students with Different Learning Styles Experience Periodic Table Trends," *Science Teacher* 64, no. 3 (March 1997): 34; Thomas R. Hoerr, "It's No Fad: Fifteen Years of Implementing Multiple Intelligences," *Educational Horizons* 81, no. 2 (Winter 2003): 92.

31. Teacher quoted in Mary Carole McCauley, "Camp Creativity: Could Your Child Be the Next Primary Ballerina or Painting Genius: Summer Arts Camps Offer a World of Possibility," *Baltimore Sun*, June 26, 2022, R1.

32. David Ebeling, "Adapting Your Teaching to Any Learning Style," *Phi Delta Kappan* 82, no. 3 (November 2000): 247.

33. Harvey Silver, Richard Strong, and Matthew Perini, "Integrating Learning Styles and Multiple Intelligences," *Educational Leadership* 55 (1997): 25.

34. Rita Dunn, Stephen Denig, and Maryann Kiely Lovelace, "Two Sides of the Same Coin or Different Strokes for Different Folks?," *Teacher Librarian* 28, no. 3 (February 2011): 9, 10.

35. Stephen J. Denig, "Multiple Intelligences and Learning Styles: Two Complementary Perspectives," *Teachers College Record* 106, no. 1 (January 2004): 107.

36. Alan Pritchard, *Ways of Learning: Learning Theories for the Classroom*, 4th ed. (Routledge, 2017), 71.

37. E. D. Hirsch Jr., *The Schools We Need and Why We Don't Have Them* (Anchor, 1999), 104, 256. Gardner responded directly to Hirsch's provocation in *The Disciplined Mind*, declaring that his book—which recommended deep interdisciplinary studies into fewer topics—was a refutation of Hirsch. As Gardner stated unequivocally: "If this book is a sustained dialectic with any contemporary thinker, that thinker is the noted literacy analyst and educator E. D. Hirsch." Gardner

dismissed Hirsch's core knowledge approach to curriculum as an "idle pursuit" because it conveyed "a view of learning that is at best superficial and at worst anti-intellectual." Gardner, *Disciplined Mind*, 24.

38. Gardner, *Multiple Intelligences*, 44, 45, 251.

39. Gardner, *Intelligence Reframed*, 85.

40. Gardner, *Synthesizing Mind*, 164.

41. Thomas Armstrong, *Multiple Intelligences in the Classroom*, 3rd ed. (ASCD, 2009), 18.

42. Gardner, *Multiple Intelligences*, 203.

43. "Howard Gardner: Multiple Intelligences Are Not Learning Styles," Local Education: Answer Sheet, *Washington Post*, October 16, 2013, https://www.washingtonpost.com/news/answer-sheet/wp/2013/10/16/howard-gardner-multiple-intelligences-are-not-learning-styles/.

44. Howard Gardner, "Why Learning Styles Based on Sensory Organs Make No Sense" (blog post), MI Oasis, September 5, 2019, https://www.multipleintelligencesoasis.org/blog/2019/9/5/why-learning-styles-based-on-sensory-organs-makes-no-sense.

45. Yasmin Anwar, "A Map of the Brain Can Tell What You're Reading About," *Berkeley News*, August 19, 2019, https://news.berkeley.edu/2019/08/19/readingbrainmap/.

46. Gardner, "Why Learning Styles Based on Organs."

47. Gardner, *Synthesizing Mind*, 122, 164–65, 235.

48. Gardner, "Why Learning Styles Based on Organs."

49. Gardner, *Unschooled Mind*, 146. Italics added.

50. "Howard Gardner: Multiple Intelligences."

51. Gardner, preface to Armstrong, *Multiple Intelligences in the Classroom*, x.

52. Gardner's textbook, *Developmental Psychology: An Introduction* (Scott Foresman, 1982), did cover the work of Witkin, but Gardner apparently did not see any pedagogical implications to his MI theory, nor did he interpret it as learning style theory, as many educators did.

53. Traub, "Multiple Intelligence Disorder," 23.

54. Gardner quoted in Traub, 22.

55. White, "The Trouble with Multiple Intelligences," 82.

Chapter Five

1. Howard Gardner, *A Synthesizing Mind: A Memoir from the Creator of Multiple Intelligences Theory* (MIT Press, 2020), 160–61.

2. Gardner, *Synthesizing Mind*, 161.

3. Stephen Jay Gould, *The Mismeasure of Man* (Norton, 2006), 39.

4. Jonathan Kozol, *Savage Inequalities: Children in America's Schools* (HarperCollins, 1992), 2.

5. Howard Gardner, *Intelligence Reframed: Multiple Intelligences for the 21st Century* (Basic Books, 1993), 109–10.

6. Joe Kincheloe, "Twenty-First-Century Questions about Multiple Intelligences," *Counterpoints* 278 (2004): 9.

7. Kolb quoted in Rita Dunn, Thomas DeBello, "Learning Style Researchers Define Differences Differently," with Patricia Brennan, Jeff Krimsky, and Peggy Murrain, *Educational Leadership* 38, no. 5 (February 1981): 373.

8. Curry and Baldwin quoted in Noliwe Rooks, *Cutting School: Privatization, Segregation and the End of Public Education* (New Press, 2017), 59, 60.

9. Quoted in Margaret Jacobs, *White Mother to a Dark Race: Settler Colonialism, Maternalism, and the Removal of Indigenous Children in the American West and Australia, 1800–1940* (University of Nebraska Press, 2009), 132.

10. Samuel Train Dutton, *Social Phases of Education in the School and the Home* (Macmillan, 1907), 217–18.

11. Thomas Fallace, *Race and the Origins of Progressive Education, 1880–1929* (Teachers College Press, 2018); David Wallace Adams, *Education for Extinction: American Indians and the Boarding School Experience, 1875–1928* (University Press of Kansas, 1995).

12. Charles Barlett Dyke, "Essential Features in the Education of the Child Races," In *Addresses and Proceedings: National Education Association of the United States* (University of Chicago Press, 1909), 929.

13. US Department of the Interior, *America, Americanism, and Americanization* (Government Printing Office, 1919), 17, 14.

14. Lewis Terman, *Measurement of Intelligence: An Explanation and Complete Guide for the Use of the Stanford Revision and Extension of the Binet-Simon Intelligence Scale* (Houghton Mifflin 1916), xi.

15. William Bagley, *Determinism in Education* (Baltimore: Warwick and York, 1925), 125; Ruth Benedict, *Race: Science and Politics* (University of Georgia Press, 1940), 154.

16. Rooks, *Cutting School*, 70.

17. Frank Riessman, "The Strategy of Style," *Teachers College Record* 65, no. 6 (March 1964): 484.

18. Rita Dunn and Kenneth Dunn, *Educator's Self-Teaching Guide to Individualizing Instructional Programs* (Parker Publishing, 1975), 90.

19. Norma Ewing and Fung Lan Yong, "A Comparative Study of the Learning Style Preferences among Gifted African-American, Mexican-American, and American-Born Chinese Middle Grade Students," *Roeper Review*14, no. 3 (March 1992): 5; Joy M. Reid, "The Learning Style Preferences of ESL Students," *TESOL Quarterly* 21, no. 2 (March 1987): 92.

20. Harry Levin, "At Risk Students in a Yuppie Age," *Educational Policy* 4 (1990): 284.

21. National Center for Educational Statistics, *Digest of Education Statistics* (US Department of Education, 2002), table 52, https://nces.ed.gov/programs/digest/d02/dt052.asp.

22. Derrick Darby and John Rury, *The Color of Mind: Why the Origins of the Achievement Gap Matter for Justice* (University of Chicago Press, 2018), 124.

23. Sylvia Martinez and John Rury, "From Culturally Deprived to At Risk": The Politics of Popular Expression and Educational Inequality in the United States, 1960–1985," *Teachers College Record* 114, no. 6 (June 2012): 24.

24. Richard R. Valencia, ed., *The Evolution of Deficit Thinking: Educational Thought and Practice* (Falmer, 1997), 197. See also Frank Margonis, "The Cooptation of 'At Risk': Paradoxes of Policy Criticism," *Teachers College Record* 92, no. 1 (Winter 1992): 343–64.

25. Stephen J. Denig, "Multiple Intelligences and Learning Styles: Two Complementary Perspectives," *Teachers College Record* 106, no. 1 (January 2004): 106.

26. Howard Gardner, *Frames of Mind: The Theory of Multiple Intelligences*, 10th anniv. ed. (Basic Books, 1993), 206–7.

27. Howard Gardner, *Multiple Intelligences: The Theory in Practice: A Reader* (Basic Books, 1993), 203–4.

28. Gardner, *Intelligence Reframed*, 171.

29. Howard Gardner, *The Disciplined Mind: Beyond Facts and Standardized Tests: The K–12 Education That Every Child Deserves* (Penguin Books, 1999), 198.

30. Andrew Honigsfeld and Rita Dunn, "Learning Style Responsive Approaches for Teaching Typically Performing and At Risk Adolescents," *Clearing House* 82, no. 5 (2009): 220.

31. Rita Dunn, Josephine Gemake, Fatimeh Jalali, and Robert Zenhausern, "Cross-Cultural Differences in Learning Styles of Elementary-Age Students from Four Ethnic Backgrounds," *Journal of Multicultural Counseling and Development* 18, no. 2 (April 1990): 68.

32. Honigsfeld and Dunn, "Learning Style Responsive Approaches," 221.

33. Rita Dunn and Kenneth Dunn, "Thirty-Five Years of Research on Perceptual Strengths: Essential Strategies to Promote Learning," *Clearing House* 78, no. 6 (July/August 2005): 275.

34. Annette Vincent and Diane Ross, "Learning Style Awareness: A Basis for Developing Teaching and Learning Strategies," *Journal of Research on Computing in Education* 3, no. 5 (2001): 7. They cited Dunn, Gardner, Kolb, and Myers–Briggs as examples of "learning styles presently found in the literature" (2).

35. Walter Burke Barbe and Raymond H. Swassing, *Teaching through Modality Strengths: Concepts and Practices*, with Michael N. Milone Jr. (Zaner-Bloser, 1979), 44–45.

36. Dunn and Dunn, "Thirty-Five Years of Research," 275.

37. Rita Dunn, "Commentary: Teaching Students through Their Perceptual Strengths or Preferences," *Journal of Reading* 31 no. 4 (January 1988): 306.

38. Dunn, "Commentary: Teaching Students through Strengths," 305.

39. Marie Carbo, "Match the Style of Instruction to the Style of Reading," *Phi Delta Kappan* 90, no. 5 (January 2009): 375.

40. Lee Cronbach and Richard E. Snow, *Aptitudes and Instructional Methods: A Handbook for Research Interactions* (Irvington Publishers, 1977): 382.

41. Rita Dunn and Shirley A. Griggs, *Multiculturalism and Learning Style: Teaching and Counseling Adolescents* (Westport, CT: Praeger, 1995), 21.

42. See Angela Klavas, "In Greensboro, North Carolina: Learning Style Boosts Achievement and Test Scores," *Clearing House* 67, no. 3 (1994): 149–51; and Karen Burke and Rita Dunn, "Learning Style–Based Teaching to Raise Minority Test Scores," *Clearing House* 76, no. 2 (November/December 2002),: 103–6.

43. Ewing and Yong, "Comparative Study of Preferences," 5, 6; Clara C. Park, "Crosscultural Differences in Learning Styles of Secondary English Learners," *Bilingual Research Journal* 26, no. 2 (Summer 2002): 455.

44. Jawanza Kunjufu, *Understanding Black Learning Styles* (African American Images, 2011), 42, 40.

45. James A. Banks, *An Introduction to Multicultural Education* (Allyn and Bacon, 2003), 53; Janice Hale, *Black Children: Their Roots, Culture, and Learning Styles* (Johns Hopkins University Press, 1986), xii.

46. Dunn and Griggs, *Multiculturalism and Learning Style*, 52, 60, 63, 70–71.

47. Dunn and Griggs, 14.

48. Honigsfeld and Dunn, "Learning Style Responsive Approaches," 220, 221, 222.

49. Dunn and Griggs, *Multiculturalism and Learning Style*, 131.

50. Richard Gage, "Excuse Me, You're Cramping My Style: Kinesthetics for the Classroom," *English Journal* 84, no. 8 (December 1995): 52–54.

51. Marilee Sprenger, *Differentiation through Learning Styles and Memory*, 2nd ed. (Corwin Press, 2008), 113–14, 116, 123.

52. Vincent and Ross, "Learning Style Awareness," 7.

53. Howard Gardner, "Reflections on Multiple Intelligences: Myths and Messages," *Phi Delta Kappan* 77, no. 3 (November 1995): 206.

54. Dunn and Dunn, "Thirty-Five Years of Research," 275, 274.

55. Jonathan Kozol, *Shame of a Nation: The Restoration of Apartheid Schooling in America* (Three Rivers Press, 2006), 64, 65, 95, 97.

56. Xin Sun, Owen Norton, and Shaylene Nancekivell, "Beware the Myth: Learning Styles Affect Parents, Children's, and Teachers' Thinking about Children's Academic Potential," *npj Science of Learning* 8, article 46 (2023): 7.

57. "Text: George W. Bush's Speech to the NAACP" (transcript), eMediaMillWorks, July 10, 2000, available at https://www.washingtonpost.com/wp-srv/onpolitics/elections/bushtext071000.htm.

58. Carbo's Reading Styles Inventory was initially recognized by the US Department of Education in 1998 as an exemplary program in reading. However, by 2014, with much higher research standards in place after No Child Left Behind, Carbo's model was not endorsed by the Department's What Works Clearinghouse database, which concluded that it "was unable to draw any conclusions based on research about the effectiveness or ineffectiveness of the *Carbo Reading Styles Program*." See Institute of Education Sciences, "What Works Clearinghouse: Carbo Reading Styles Program," October 2014, 1, https://ies.ed.gov/ncee/wwc/Docs/InterventionReports/wwc_carbo_101514.pdf.

59. Jonathan Kozol, "Still Separate, Still Unequal: America's Educational Apartheid," *Harper's Magazine*, September 2005, 48, 49. Kozol's article was excerpted from *Shame of a Nation*.

60. John Clare, "John Clare Explains the Latest Learning Style Orthodoxy," *Daily Telegraph* (UK), May 3, 2006, 29.

Chapter Six

1. John O'Neil, "Making Sense of Style: While Critics Grumble, Advocates Make a Case for Transforming Classrooms Based on Students' Individual Learning Styles," *Educational Leadership* 48, no. 2 (October 1990): 8, 9.

2. Rita Dunn, "Commentary: Teaching Students through Their Perceptual Strengths or Preferences," *Journal of Reading* 31, no. 4 (January 1988): 305.

3. Rita Dunn and Kenneth Dunn, "Thirty-Five Years of Research on Perceptual Strengths: Essential Strategies to Promote Learning," *Clearing House* 78, no. 6 (July/August 2005): 276; Dunn, "Commentary: Teaching Students through Strengths," 304.

4. Robert Searson and Rita Dunn, "The Learning Style Teaching Model," *Science and Children* 38, no. 5 (February 2001): 25.

5. Judith Reiff, *Learning Styles: What the Research Says to the Teacher* (NEA, 1992), 14, 17.

6. Neil Fleming and Colleen Mills, "Not Another Inventory, Rather a Catalyst for Reflection," *To Improve the Academy: Professional and Organization Development Network in Higher Education* 11, no. 1 (1992): 138, 140.

7. Kelli Allen, Jeanna Scheve, and Vicki Nieter, *Understanding Learning Styles: Making a Difference for Diverse Learners* (Shell Education, 2011).

8. See Neil D. Fleming, *Teaching and Learning Styles: VARK Strategies* (published by author, 2001); Neil D. Fleming, *VARK Strategies: The Definitive Guide to VARK* (published by author,

2019); and Neil D. Fleming, *How Do I Learn Best? A Student's Guide to Improved Learning* (published by author, 2019).

9. National Center for Educational Statistics, *Internet Access in U.S. Public Schools and Classrooms: 1994–2000* (US Department of Education, Office of Educational Research and Improvement, 2001), 2.

10. Olga Khazan, "The Myth of 'Learning Styles,'" *Atlantic*, April 11, 2018, https://www.theatlantic.com/science/archive/2018/04/the-myth-of-learning-styles/557687/.

11. Neil Fleming and David Baume, "Learning Styles Again: VARKing Up the Right Tree!," *Educational Developments* 7, no. 4 (November 2006): 5.

12. NAASP assessment report quoted in Laura Shea Doolan, *The History of the International Learning Styles Network and Its Impact on Instructional Innovation* (Edwin Mellon Press, 2004), 72, 77.

13. Rita Dunn, David P. Cavanaugh, Betty M. Eberle, and Robert Zenhausern, "Hemispheric Preference: The Newest Element of Learning Style," *American Biology Teacher* 44, no. 5 (May 1982): 293.

14. These findings—some published, some not—were compiled in Doolan, *History of International Network*, 31–44.

15. See, for example, Joan Della Valle, Kenneth Dunn, Rita Dunn, Gene Geisert, Richard Sinatra, and Robert Zenhausern, "The Effects of Matching and Mismatching Students' Mobility Preferences on Recognition and Memory Tasks," *Journal of Educational Research* 79, no. 5 (1986): 267–72; and Rita Dunn, Ronald Sklar, Jeffrey S. Beaudry, and Jean Bruno, "Effects of Matching and Mismatching Minority Developmental College Students' Hemispheric Preferences on Mathematics Scores," *Journal of Educational Research* 83, no. 5 (1990): 283–88.

16. See Rita Dunn, Jeffrey S. Beaudry, and Angela Klavas, "Survey of Research on Learning Styles," *Educational Leadership* 46, no. 6 (March 1989): 50–58.

17. Dunn and Dunn, "Thirty-Five Years of Research," 276.

18. Dunn, "Commentary: Teaching Students through Strengths," 305.

19. See Karen Burke and Rita Dunn,"Learning Style–Based Teaching to Raise Minority Student Test Scores: There's No Debate!," *Clearing House* 76, no.2 (2002), 103–6; Dunn and Dunn, "Thirty-Five Years of Research"; and Rita Dunn, Shirley A. Griggs, Jeffrey Olson, Mark Beasley, and Bernard S. Gorman, "A Meta-analytic Validation of the Dunn and Dunn Model of Learning Style Preferences," *Journal of Educational Research* 88, no. 6 (1995): 353–62.

20. Rita Dunn and Marie Corbo, "Modalities: An Open Letter to Walter Barbe, Michael Milone, and Raymond Swassing," *Educational Leadership* 38 no. 5 (February 1981): 382. See also Randall A. Silverston and John W. Deichman, "Sense Modality Research and the Acquisition of Reading Skills," *Review of Educational Research* 45 (Winter 1975): 166.

21. O'Neil, "Making Sense of Style," 7.

22. Dunn quoted in Allen, Scheve, and Nieter, *Understanding Learning Styles*, 61.

23. Rita Dunn, "Rita Dunn Answers Questions on Learning Styles," *Educational Leadership* 48, no. 2 (October 1990): 15.

24. Sternberg quoted in Erica Goode, "His Goal: Making Intelligence Tests Smarter," *New York Times*, April 3, 2001, F1.

25. Robert Sternberg, "Mental Self-Government: A Theory of Intellectual Styles and Their Development," *Human Development* 31, no. 4 (July/August 1988): 198.

26. Howard Gardner, *A Synthesizing Mind: A Memoir from the Creator of Multiple Intelligences Theory* (MIT Press, 2020), 137.

27. Sternberg, "Mental Self-Government," 203, 206–7, 214.

28. Robert J. Sternberg, "Intellectual Styles: Theory and Classroom Implications," in *Thinking Styles: Classroom Interaction*, ed. Barbara Z. Presseisen, Robert J. Sternberg, Kurt W. Fischer, and Catharine C. Knight (National Education Association), 34, 38.

29. Later, Sternberg and his coauthor, Li-fang Zhang, administered their Thinking Styles Inventory to more than three thousand students in the US, Hong Kong, and mainland China, and discovered that culture interacted with thinking styles in complicated ways that belied simple generalizations. See Li-fang Zhang and Robert Sternberg, "Thinking Styles across Cultures: Their Relationship with Student Learning," in *Perspectives on Thinking, Learning, and Cognitive Styles*, ed. Sternberg and Zhang (Routledge, 2001), 197–226.

30. Robert J. Sternberg and Elena L. Grigorenko, "Are Learning Styles Still in Style?," *American Psychologist* 52, no. 7 (July 1997): 701.

31. See Robert Sternberg, "Thinking Styles: Keys to Understanding Student Performance," *Phi Delta Kappan* 71, no. 5 (1990): 366–71; and Robert Sternberg, "Allowing for Thinking Styles," *Educational Leadership* 52, no. 3 (November 1994): 36–40.

32. See Robert Sternberg and Li-fang Zhang, eds., *Perspectives on Thinking, Learning, and Cognitive Styles* (Routledge, 2001); and Li-fang Zhang, Robert Sternberg, and Stephen Rayner, eds., *Handbook of Intellectual Styles: Preferences in Cognition, Learning and Thinking* (Springer, 2012).

33. Preface to Sternberg and Zhang, *Perspectives on Thinking*, viii.

34. Gardner quoted in Jack Schneider, *From the Ivory Tower to the Schoolhouse: How Scholarship Becomes Common Knowledge in Education* (Harvard Education Press, 2014), 156.

35. Frank Coffield, David Moseley, Elaine Hall, and Kathryn Ecclestone, *Should We Be Using Learning Styles? What Research Has to Say* (Learning and Skills Research Centre, 2004), 34.

36. Erik Gilbert, "How Ed Schools Became a Bastion of Bad Ideas: A Tale of Assessment, Learning Styles and Other Notorious Concepts," *Chronicle of Higher Education* 66, no. 13 (2019), https://www.chronicle.com/article/how-ed-schools-became-a-bastion-of-bad-ideas/.

37. Philip M. Newton, "The Learning Styles Myth Is Thriving in Higher Education," *Frontiers in Psychology* 6 (December 2015): 4.

38. Jeffrey J. Kuenzi, *Teacher Preparation Policies and Issues in the Higher Education Act* (Congressional Research Service, 2018), 2, https://sgp.fas.org/crs/misc/R45407.pdf.

39. See Martha C. Grindler and Beverly D. Stratton, "Type Indicator and Its Relationship to Teaching and Learning Styles," *Action in Teacher Education* 12, no. 1 (1990): 31–34; Andrea Honigsfeld and Marjorie Schiering, "Diverse Approaches to the Diversity of Learning Styles in Teacher Education," *Educational Psychology* 24, no. 4 (2004): 487–507; Doris B. Matthews, "Learning Styles Research: Implications for Increasing Students in Teacher Education Programs," *Journal of Instructional Psychology* 18, no. 4 (1991): 228; Doris B. Matthews and Miriam C. Jones, "An Investigation of the Learning Styles of Students in Teacher Education Programs," *Journal of Instructional Psychology* 21, no. 3 (1994): 234; Frank Pettigrew and Cathy Buell, "Preservice and Experienced Teachers' Ability to Diagnose Learning Styles," *Journal of Educational Research* 82, no. 3 (1989): 187–89; Chris Perry, "Students' Learning Styles: Implications for Teacher Education," ERIC 375 136 (1994), 1–10.

40. See Jill Hadfield, "Teacher Education and Trainee Learning Style," *RELC Journal* 37, no. 3 (2006): 367–86.

41. James W. Fraser, *Preparing America's Teachers: A History* (Teachers College Press, 2007), 223–26.

42. National Academy of Education, *A Good Teacher in Every Classroom: Preparing the Highly Qualified Teachers Our Children Deserve* (San Francisco: Jossey-Bass, 2005), 22.

43. Council of Chief State School Officers, *InTASC Model Core Teaching Standards: Resource for State Dialogue* (CCSSO, 2011), 21.

44. Geraldine Jonçich Clifford and James W. Guthrie, *Ed School: A Brief for Professional Education* (University of Chicago Press, 1988), 3–4.

45. Charles S. Claxton and Patricia H. Murrell, *Learning Styles: Implications for Improving Educational Practices* (Association for the Study of Higher Education, 1987), 7.

46. Linda J. Swanson, *Learning Styles: A Review of the Literature* (ERIC ED 387 067, July 1995), 11.

47. Adriana Kezar, "Theory of Multiple Intelligences: Implications for Higher Education," *Innovation Higher Education* 26, no. 2 (2001), 141–54.

48. See Rita Dunn and Shirely A. Griggs, eds., *Practical Approaches to Using Learning Styles in Higher Education* (Bergin and Garvey, 2000).

49. Alice Y. Kolb and David A. Kolb, "Learning Styles and Learning Spaces: A Review of the Multidisciplinary Application of Experiential Learning Theory in Higher Education," in *Learning Styles and Learning: A Key to Meeting the Accountability Demands in Education*, ed. Ronald R. Sims and Serbrenia J. Sims (Nova Science Publishers, 2006), 63–79.

50. Newton, "Learning Styles Myth Is Thriving."

51. Doug Roher and Harold Pashler, "Learning Styles: Where's the Evidence?," *Medical Education* 46 (2012): 35.

52. Philip Newton and Mahallad Miah, "Evidence-Based Higher Education—Is the Learning Styles 'Myth' Important," *Frontiers of Psychology* 27 (2017): 444, https://doi.org/10.3389/fpsyg.2017.00444.

53. Frank Coffield, David Moseley, Elaine Hall, and Kathryn Ecclestone, *Learning Styles and Pedagogy in Post-16 Learning: A Systematic and Critical Review* (Learning and Skills Research Centre, 2004), 3, 2.

54. Coffield et al., 33, 34.

55. Coffield et al., 51, 70, 117.

56. Frank Coffield, "Further: Comment: Next Time You See a Learning Styles Questionnaire, Burn It," Education, *Guardian*, July 25, 2006, 8.

57. Jack Schneider, *From the Ivory Tower to the Schoolhouse: How Scholarship Becomes Common Knowledge in Education* (Harvard Education Press, 2014), 155; Newton, "Learning Styles Myth Is Thriving," 4.

Chapter Seven

1. Matt Huston, "Ten Myths about the Mind: It's High Time We Put the Most Enduring Myths about Human Behavior to Bed and See the Mind—and the World—As It Is," *Psychology Today*, September 2019, 57.

2. Frank Coffield, "Further: Comment: Next Time You See a Learning Styles Questionnaire, Burn It," Education, *Guardian*, July 25, 2006, 8. See also chapter 6.

3. Grace M. Fernald, *Remedial Techniques in Basic School Subjects* (New York; McGraw-Hill, 1943), 168.

4. Max Raymond Rennels, "The Effects of Instructional Methodology in Art Education upon Achievement in Spatial Tasks by Disadvantaged Negro Youths," *Journal of Negro Education* 39, no. 2 (Spring 1970): 123.

5. Randall A. Silverston and John W. Deichman, "Sense Modality Research and the Acquisition of Reading Skills," *Review of Educational Research* 45 (Winter 1975): 149–72

6. Lee Cronbach and Richard E. Snow, *Aptitudes and Instructional Methods: A Handbook for Research Interactions* (Irvington Publishers, 1977), 391.

7. Sara G. Tarver and Margaret M. Dawson, "Modality Preference and the Teaching of Reading," *Journal of Learning Disabilities* 11, no. 1 (January 1978): 5.

8. Lynn Curry, *An Organization of Learning Styles Theory and Constructs* (paper presented at the Annual Meeting of the American Educational Research Association, Montreal, Quebec, April 11–15, 1983), 2; Kenneth Kavale and Steven Forness, "Substance over Style: Assessing the Efficacy of Modality-Based Instruction," *Exceptional Children* 56, no. 4 (1987): 228, 237.

9. Edmund W. Gordon, *Report of the New York State Board of Regents' Panel on Learning Styles* (State Board of Regents, 1988), 8.

10. Jacqueline Jordan Irvine and Darlene Eleanor York, "Learning Styles and Culturally Diverse Students: A Literature Review," in *Handbook of Research on Multicultural Education*, ed. James A. Banks and Cherry McGee Banks (MacMillan, 1995), 485.

11. Gregorc and Snow quoted in John O'Neil, "Making Sense of Style: While Critics Grumble, Advocates Make a Case for Transforming Classrooms Based on Students' Individual Learning Styles," *Educational Leadership* 48, no. 2 (October 1990), 7. Keefe and Slavin are also discussed in article.

12. Lynn Curry, "A Critique of the Research on Learning Styles," *Educational Leadership* 48, no. 2 (October 1990): 50.

13. Richard Riding and Indra Cheema, "Cognitive Styles—an Overview and Integration," *Educational Psychology* 11, no. 3–4 (1991): 193–215; Simon Cassidy, "Learning Styles: An Overview of Theories, Models, and Measures," *Educational Psychology: The International Journal of Experimental Psychology* 24, no. 4 (August 2004): 419–44.

14. Coffield et al., *Learning Styles and Pedagogy*, 2.

15. Curry, "Critique of the Research," 50.

16. Curry, ," 51, 52.

17. Curry, 54.

18. J. J. Kramer and J. C. Conoley, eds., *The Eleventh Mental Measurements Yearbook* (University of Nebraska Press, 1992), 455, 456, 464.

19. "Howard Gardner: Multiple Intelligences Are Not Learning Styles," Local Education: Answer Sheet, *Washington Post*, October 16, 2013, https://www.washingtonpost.com/news/answer-sheet/wp/2013/10/16/howard-gardner-multiple-intelligences-are-not-learning-styles/.

20. Stephen J. Ceci and Robert Bjork, "Announcement: Psychological Science in the Public Interest: The Case for Juried Analyses," *Psychological Science* 11, no. 3 (May 2000): 177, 178.

21. Harold Pashler, Mark McDaniel, Doug Rohrer, and Robert Bjork, "Learning Styles: Concepts and Evidence," *Psychological Science in the Public Interest* 9, no. 3 (2009): 105.

22. David Glenn, "Matching Teaching Style to Learning Style May Not Help Students," *Chronicle of Higher Education*, December 15, 2009, https://www-chronicle-com.ezproxy.wpunj.edu/article/matching-teaching-style-to-learning-style-may-not-help-students/.

23. Glenn, "Matching Teaching Style."

24. Debra Viadero, "Cognitive Scientists Debunk Learning-Style Theories," *Education Week*, December 17, 2009, https:/www.edweek.org/education/cognitive-scientists-debunk-learning-style-theories/2009/12.

25. Peter DeWitt, "The Myth of Learning Styles," *Education Week*, April 29, 2014, https://www.edweek.org/teaching-learning/opinion-the-myth-of-learning-styles/2014/04.

26. Beth A. Rogowsky, Barbara Calhoun, and Paula Tallal, "Matching Learning Style to Instructional Methods: Effects on Comprehension," *Journal of Educational Psychology* 107, no. 1 (2014): 64.

27. Joshua Cuevas, "Is Learning Styles-Based Instruction Effective? A Comprehensive Analysis of Recent Research on Learning Styles," *Theory and Research in Education* 13, no. 3 (2015): 328.

28. Bruce Hood, Paul Howard-Jones, Diana Laurillard, Dorothy Bishop, Frank Coffield, Dame Uta Frith, Steven Pinker, Sire Olin Blakemore, Hal Pashler, Peter Etchells, et al., "Letter: No Evidence to Back Idea of Learning Styles," *Guardian*, March 12, 2017, https://www.theguardian.com/education/2017/mar/12/no-evidence-to-back-idea-of-learning-styles; Sally Weale, "Teachers Must Ditch Neuromyth of Learning Styles, Scientists Say: Eminent Academics from Worlds of Neuroscience, Education, and Psychology Voice Concerns Over Popularity of Method," *Guardian*, March 12, 2017, https://www.theguardian.com/education/2017/mar/13/teachers-neuromyth-learning-styles-scientists-neuroscience-education.

29. Benjamin Riley, "The Value of Knowing How Students Learn," *Phi Delta Kappan* 97, no. 7 (April 2016): 37.

30. Polly R. Hushmann and Valerie Dean O'Loughlin, "Another Nail in the Coffin for Learning Styles? Disparities among Undergraduate Anatomy Students Study Strategies, Class Performance, and Reported VARK Learning Styles," *Anatomical Sciences Education* 12, no. 1 (January/February 2018): 6.

31. Olga Khazan, "The Myth of 'Learning Styles,'" *Atlantic*, April 11, 2018, https://www.theatlantic.com/science/archive/2018/04/the-myth-of-learning-styles/557687/.

32. Michael Zwaagstra, "Is the Theory of Unique Learning Styles Dragging Down Our Education System?," *Globe and Mail*, July 20, 2022, A11.

33. Daniel T. Willingham, "Ask the Cognitive Scientist: Do Visual, Auditory, and Kinesthetic Learners Need Visual, Auditory, and Kinesthetic Instruction?," *American Educator*, Summer 2005, https://www.aft.org/ae/summer2005/willingham.

34. Daniel T. Willingham, "Reframing the Mind: Howard Gardner Became a Hero Among Educators Simply by Redefining Talents as Intelligences," *Education Next* (Summer 2004): 22.

35. Willingham, "Reframing the Mind," 24.

36. See Jay Matthews, "21 Years Later: Multiple Intelligences Still Debated: Education Pushes Appealing to All Types of Learners," *Washington Post*, September 7, 2004, A9.

37. Correspondence with the author, July 6, 2023.

38. Daniel T. Willingham, *Why Don't Students Like School? A Cognitive Scientist Answers Questions about How the Mind Works and What It Means for the Classroom* (Jossey-Bass, 2009), 147, 164.

39. Cedar Riener and Daniel Willingham, "The Myth of Learning Styles," *Change* 42, no. 5 (September/October 2010): 34.

40. Daniel Willingham, Elizabeth M. Hughes, and David G. Dobolyi, "The Scientific Status of Learning Styles Theories," *Teaching of Psychology* 42, no. 2 (2015): 268.

41. Deans for Impact, *Science of Learning*, 8, https://deansforimpact.org/wp-content/uploads/2016/12/The_Science_of_Learning.pdf.

42. Daniel Willingham, "You Are Not a Visual Learner," *New York Times*, October 7, 2018, SR6.

43. Daniel Willingham, "Ask the Cognitive Scientist: Does Tailoring Instruction to Learning Styles Help Students Learn?," *American Educator* 42, no. 2 (Summer 2018): 32.

44. David Kraemer, Lauren M. Rosenberg, and Sharon L. Thompson-Schill, "The Neural Correlates of Visual and Verbal Cognitive Styles," *Journal of Neuroscience* 29, no. 12 (2009): 3792–98.

45. Willingham quoted in Khazan, "Myth of 'Learning Styles.' "

46. Paul A. Howard-Jones, "Neuroscience and Education: Myths and Messages," *Nature Reviews Neuroscience* 15 (2014): 2, available at https://scottbarrykaufman.com/wp-content/uploads/2014/10/nrn3817.pdf; Steven R. Wininger, Jenni L. Redifer, Antony D. Norman, and Mary K. Ryle, "Prevalence of Learning Styles in Educational Psychology and Introduction to Education Textbooks: A Content Analysis," *Psychology Learning & Teaching* 18, no. 3 (2019): 221.

47. Philip M. Newton and Atharva Salvi, "How Common Is the Belief in the Learning Styles Neuromyth, and Does It Matter? A Pragmatic Systemic Review," *Frontiers in Education* 5 (2020), https://doi.org/10.3389/feduc.2020.602451.

48. Madeline Will, "Teachers Still Believe in Learning Styles and Other Myths about Cognition," *Education Week*, September 5, 2019, https://www.edweek.org/teaching-learning/teachers-still-believe-in-learning-styles-and-other-myths-about-cognition/2019/09.

49. Carol Lethaby and Patricia Harries, "Learning Styles and Teacher Training: Are We Perpetuating Neuromyths?," *ELT Journal* 70, no. 1 (October 2015): 17.

50. Wininger, Redifer, Norman, and Ryle, "Prevalence of Learning Styles," 221.

51. Alan Pritchard, *Ways of Learning: Learning Theories for the Classroom*, 4th ed. (Routledge, 2017), 75.

52. Philip M. Newton, "The Learning Styles Myth Is Thriving in Higher Education," *Frontiers in Psychology* 6 (December 2015): 1908, https://doi.org/10.3389/fpsyg.2015.01908.

53. Jesse Signal, "One Reason the Learning Style Myth Persists," *Cut*, December 28, 2015, https://www.thecut.com/2015/12/one-reason-the-learning-styles-myth-persists.html.

54. Catherine Scott, "The Enduring Appeal of Learning Styles," *Australian Journal of Education* 54, no. 2 (April 2010): 12, 14.

55. Riener and Willingham, "Myth of Learning Styles," 34–35.

56. Michael Pershan and Benjamin Riley, "Why Mythbusting Fails: A Guide to Influencing Education with Science," Deans for Impact, June 29, 2017, https://www.deansforimpact.org/about/news-and-blog/2017/06/29/why-mythbusting-fails-a-guide-to-influencing-education-with-science.

57. Mindy Kornhaber, "Multiple Intelligences: From the Ivory Tower to the Dusty Classroom—but Why?," *Teachers College Record* 106, no. 1 (January 2004): 68.

58. Lenna Ojure and Thomas M. Sherman, "Learning Styles: Why Teachers Love a Concept Research Has Yet to Embrace," *Education Week*, November 28, 2001, https://www.edweek.org/education/opinion-learning-styles/2001/11.

59. Dylan Kane, "Talking about Learning Styles," *Five Twelve Thirteen* (blog), April 29, 2017, https://fivetwelvethirteen.wordpress.com/2017/04/29/talking-about-learning-styles/.

60. Heather Wolpert-Gawron, "The Bunk of Debunking Learning Styles," *Education Week*, February 17, 2010, https://www.edweek.org/education/opinion-the-bunk-of-debunking-learning-styles/2010/02.

61. Cedar Riener, "Learning Styles: What's Being Debunked," *Education Week*, February 24, 2010, https://www.edweek.org/education/opinion-learning-styles-whats-being-debunked/2010/02.

62. Ellen Condliffe Lagemann, *An Elusive Science: The Troubling History of Education Research* (University of Chicago Press, 2000), 219–25.

63. Kelli Allen, Jeanna Scheve, and Vicki Nieter, *Understanding Learning Styles: Making a Difference for Diverse Learners* (Shell Education, 2011), 62.

64. Glenn, "Matching Teaching Style."

65. Robert Sternberg, "Book Reviews: Styles of Thinking and Learning: Personal Mirror or Personal Mirage?," *American Journal of Psychology* 128, no. 1 (Spring 2015): 118, 120.

66. Harold Pashler, Robert Bjork, Mark McDaniel, and Doug Rohrer, "Comment on Sternberg's Review of Zhang," *American Journal of Psychology* 128, no. 1 (Spring 2015): 122.

67. See Li-fang Zhang and Robert Sternberg, *The Nature of Intellectual Styles* (Lawrence Erlbaum, 2006); Li-fang Zhang, *The Malleability of Intellectual Styles* (Cambridge University Press, 2013); and Li-fang Zhang, *The Value of Intellectual Styles* (Cambridge University Press, 2017).

68. Li-fang Zhang and Robert Sternberg, "A Threefold Model of Intellectual Styles," *Educational Psychology Review* 17, no. 1 (March 2005): 34, 36.

69. Zhang, *Value of Intellectual Styles*, 35, 85.

70. Zhang, 141.

71. Zhang, 8.

Conclusion

1. *Abbott Elementary*, season 1, episode 6, "Gifted Program," 15:02.

2. *Girls5eva*, season 2, episode 3, "Who U Know," 13:08. In this case, the writers were clearly making fun of the learning style idea and may have deliberately conflated social learning with Gardner's interpersonal learning.

3. Matt Hudson, "Ten Myths about the Mind," *Psychology Today*, October 2019, 57.

4. Gordon Allport, *Personality: A Psychological Interpretation* (Henry Holt, 1937), 296; Gordon Allport, *Pattern and Growth in Personality* (Holt, Rinehart, and Winston, 1961), 350.

5. Kolb quoted in Rita Dunn and Thomas DeBello, "Learning Style Researchers Define Differences Differently," with Patricia Brennan, Jeff Krimsky, and Peggy Murrain, *Educational Leadership* 38, no. 5 (February 1981): 373.

6. Kris D. Gutierrez and Barbara Rogoff, "Cultural Ways of Learning: Individual Traits or Repertoires of Practice," *Educational Researcher* 32, no. 5 (June/July 2003): 20, 23.

7. Peter DeWitt, "Learning Strategies, Not Learning Styles," *Education Week*, https://www.edweek.org/education/opinion-learning-strategies-not-learning-styles/2016/08.

8. This is the approach suggested in Diane Ravitch, *Left Back: A Century of Failed School Reform* (Simon and Schuster, 2000); E. D. Hirsch Jr., *The Schools We Need and Why We Don't Have Them* (Anchor, 1999); and David Angus and Jeffrey E. Mirel, *The Failed Promise of the American High School, 1890–1995* (Teachers College Press, 1999).

9. Angeline Stoll Lillard, *Montessori: The Science behind the Genius*, 3rd ed. (Oxford University Press, 2017); Thomas Fallace, "The Racism of Marie Montessori," *Journal of Curriculum Studies* 55, no. 5 (2023): 619–31. See also Marie Montessori, *Pedagogical Anthropology* (Frederic Stokes, 1913).

Index